P9-CQJ-022

# THE KARANKAWA INDIANS OF TEXAS

*Texas Archaeology and Ethnohistory Series,*
*Thomas R. Hester, Editor*

# THE
# KARANKAWA
# INDIANS
# OF TEXAS

## AN ECOLOGICAL STUDY OF CULTURAL TRADITION AND CHANGE

Robert A. Ricklis

 University of Texas Press, Austin

Requests for permission to reproduce material from this work should be sent to
Permissions, University of Texas Press, P.O. Box 7819, Austin, TX 78713-7819.

⊗ The paper used in this publication meets the minimum requirements of
American National Standard for Information Sciences—Permanence of Paper for
Printed Library Materials, ANSI Z39.48-1984.

**Library of Congress Cataloging-in-Publication Data**

Ricklis, Robert A. (Robert Arthur)
    The Karankawa Indians of Texas: an ecological study of cultural
tradition and change / by Robert A. Ricklis.—1st ed.
        p.     cm.—(Texas archaeology and ethnohistory series)
    Includes bibliographical references (p.     ) and index.
    ISBN 0-292-77073-1 (cloth : alk. paper).—ISBN 0-292-77077-4
(pbk : alk. paper)
        1. Karankawa Indians—History—Sources.   2. Karankawa Indians—
Government relations.   3. Karankawa Indians—Antiquities.
4. Excavations (Archaeology)—Texas—Gulf Coast.   5. Ethnohistory—
Texas—Gulf Coast.   6. Gulf Coast (Tex.)—Antiquities.   I. Title.
II. Series.
E99.K26R53   1996
976.4'1—dc20                                            95-30404

# Contents

# Foreword

The Karankawas are certainly the most maligned and misunder-
stood Native American peoples who once inhabited Texas. Moreover, much of what has been written about them, especially in
newspapers and popular magazines, is either greatly exaggerated or
wholly without merit. As an archaeologist who has worked on the
central coast of Texas, I am used to hearing descriptions of the Karankawas as "cannibals" and "giants." Most prehistoric burials or
cemeteries found on the coast, through construction or looting,
are usually attributed to the "Karankawas." And the bones, when
viewed in the ground, often appear to the untrained eye to be of
large individuals. Furthermore, fertile imaginations and unsupported
linguistic studies have suggested that the Karankawas were of Carib
derivation, landing on the Texas coast in the sixteenth century. No
ethnographic or archaeological data lend credence to this tale. There
is evidence that the Karankawas practiced ritual cannibalism, like
most native peoples of the New World, and the Karankawas do seem
to have been taller than the average precontact Native Americans.
(Although, a 1720 account of the Karankawas at present-day Aransas
Pass reports some males at six feet, two inches in height, further
notes indicate that they were usually five and a half feet tall.)
    What generated all of the negative views of the Karankawas?
William W. Newcomb in his classic volume, *The Indians of Texas*,
writes:

> Some of the atrocities attributed to these Indians are undoubt-
> edly rationalizations growing out of the inhuman, unfair treat-
> ment the Spaniards and Texans accorded them. It is much easier
> to slaughter men and appropriate their land if you can convince
> yourself that they are despicable, inferior, barely human crea-
> tures. (1961:78)

Fortunately, we now have the present book by Robert Ricklis that provides a considerably more balanced view of Karankawan history and prehistory. His ethnohistoric description of the Karankawas deals with their interactions with the Spanish as well as their confrontations with Anglo-American settlers. Through Ricklis' use of archival records, we get to see the Karankawas as a native population responding to normal human patterns of adaptation, integrating their traditional lifeway with the new realities of the Spanish Colonial missions.

Perhaps more important, Ricklis is able to trace the Karankawas, or at least their mode of adaption, back at least 2,000 years. He links them with the long-defined Rockport Complex known from archaeological sites on the central coast. Through his own innovative fieldwork and material culture studies, he defines their territorial boundaries as extending inland about 40 kilometers. It is clear from his work and that of other archaeologists working in southern Texas that at least one other major cultural pattern was contemporary with the Rockport Complex. This is the Toyah Horizon, typical of late prehistoric South and Central Texas. Interaction between these two peoples (if we assume that the Toyah Horizon represents Coahuilteco speakers or similar groups) has been recognized in artifact assemblages studied by other archaeologists. But Ricklis' research at Site 41RF21, in Refugio County, is the first to document what are apparently the contemporary camping localities of Rockport (Karankawan) peoples at one end of the site and Toyah (Coahuilteco) peoples at the other.

Finally, Ricklis' review of past and present archaeological studies on the central coast of Texas reveals seasonal use of shoreline sites and interior coastal prairie sites, part of an established Rockport/Karankawan lifeway. This research reflects the value of ecologically oriented research, especially in an area with such distinctive environmental niches. I believe this volume will be a baseline for all future work on the aboriginal history and prehistory of the central coast of Texas and, moreover, will be a model for similar investigations that should be conducted in other regions.

Thomas R. Hester

# Preface

The findings presented in this book began as an archaeological study of prehistoric settlement patterns on the central coast of Texas and evolved into an interdisciplinary exploration of how one Native American society adapted to its environment and to conditions of rapid change brought about by early historic Euro-American colonization. If one believes popular folklore, the Native Americans known historically as the Karankawas were the most primitive of people, living from day to day without fixed abodes and more or less scavenging a living from a harsh and inhospitable environment. As I began to look at the actual archaeological evidence, it became increasingly difficult to entertain such notions, much less to subscribe to such a simplistic—and denigrating—perspective on the extinct culture of these native people. The commonly held notion, for example, that the Karankawas were constantly moving about in small groups to eke out a bare living did not seem, on the face of it, to explain why some of the region's archaeological sites were so large, with such dense deposits of cultural debris. Large sites, highly productive of cultural materials, often indicate intensive occupations, perhaps by rather large groups of people and perhaps for extended periods of time. Where people congregate in large numbers for any length of time, it can be assumed that they have the know-how with which to procure rich and abundant resources and the ability to process the resources and distribute them among members of their society, and that they employ rather sophisticated social mechanisms with which to maintain group cohesion. Certainly, the ethnography of hunting and gathering peoples (and the Karankawas were in fact nonagricultural hunter-gatherer-fishers) shows that so-called primitive peoples possess intimate knowledge of their environments and fine-tuned adaptive strategies, not to mention rich mythologies and folklore.

The key to defining Karankawan adaptive patterns logically seems to be to look at the range of archaeological sites with an eye to determining what resources were used and how intensively the sites were occupied—and then to assess how well the archaeological data seemed to "fit" with the spatial and seasonal patterns of resource availability in the central coast environment. A measure of success was realized with this approach, to the extent that we can now begin to understand how the Karankawas used and moved within their environment, as well as to make some strong inferences about basic patterns of socioeconomic organization.

Perhaps the most interesting insights that emerge from this study come out of a synthesis of the archaeological and ethnohistorical data. Study of historical documents, mainly Spanish archival materials from the eighteenth century, has yielded a fascinating look at how the Karankawas dealt with Euro-American colonization of their homeland. We see that the Karankawas were neither hapless victims of colonization nor intractably confrontational toward newcomers to their homeland. Rather, they drew upon their own cultural tradition—rooted in the long-lived adaptive patterns indicated archaeologically—to develop what was ultimately a viable and peaceful interaction with the political, social, and religious dimensions of colonial Spanish culture. We see that the Karankawas, like various other relatively small-scale societies, were able to cope with rapid change once the foreign elements of colonization were integrated within traditional cultural ecological patterns.

All of this is not, and should not be, presented as the final word on the archaeology and ethnohistory of the Karankawas. Certainly, much work still needs to be accomplished in further explorations into the nature of Karankawan culture. Nonetheless, the research results presented here begin to elucidate, for the first time, some fundamental aspects of the culture as a human adaptive system and to show that Karankawan life was strategically organized to successfully respond to the opportunities and constraints afforded by a resource-rich environment. Importantly, it is now possible to begin to understand the Karankawas as a real people worthy of our interest, to the extent that we have some insight into how they lived and how they successfully coped with a changing world in the context of deeply rooted tradition.

None of this would have been possible without the help of many individuals. Most of the research reported here was carried out within the framework of my graduate studies at the University of Texas at Austin. My thanks are extended to the faculty members who offered scholarly input during the course of the project: Karl W. Butzer, Terry G. Jordan, William E. Doolittle, and Gregory W. Knapp (Department of Geography), and Jeremiah F. Epstein, E. Mott Davis, and James A. Neely (Department of Anthropology). Particular appreciation goes to Karl Butzer, whose broad interdisciplinary perspective and knowledge helped to inspire a synthetic approach involving archaeological, environmental, and historical data. Several discussions with Thomas N. Campbell, Professor Emeritus of Anthropology, provided valuable insights into the ethnohistorical records of aboriginal peoples in Texas. Dee Ann Story, Professor of Anthropology and former Director of the Texas Archeological Research Laboratory (TARL), was most helpful in providing me access to comparative collections and archaeological site files housed at TARL.

Many people helped with the labor-intensive archaeological fieldwork. Particularly steadfast in their interest and assistance were Jerry Bauman, Nancy and Larry Beaman, Jim and Marion Craft, Kim and Susan Cox, Skip Kennedy, and John and Arlene McGee. Access to an important series of archaeological sites along the Aransas River was provided by the Welder Wildlife Refuge, Sinton, Texas; my thanks go to Dr. James Teer, the refuge director, and his friendly staff.

Financial assistance from a University of Texas Graduate Fellowship, awarded through the Department of Geography, greatly facilitated preparation of the doctoral dissertation of which this book is a revised and condensed version. Funds for radiocarbon dates were provided by the Donors Fund of the Texas Archeological Society, Sigma Xi, the Scientific Research Society, and the James R. Dougherty Foundation, Beeville, Texas.

Finally, very special thanks go to my wife, Madeleine-Sophie Ricklis, for her affection and patient support throughout the several years of this project.

Robert A. Ricklis
Corpus Christi, Texas

# THE KARANKAWA INDIANS OF TEXAS

# Chapter 1
# Who Were the Karankawas?

In the winter of 1685, two ships under the command of the re-
nowned French explorer Robert Sieur de La Salle sailed into the
shallow waters of Matagorda Bay, on what is today the central coast
of Texas. The expedition encountered several hundred native people
who were living at a nearby fishing camp and who may have never
before set eyes on Europeans. At first the Indians were friendly and
even invited the Frenchmen to join them in a hunting expedition.
But Monsieur La Salle, not known for his humility, quite arrogantly
ordered his men to steal several of the Indians' dugout canoes. After nightfall, the Indians tracked down the thieves and killed or
wounded several of them (Cox 1905).

So began the history of relations between Euro-American colonists and the Karankawas. For more than a century and a half, the
Karankawas would find themselves confronted by French and
Spaniards, and later by Mexicans and Texans, all interlopers in what
for countless generations had been the Karankawa homeland. Much
of the time, relations were fraught with conflict, first with La Salle
and his compatriots, then with Spanish colonists of the eighteenth
century, and finally with the Mexican and Anglo ranchers who
began to settle the coastal prairies after 1820. With time the Karankawas came to be condemned as a warlike and treacherous people,
predisposed to conflict and incapable or unwilling to interact peace-
fully with outsiders. Along with a reputation for fierceness, these
Native American people acquired infamy as vile, cannibalistic savages who perpetually roamed the coastline looking for their next
meal—or their next victim.

It is historical fact that the Karankawas were chronically at war
with Spanish colonists during much of the eighteenth century. It is
also true that they fought bitterly, as did so many Native American
peoples, to keep their homeland when it was thrown open to aggressive Anglo-American settlement. But the image of the ferocious

savage, incapable of peaceful interaction with foreign cultures, is not supported by the synthesis of archaeological and historical information presented in this book.

The archaeological record now shows that the Karankawas, far from primitive scavengers, possessed an intimate knowledge of their environment. They knew where to find the key resources they needed to sustain a viable subsistence economy, and they understood how to move strategically within their environment so that those resources could be obtained when and where they were most abundant. Because they had expert knowledge of the time and places of greatest availabilities of important subsistence resources, they were able to adjust the size and duration of encampments with minimal risk of food shortages.

Setting aside the more sensational interpretations of some contemporary observers, the historical record shows that the Karankawas were neither predisposed to indiscriminate conflict nor incapable of peaceful interactions with newcomers to their lands. Indeed, the evidence indicates that they were generally willing to meet intruders with open attitudes. When the Spaniards established their first mission near the coast in 1722, the Karankawas showed considerable interest in what the foreigners had to offer. It was only after the apparently intolerant commander of the mission's military garrison ordered his soldiers to ambush Indian men, women, and children that the Karankawas, feeling deeply betrayed, viewed Spanish colonial settlement with hostility.

Decades of fighting followed the 1722 debacle, and warfare between the Karankawas and Spanish colonial soldiers had become a chronic condition by the 1780s (e.g., Gilmore 1984). Nonetheless, in 1789 the Karankawas established a peace that was to endure, for the most part, right up to the closing of the last of the Spanish missions some forty years later. During this period, largely unrecognized by historians, the Karankawas succeeded in integrating the foreign presence into their world, adjusted to colonial culture, and even became political allies of the Spaniards. Although later Anglo-American settlement of Texas forced the Karankawas to abandon their homeland, these decades of successful adjustment to colonial culture represent a remarkable story of human adaptability that belies simplistic notions of stubbornly intractable savages.

Given that most of the eighteenth century was marked by hostility and animosities, the question arises as to how the Karankawas managed to maintain the peace and come to terms with the fundamental changes in their world brought about by Euro-American colonization. What were the conditions that empowered a people with a highly traditional way of life to change attitudes and patterns of behavior and to shift from a relationship of resistance and conflict to one of acceptance and peaceful interaction with a foreign culture? The answers to these questions emerge from an examination of the interrelation between cultural tradition and change, which is the central theme of this book.

In order to explore these questions, it is necessary to identify the main features of the traditional native lifeway as it existed prior to the effects of Euro-American colonization. This inquiry requires insight into the human ecology of the Karankawas—how they adapted to the opportunities and constraints afforded by their environment using a limited but effective technology. To gain such insight, we must rely on archaeological evidence, augmented by relevant information from historical documents. Then a careful examination of the historical record sheds light on how colonization affected the traditional Karankawan lifeway and upon what store of collective experience these people ultimately relied to effectively respond to profound changes that began in 1685 and continued for over 150 years.

The combined archaeological and ethnohistorical records show that fundamental Karankawan adaptive patterns had been operating for centuries when the first Europeans came to the shores of Texas. And, in spite of the various pressures on the Karankawas resulting from Euro-American colonization of the coastal plain—chronic conflicts, introduction of European diseases, and changes in regional ecology—the traditional native lifeway was sufficiently resilient to persist in modified form throughout the colonial era. Most important for an understanding of how traditional native society adapted to the pressures of rapid change is a juxtaposition of archaeological and ethnohistorical information that shows that the Karankawas made a viable response to change by integrating the Spanish colonial mission-presidio complex into their traditional patterns of land use and seasonal settlement mobility. Workable intercultural relations were achieved not through the abandonment of established cultural patterns and submission to Spanish colonial culture but through a strategic integration of the new colonial presence into traditional Karankawan cultural-ecological patterns. The mission, the focal point of contact between two entirely different worlds of human cultural experience, was drawn into the native lifeway at the basic level of an ecological resource. Thus finding a measure of acceptance within the framework of traditional native culture, the missions became the focal points for a degree of Karankawan acculturation to the Spanish colonial world.

Before beginning our archaeological and historical explorations of patterns of continuity and change in the Karankawan world, some of the generally recognized characteristics of the native people and their culture can be summarized. The Karankawas were a nonagricultural people whose subsistence economy relied heavily on the abundant fish and shellfish resources of the coastal estuaries (Newcomb 1961, 1983; Schaedel 1949; Gatschet 1891). As Newcomb (1983: 362) has pointed out, they were not a maritime people, since their livelihood was based upon resources of the shallow bays and lagoons found behind the protective chain of barrier islands that parallels the mainland shoreline. The Karankawas made and used dugout canoes that were not designed for travel in the open Gulf of Mexico. Fish were often taken with the bow and arrow (Berlandier 1980; Carroll 1983), and nets, weirs, and fish traps were likely used as well. Hunting, a male activity, was of considerable importance. Plant foods such as tubers, fruits, roots, and nuts were gathered. Socioeconomic groups—bands of probably kin-related individuals—were mobile, camping at locales that provided ready access to important resources according to their seasonal availabilities. Houses were simple, wigwamlike circular pole frame structures covered with mats or hides. The simple design facilitated efficient set up, and the component parts could be transported in canoes when camps were abandoned (see Newcomb 1983). Other salient behavioral and organizational features of Karankawan life are discussed at some length further on, in the context of pertinent archaeological and historical information.

The term "Karankawa" can be somewhat misleading, since it includes several historically documented groups, only one of which was the Karankawa proper (in this book, however, unless otherwise indicated, the term Karankawa refers to the larger inclusive cultural group). Five principal groups, related by language and culture, made up the larger Karankawan cultural entity during colonial times. Known by the Spaniards since as early as the 1720s (Castañeda 1936:168), these were the Carancaguases (Karankawa proper), Cocos, Cujanes, Guapites, and Copanes. These names recur in documentary references throughout the eighteenth century, and colonial Spanish missionaries and military officials regarded the five groups as closely related. By the mid-eighteenth century, the Spaniards had come to subsume the various groups under the term Coxanes; Captain Manuel Ramírez de la Piszina, commandant at Presidio La Bahía at present-day Goliad, noted that "the four nations included under the name Coxanes are the Cojanes, Guapites, Carancaguases, and Copanes" (Piszina to the Viceroy, December 26,

1751, author's translation). Later, in 1797, Juan Elquezabal, interim commander at La Bahía, wrote that "they [referring specifically to the Carancaguases and Cocos] are all one nation, and of one language, which is nothing new" (Elquezabal to Muñoz, July 3, 1797, author's translation). In 1791 Fray Juan Garza of the Refugio mission wrote to Muñoz (letter of December 15, 1791) that "the Indians who are now asking for a mission [Carancaguases and Copanes] are peaceful, and have communication with, and are reputed to be of one nation with, those of the Colorado River and the Brazos de Dios, and they keep up communication with these, as well as friendship with the Orcoquisacs and the Atacapas" (author's translation). For reasons to be discussed shortly, it is probable that the group living near the mouths of the Colorado and Brazos Rivers were Cocos.

Although the several groups were consistently differentiated by the Spaniards, they seem to have mixed rather freely with one another. In 1788 the commandant at Presidio La Bahía wrote to Governor Rafael Martinez Pacheco that "the majority of those [Indians] who were at that ranchería [encampment, near the Nueces River] would be mission [Indians] mixed with Copanes, among which there are always some Carancaguases" (Cazorla to Pacheco, May 2, 1788). In 1791 Fray Manuel Silva, superior of the Franciscan missions of the College of Zacatecas, directed Fray Juan Garza to visit the numerous rancherías from Copano to La Vaca and thus to visit "all the Carancaguases." Silva accompanied Garza on this trip and noted in a letter to Muñoz (April 26, 1791) that "those [Indians] we have seen were mixed with Cujanes, Copanes, and Carancaguases" (author's translation).

Despite this mixing, distinctions between the several Karankawan groups were apparently made quite readily by Spaniards during the eighteenth century. In earlier times, under conditions of greater population densities (before the population decline that was to result from introduced European diseases), group territories may have been more clearly defined, thus providing geographic constraints in which group identities were fairly clear-cut. It is interesting, for instance, that Juan Cazorla, writing in 1788 from La Bahía to Governor Pacheco in San Antonio de Bexár, and referring to the year 1778, stated, "At that time the aforesaid Indians [Carancaguases] were less dispersed than they are today, for which reason other measures than those of the past are necessary [to effect their reduction]" (letter of May 2, 1788). Also suggesting a tendency to dispersal during later historic times are observations of Karankawan camps located considerably further up the coast in the early nineteenth century than was earlier the case. The Karankawas were reported in the Galveston area in the 1820s (Dyer 1916:2), and their camps were seen in the early 1800s as far east as the mouth of the Sabine River (Dyer 1917:1), during which time some of the Cocos were said to be residing in Louisiana (Morse 1922). These areas were, in the eighteenth century, the traditional homelands of the ethnically and linguistically distinct Akokisan and Atakapan groups (Aten 1983a).

The historical documents allow only an approximate geographical placement of each of the several Karankawan groups (Figure 1). The Cocos were apparently the northeasternmost group. These people were reported to have their camps primarily around the lower Colorado River in 1768, though some Cocos were present on the lower Brazos along with people of various other native groups (Kress and Hatcher 1931). The mixing of peoples along the lower Brazos suggests that this drainage may have been an ethnic boundary zone between Karankawas and non-Karankawas in the 1760s. In the eighteenth century, the Carancaguases, or Karankawa proper, lived around Matagorda Bay, as evidenced by references to groups of that "nation" under the leadership of the "chief," Frasada Pinta (e.g., Silva to Viceroy, March 10, 1792; Muñoz to Castro, February 8, 1793). Although no precise location is given for the Copanes, it is generally assumed that they resided around Copano Bay and the northern shore of Corpus Christi Bay (Bolton 1915:282). The historian Herbert Bolton placed the Cujanes and Guapites (or Coapites) on either side of Matagorda Bay, "particularly to the west of it," though he did not reveal the basis for his conclusions on group locations (ibid.).

More recently, W. W. Newcomb (1983) has attempted to locate group territories of the colonial era by reference to the early sixteenth-century group names recorded by Alvar Núñez Cabeza de Vaca, survivor of a 1528 Spanish shipwreck on the Texas coast. Newcomb accepts the locations inferred by T. N. Campbell and T. J. Campbell (1981), which in turn are derived from Cabeza de Vaca's general listing of coastal groups and their relative locations along the coast. Newcomb suggests that Cabeza de Vaca made landfall in the area just west of Galveston Bay, where he resided with a group that he called the "Capoques." Newcomb equates this group with the eighteenth-century Cocos. The later Cujanes are equated with Cabeza de Vaca's Deguenes; the Karankawa proper, with his Quevenes; the Coapites, with his Guayacones; and the Copanes, with his Quitoles. In the case of the Capoque-Coco correlation, it is assumed that the two names have sufficient phonetic similarity that the two documented groups were the same. The other

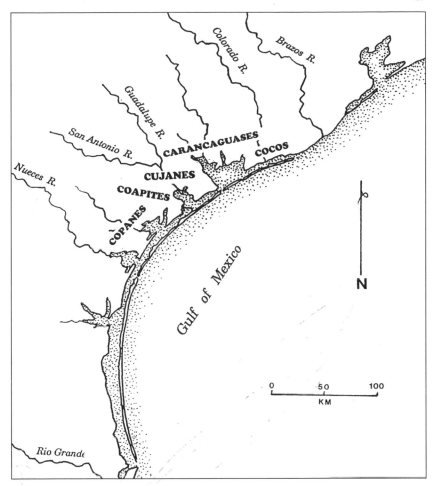

*Figure 1.* Map of the Texas coast showing approximate locations of the five major Karankawan groups.

correlations are made primarily on the basis of geographical correspondences between the Campbells' placement of group territories and the general locations of the eighteenth-century groups. Thus the Karankawa proper are equated with the Quevenes because the latter are believed to have resided around Matagorda Bay (see Campbell and Campbell 1981:11). The Campbells' placements take, as their point of departure, the inference that Cabeza de Vaca's Mariames, a slightly inland group, lived along the lower Guadalupe River, adjacent to the territory of a coastal group or groups.

These arguments seem to be well founded, since they are based on a careful scrutiny of Cabeza de Vaca's descriptions of distances and topographical features. However, much in Newcomb's geographical placements of the various groups is conjectural. The assumption that the Cocos and the Capoques are one and the same is open to question, since it is not known with certainty exactly where on the Texas coast Cabeza de Vaca landed. If it were as far north as the western end of Galveston Island, there is an incongruity with the eighteenth-century placement of the Cocos around the mouth of the Colorado River and the adjacent east end of Matagorda Bay (though this would not necessarily rule out occasional forays outside the more usual territorial boundaries). It should be mentioned, too, that a group called the Quoaquis were said to have lived in the vicinity of Matagorda Bay in the late seventeenth century, and this could be the same group known as the Coacozis and identified by the Mexican historian José Antonio Pichardo in the early nineteenth century as the Cocos (Hackett 1934:147, 176). Similarly, all other correlations between Cabeza de Vaca's group locations and later ones have the inherent problem that placements in both cases are, for the most part, far from precise, and phonetic synonymies of group names are tenuous at best.

Despite these ambiguities, there is an important point that emerges from comparison of Cabeza de Vaca's group names, and their inferred locations, with later eighteenth-century observations. This is the simple fact that observers in both centuries indicated that there were five groups between Matagorda Bay and Corpus Christi Bay. Cabeza de Vaca listed the Deguenes, Quevenes, Guaycones, Quitoles, and Camolas. Campbell and Campbell (1981:11–13) place these groups along the coast with the Quevenes around Matagorda Bay and the Camolas around Corpus Christi Bay. Newcomb (1983:Table 1) reasonably puts the Deguenes around the mouth of the Colorado River, since this group was noted by Cabeza de Vaca as living just up the coast from the Quevenes. The eighteenth-century documents indicate the northernmost Karankawan group, the Cocos, living primarily around the mouth of the Colorado River and as far up the coast as the Brazos River, and the other four group locations extending southward to the Corpus Christi Bay area. This general correlation suggests that there was, at a very basic level, continuity in sociocultural organizational patterns and territories from the early sixteenth through the eighteenth centuries.

In addition to the generalizations made by eighteenth-century and later writers that the five groups were of the same language and culture (*"del mismo nación"*), there is also some limited but re-

*lang*

vealing linguistic evidence. Three short but useful lists of Karanka-wan words have survived. The first, containing thirty-three words (Troike 1987), dates from the late seventeenth century and was recorded during the interrogations of Jean Baptiste and Pierre Talon at Brest, France, in 1698 (Weddle 1987:225–258). The Talon broth-ers were boys living at La Salle's Fort Saint Louis, located on Garcitas Creek near its mouth at Matagorda Bay, when the settle-ment was sacked by the Karankawas in late 1688. Jean Baptiste was captured and adopted by a group he called "Clamcoet" and subse-quently learned the language ("Clamcoet" is probably one of at least three French renditions of "Carancaguase"; T. N. Campbell, pers. comm. 1988). A second list of 106 words was recorded by the French navigator Jean Beranger in 1720 near Aransas Pass, in the vicinity of Corpus Christi Bay (Carroll 1983). The third list, consisting of 263 words, was recorded in 1888 by Albert Gatschet, mostly from Alice Oliver, who as a girl had lived with her family near a Karankawan camp at Matagorda Bay. These lists have been examined by Rudolph Troike (1987), who concludes that, while suggesting differences and possible areal dialects, they all clearly represent the same language.

The Karankawan language was linked by J. R. Swanton (1952: 320) with the neighboring Coahuiltecan linguistic stock of interior southern Texas and northeastern Mexico. However, according to I. Goddard (1979), the available word lists are inadequate to confi-dently determine the larger affiliation of the language. One linguist (Landar 1968) has argued that the Karankawan language is of Caribe stock and that the Karankawas were latecomers to the Texas coast, invading the region in the fifteenth century after migrating from the Antilles. This hypothesis has not received support, however (Goddard 1979; Newcomb 1983:362), and, as is shown further on, there is considerable archaeological evidence showing that Karankawan culture has prehistoric antecedents on the Texas coast.

In addition to language, a Karankawan characteristic that re-peatedly set them apart from neighboring Indian groups was their physical stature. It is clear that the Karankawas were unusually tall for Native Americans; men not infrequently attained statures approaching or reaching six feet and were noted for their strong and robust physiques (e.g., Gatschet 1891:17; Carroll 1983:21; Berlan-dier 1980:381; Barroto 1987:174). The historical observations on this point are corroborated by limited data derived from prehistoric skele-tal samples. Estimates of stature based on human femurs from the *thighbone* Palm Harbor Site (41AS80), a coastal prehistoric cemetery site north of Corpus Christi, indicate a mean group stature of 167 centimeters

(5′5″). At least seven individuals are represented. The tallest is estimated to have had a stature of 183.4 centimeters (6′0″) (Comuzzie
et al. 1986). Because the bones were recovered in disarticulated condition in an emergency salvage excavation, it was impossible to determine with certainty the sex of the various skeletal elements. Presumably, however, the mean figure represents both male and female
individuals, and the greatest figure, a male individual. Estimates
based on other long bones were of comparable sizes. Also noted in
the sample was a marked skeletal robusticity, "best expressed in the
marked development of the sites for muscle attachment, the marked
development of nuchal cresting, the well-defined cranial and facial
features such as browridges and occipital protuberences, and also
the massiveness of the postcranial remains" (ibid.:241).

These features are also found in a series of skeletons excavated in
the 1930s at a large prehistoric cemetery site (41NU2) on Oso Bay,
an extension of Corpus Christi Bay (Comuzzie et al. 1986; Woodbury and Woodbury 1935; see also Neumann 1952). Similar robusticity was in evidence at this site, which is believed to pertain
mainly to the late Archaic Period (Jackson et al. 1987). Further up
the coast, around Galveston Bay, skeletal materials again exhibit
robusticity (Comuzzie et al. 1986:241). Mean statures, however, are
somewhat less than in samples from nearby sites to the south of
Galveston Bay (Powell 1989). This may reflect the difference
between populations: that around Galveston Bay correlating with
Akokisan and/or Atakapan groups; that to the southeast of the bay
with the Karankawas.

With our present knowledge, however, any correlation between
physical stature and ethnic identity is premature at best, considering the small size of available skeletal samples and the vagaries,
already alluded to, of defining ethnic territorial boundaries along
the coast. Moreover, we do not know for certain to what extent the
stature of the Karankawas can be attributed to genetics, a year-
round high protein diet (as will be shown further on), or some combination of the two. Interestingly, Powell (1988) found evidence of
markedly greater stress pathologies, possibly related to dietary
deficiencies, in Late Prehistoric skeletal materials from interior
Texas than in samples from the coastal zone. The possibility that
physical stature resulted in part from dietary factors rather than
strictly from a culturally maintained gene pool must be kept in
mind.

# Chapter 2
# The Karankawan Environment

To the newcomer, the central coast of Texas can be a bewildering maze of islands, lagoons, and salt marshes. Topography is low and flat, and thick marsh and riverine floodplain vegetation often obscures the terrain. During the eighteenth century, the Karankawas found safe sanctuary among the many lagoons and islands, since the Spaniards had only a poor understanding of what was, for them, a confusing coastal geography. The Karankawas had an intimate knowledge of the lay of the land and, importantly, a fine-tuned understanding of the rich mosaic of resources offered by the bays, river valleys, and coastal prairies. How they integrated the use of these resources into their lives, as an adaptive system (*sensu* Butzer 1982) defines the nature of the human ecology of the Karankawas.

The central coast of Texas is marked by five major, nearly contiguous estuarine bays (Figure 2). These are separated from the open Gulf of Mexico by a protective chain of narrow barrier islands that are made up of sands and shells deposited by wave action and longshore drift. A number of narrow tidal passes connect the bay/lagoon estuaries with the Gulf. Immediately inland of the shoreline zone is the coastal prairie, part of the western Gulf coastal plain physiographic province (Fenneman 1938). Topography throughout the region is essentially flat, significantly broken only by eolian dune formations and stream channels. The region's climate is characterized by hot summers and mild winters. Mean annual temperatures from 1931 to 1960 ranged from 70 degrees Fahrenheit at Matagorda Bay to 73 degrees at Baffin Bay (Carr 1967). While winters are not severe, and snowfall and extended hard freezes are rare, the months of December, January, and February generally see between fifteen and twenty rapidly moving polar cold fronts pass through the area (Hayes 1965). During these so-called blue northers, temperatures drop rapidly and often fall below freezing. Frequently, these fronts arrive in fairly rapid succession, so that the winter months are generally characterized by cool or cold temperatures for periods extending up to several weeks. From March through September, a persistent southeasterly wind regime predominates, bringing to the area high temperatures and humidity from the Gulf of Mexico. Once every decade or so, a major tropical storm or hurricane makes landfall somewhere within the region, usually during August or September. In October the winds shift to a generally northeasterly pattern as the first polar cold fronts begin to push into southern Texas.

Average annual precipitation shows a clinal gradient from northeast to southwest along the coast, averaging 40 inches at Matagorda Bay and 28 inches at Baffin Bay (Carr 1967). However, high evaporation rates produce precipitation deficits averaging 0–4 inches at Matagorda Bay and 20–24 inches at Baffin Bay (Orton 1969). Rainfall is generally highest during the late summer and early fall, with secondary and tertiary precipitation peaks occurring in midsummer and late winter, respectively (Shew et al. 1981). Periods of extended drought are documented historically, and these are known to have significant effects on the distributions of terrestrial plant communities (Drawe et al. 1978). Estuarine shellfish populations can also be affected due to increased salinities in bays and lagoons resulting from reduced freshwater stream discharge (see Parker 1959).

The regional resource mosaic can be appreciated by examining the area that is the stage for most of the archaeological investigations discussed further on. Our study area encompasses the coastal and adjacent prairie environment from San Antonio Bay southward to the Corpus Christi Bay area. The nearly flat Gulf coastal plain rises in elevation only very gradually from the coast to the interior. Maximum elevations at the inland margin of the present study area, some 40–50 kilometers from the mainland shoreline, are around 50–60 feet above sea level. The coastal plain consists geologically of sandy clay and clayey sand deposits of the Beaumont and Lissie Formations, which were laid down during Pleistocene interglacials. During these periods, when sea level approximated that of the present, the region was traversed by several large riverine deltaic systems, depositing muds and fine-grained sands (Brown et al. 1976). In profile, the area's geology shows a macrostratigraphic pattern, with older deposits underlying younger ones in a general pattern of west-to-east downdip. From the coast to the interior, progressively older formations are exposed at the surface. At the present coastal margin of the Beaumont Formation, parallel to the modern shoreline, is the Ingleside Strandplain, a geologic unit several kilometers in width.

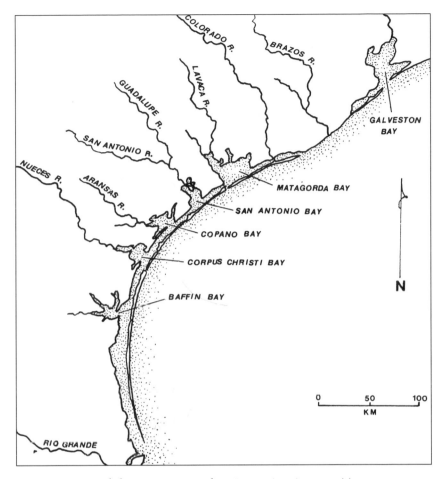

*Figure 2.* Map of the Texas coast showing major rivers and bays.

This deposit represents either a Pleistocene strandplain produced by accretion of wave-reworked sediments along the front of the deltaic sediments (Brown et al. 1976:18) or a relict Pleistocene barrier island chain (Price 1933).

During the last glacial period, sea levels were about 100 meters lower than today because much of the world's water supply was captured by greatly expanded polar ice caps and mountain glaciers. The continental shelf, now under Gulf waters, was dry land, and coastal rivers cut deep channels into the older geologic deposits, creating a series of deep valleys along the coast. At the glacial maximum, some 20,000 years ago, the coastline was as much as 200 kilometers to the east of the present shoreline, and major river systems, portions of whose relict valleys now form embayments along the central coast of Texas, flowed eastward and southward.

As global climate warmed between 18,000 and 9,000 years ago, these valleys were drowned by rising sea level, creating the bays that, in modified form, are seen today along the coast (Brown et al. 1976; Wright 1980). Sea level continued to rise, with periods of still-stand or perhaps minor reversals, until about 3,000 years ago. Wave action and longshore drift deposited the sand and shell that constitute the present barrier islands, which may have approximated their present configuration as little as 2,000 years ago (Brown et al. 1976; McGowen et al. 1976).

Continuing wave action in Corpus Christi and Copano Bays, undercutting Pleistocene valley margins, has resulted in the modern bayshore configurations. Water-transported sediments of varying texture accumulated within the bay/lagoon systems, filling in the deeper Pleistocene valleys, to the extent that the deep river channels of the late Pleistocene have been largely filled in, creating the present shallow bays.

### Estuarine Resources of the Coastal Bays and Lagoons

The fish and shellfish resources of the estuarine bays and lagoons of the Texas central coast provided rich harvests that were important mainstays in the subsistence economy of the Karankawas. To understand how the Karankawas strategically exploited these resources, the patterns of their spatial and seasonal abundance need to be examined.

The Texas coast has historically produced a bountiful supply of shellfish. Oysters have been harvested from all the bays, with the exception of Baffin Bay, where hypersaline waters cannot support viable populations of economically useful shellfish species. The abundance of oysters in the other bays was clearly the case in prehistoric times, since oyster shells are found in profusion at shoreline archaeological sites from Corpus Christi Bay northward (cf. Fritz 1975; Steele 1988). Other species of shellfish were also important but varied in economic significance according to local availabilities. Generally speaking, distributions of mollusks vary according to species salinity requirements. Gastropods such as lightning whelk (*Busycon perversum*), shark eye (*Polinices duplicatus*), and banded tulip (*Fasciolaria lilium*) are found in relatively high-salinity areas near the tidal passes that separate the several barrier islands of the central coast. Bivalves such as oyster (*Crassostrea virginica*), bay scallop (*Argopectin irradians*), quahog (*Mercenaria campechensis*), and cross-barred venus (*Chione cancellata*) inhabit areas of moderate salinity within the bays and lagoons. The low-salinity clam, *Rangia cuneata*, lives in brackish water environments in river-influenced areas of bays and in the lower reaches of streams where tidal influence results in salinities of approximately 2–10 parts per thousand.

Fish species of economic importance in the coastal bays of Texas are black drum (*Pogonias cromis*), redfish (*Sciaenops ocellata*), speckled sea trout (*Cynoscion nebulosus*), Atlantic croaker (*Micropogonius undulatus*), sea catfish (*Aurius felis*), southern flounder (*Paralichthys lethostigma*), sheepshead (*Archosargus probatocephalus*), silver perch (*Bairdiella chrysura*), and mullet (*Mugil cephalus*). Fish bones excavated from archaeological sites indicate that the species most commonly exploited by aboriginal peoples were black drum, redfish, speckled sea trout, sheepshead, Atlantic croaker, and sea catfish. Black drum is the largest of the major economic species. Adult fish commonly are 400 to 500 millimeters in length and weigh several kilograms (cf. Matlock and Weaver 1979; Harrington et al. 1979). Fish up to 60 centimeters in length and weighing 5 to 6 kilograms are not uncommon, and occasional specimens, the so-called bull drum, can reach lengths of over 100 centimeters and weights of over 30 kilograms. Black drum feed upon mollusks and have large grinding molars for crushing protective shell casings. Spawning occurs during the winter through early spring in the shallower parts of bays and lagoons (Simmons and Breuer 1962).

Redfish, sometimes called red drum, are about the same size as black drum, though the largest individuals may not quite reach the weight of black drum. Adults frequently are 30 to 60 centimeters in length and weigh 3 to 5 kilograms. The bottom-feeding redfish do not generally move in schools, but during the spawning season in the late summer and fall, they aggregate in large numbers as they move to spawning areas around tidal passes.

Speckled sea trout spawn in the bays during the warmer months, mainly in April and May, but spawning can continue as late as October (Pearson 1929). This fish is not as large as black drum or redfish; commonly, specimens range in length from 20 to 40 centimeters and weigh 0.2 to 1.0 kilograms (cf. Matlock and Weaver 1979; Harrington et al. 1979). Although found in the Gulf, speckled sea trout are most abundant in protected bays and lagoons, especially in the vicinity of tidal passes (Henley and Rauschuber 1981: 103–104).

Sheepshead is a good-sized fish that reaches adult lengths of about 50 centimeters and weights of approximately 2 kilograms. Occasionally, individuals reach lengths of over 75 centimeters and weights of over 13 kilograms (Hoese and Moore 1977). Like black drum and redfish, sheepshead are bottom feeders. Heavy molars for crushing, similar to those of black drum, are adapted to a diet that includes shellfish. Spawning takes place in bay and lagoon shallows during winter through early spring.

Atlantic croaker is a relatively small fish that may live only four or five years (Lassuy 1983). Adults commonly weigh less than 0.4 kilogram and are 20–40 centimeters in length. Spawning takes place during the fall and winter (Henley and Rauschuber 1981:102). In the Corpus Christi Bay system, croaker is most abundant in areas around tidal passes and along the north shore of the bay.

Sea catfish, another relatively small fish, is a slender species that commonly weighs less than 0.5 kilogram. A carnivorous scavenger, sea catfish spawn during the summer months, at which time they are most abundant in the bays (Compton 1975; Hoese and Moore 1977).

These observations indicate that the most concentrated fish biomass in the central coastal bays should be available during the fall and winter months. It is during this time of year that the largest species, black drum and redfish, are most readily harvested, inferably because they are in concentrated and predictably large quantities corresponding to their respective fall and winter spawning cycles. These inferences for a fall-winter peak in fish biomass are supported by relatively high fall-winter/early spring peaks in monthly commercial catch rates within the study area for black drum, redfish, sheepshead, and speckled sea trout (see representative data in graphic form, Figure 3). Thus, while fish can be taken in the bays year-round, the largest and most economically useful species will be predictably most concentrated in shallow bay waters or around tidal passes during the fall and winter. During this time of the year, the Karankawas could have harvested fish in largest quantities, with least effort and least risk of subsistence failure.

## Plant Communities

Primary productivity in estuaries is high due to the abundance of mineral nutrients derived from riverine discharge and due to optimal conditions for photosynthesis in shallow coastal waters (e.g., Odum 1971; Whittaker 1975). A rich phytoplanktonic life, consisting most abundantly of diatoms, as well as benthic and drift algae and various sea grasses, is supported in this study area because of

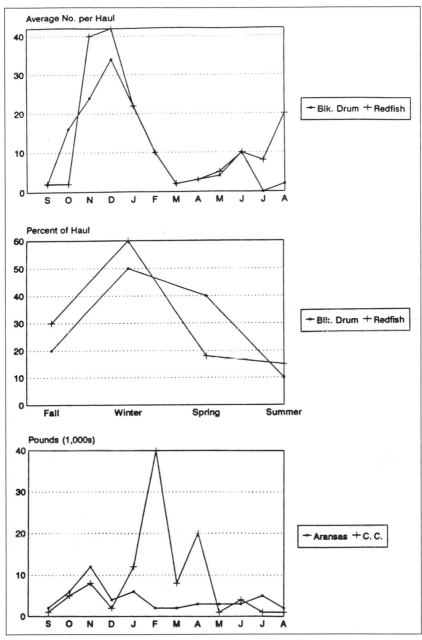

*Figure 3.* Data showing seasonal peaks in commercial catches for two major fish species, black drum and redfish, on the central coast of Texas. Note that, while various measures are used to indicate amount of fish harvested, greatest peaks tend to occur from fall to early spring. Top graph is based on data from Copano Bay (Gunter 1945); middle graph, on data from San Antonio Bay (Heffernan et al. n.d.); bottom graph, on data for black drum and redfish from Aransas and Corpus Christi Bays (Quast et al. 1988).

the shallow bays and lagoons as well as the nutrients transported by the Nueces, Aransas, Mission, and Guadalupe Rivers. Primary productivity is somewhat greater in the San Antonio and Matagorda Bays systems, since these receive higher nutrient influx from rivers with generally higher rates of discharge (Shew et al. 1981). Extensive salt marshes are found around the Nueces River and Aransas Bay and in a narrower, more restricted form along the margins of Copano and Corpus Christi Bays and the lagoonal margins of San Jose, Mustang, and Padre Islands. The most abundant species of salt tolerant grasses are smooth cordgrass (*Spartina alkiniflora*), maritime saltwort (*Baltis maritima*), glasswort (*Salicornia bigelovii*), and salt grass (*Distichlis spicata*).

Terrestrial plant species, whose distributions are determined primarily by factors of soil type and moisture availability, can be grouped into several major associations. Oak mottes are concentrated on the Ingleside sands that fringe the mainland shoreline. Several species are present, though by far the most abundant is the live oak (*Quercus virginiana*), which yields edible acorns annually in the fall. Characteristically associated with the oaks in this area are various short grasses and shrubs (Jones 1983). A variety of salt tolerant plants grow on the barrier islands and in marshy areas along bay and lagoon margins. Common species are spikerush, fimbry, and sea purslane. Extensive stands of salt tolerant cattail, whose roots provide edible starch during the fall and winter (Tull 1983), are found along the lagoonal margins of the barrier islands and in protected and shallow bayshore locations (Jones 1983).

On the river floodplains, upstream of the estuarine salt marshes, is found dense arboreal vegetation. Common trees are hackberry (*Celtis laevigata*), anacua (*Ehretia anacua*), huisache (*Acacia smallii*), elm (*Ulmus crassifolia*), and pecan (*Carya illinoensis*). Tree limbs are frequently draped with vines of mustang grape (*Vitis mustangensis*). Larger trees form a partial canopy, under which is found a shrub understory of smaller live oaks and mesquite (*Prosopis glandulosa*). Various short-to-medium grasses and shade tolerant forbs form the ground cover (Drawe et al. 1978; Jones 1983). Small lakes and ponds, relicts of old stream channels, hold fresh water except during periods of prolonged drought and support floating vegetation such as lotus (*Nelumbo lutea*) and freshwater marsh plants such as bulrushes (*Scirpus* spp.), cattails (*Typha* spp.), and sedges (*Carex* spp.).

On the level uplands between stream channels is the extensive coastal prairie. Prior to historic settlement and related land-use patterns, this was an extensive grassland with some areas of oak savanna. Since the beginning of cattle grazing in the mid-nineteenth century, thornbrush chaparral, primarily mesquite and acacia (spp.), has expanded greatly (Bogusch 1952), though these species were present in more restricted distributions during earlier times (Johnston 1963).

## Terrestrial Fauna  ~animals

The marshes and prairies of the Texas central coastal zone support a diversity of faunal species (see Blair 1950 for a complete list). Reptiles include aquatic and terrestrial turtles, lizards, and snakes; the American alligator inhabits fresh-to-brackish water areas of the rivers and coastal marshes. Amphibians include a variety of frogs and toads. Several species of migratory birds frequent the area seasonally, including a variety of ducks and the Canada goose (*Branta canadensis*) and snow goose (*Chen caerulescens*), most of which feed on seeds and grasses in both aquatic and freshwater marshes. Sandhill and whooping cranes are found in the Copano Bay area from late fall through early spring. Along bay and lagoon margins are brown pelican (*Pelecanus occidentalis*), great blue heron (*Ardea herodias*), and the little blue heron (*Florida caerulea*). A variety of gulls and terns frequent the beaches. Inland from the shoreline, there is a wide variety of birds along the floodplain and upland prairie habitats. Predatory birds include a variety of hawks and owls, feeding on the different species of rats, mice, and gophers found on floodplains and uplands. Scavengers include both the black vulture (*Coragyps atratus*) and the turkey vulture (*Cathartes aura*). The wild turkey (*Meleagris gallopavo intermedia*) inhabits mixed grassland/arboreal vegetation on both floodplains and uplands (Shew et al. 1981).

Smaller mammalian fauna include rodents (mice, rats, and pocket gophers) and lagomorphs (cottontail rabbit and jackrabbit). The javelina, or collared peccary (*Dicotyles tajacu*), has been expanding its range northward during historic times and may not have been abundant in prehistory. Black bear (*Ursus americanus*), wolves (*Canis lupus*), and pumas (*Felis concolor*) are absent from the area today but were present in early historic and presumably late prehistoric times. Carnivores now present include the bobcat (*Lynx rufus*), gray fox (*Urocyon cinereoargenteus*), coyote (*Canis latrans*), raccoon (*Procyon lotor*), and opossum (*Didelphis marsupialis*) (Shew et al. 1981).

By far, the most economically important mammals for the Karankawas were the white-tailed deer (*Odocoileus virginianus*) and buffalo, or bison (*Bison bison*). White-tailed deer are, and presumably were in aboriginal times, abundant on the coastal prairies and marshes, where current population density is roughly one animal per four hectares (extrapolated from data in Schmidly 1983). The presence of this species in any given area would have been fairly predictable for aboriginal hunters, since white-tailed deer are highly territorial and range within radii of 2 kilometers or so (ibid.:297). But since deer do not generally aggregate in large numbers and are highly mobile within their territories, the species should be viewed as a dispersed rather than concentrated resource.

Bison are known to have been present in the area in early historic times, and judging by the frequent references to herds on the coastal prairies, they must have been abundant. It has been suggested that this large grazer was present only on a seasonal basis (e.g., Newcomb 1983), but seventeenth- and eighteenth-century observers saw bison during all seasons of the year (cf. West 1905:207, 216; Folmer 1940:216, 219; Carroll 1983:21). These large herd animals would have been a highly concentrated resource, but, because of their mobility, native hunters may have had to range over some distance to locate herds at any given time.

### Resource Availabilities and Karankawan Subsistence Patterns

The general patterns of spatial and seasonal occurrence of the key economic resources in the Karankawan environment are summarized in Table 1. These patterns are critical for understanding aboriginal Karankawan ecology, assuming that dependable subsistence was achieved and maintained through strategies that yielded an efficient ratio between procurement costs and benefits (e.g., Smith 1981; Winterhalder 1981), along with an acceptably low level of risk of failure to procure food resources.

Subsistence activities involve the least risk when resources are predictable in both time and space, and procurement activities have the greatest likelihood of success in terms of a favorable cost-benefit ratio when, in addition to predictability, resources are spatially concentrated. As indicated by Table 1, estuarine resources, such as fish and shellfish, best meet the key criteria of predictability and concentration. Since shellfish are not seasonally mobile and were probably of only supplemental dietary significance (Parmalee and Klippel 1974; Aten 1983b), and since the biomass of economically significant fish is predictably most concentrated during the fall-winter period, an aboriginal emphasis on fall-winter marine resource exploitation is predictable. Such activities would have taken place

**Table 1.** *Availability Factors of Significant Food Resources in the Karankawan Environment*

| Resource Category | Spatial Occurrence | Temporal Occurrence |
|---|---|---|
| Mollusks | Concentrated (bay/ lagoon margins) | Predictable, year-round |
| Fish | Concentrated (bay shallows, inlet areas) | Predictable, peak in fall-winter |
| Mammals | | |
| Deer | Dispersed (prairies, wooded areas) | Predictable, year-round |
| Bison | Concentrated but mobile (prairies) | Predictable, year-round |
| Plants | | |
| Greens | Variable | Predictable, spring |
| Fruits, seeds | Variable | Predictable, summer |
| Nuts | Concentrated (coastal fringe, wooded floodplains) | Predictable, fall |
| Roots | Variable | Predictable, fall-winter |

in areas where both fish and shellfish distributions overlapped, around the margins of primary bays where either sandy bottoms or shallow and accessible oyster reefs are found. In this study area, such optimal locales are mainly near the tidal passes and along the seaward margins of the bays.

Generally speaking, the major terrestrial resources are, though seasonally predictable, more spatially dispersed. White-tailed deer, usually not found in large concentrations, can feed on different kinds of vegetation by either grazing or browsing (Shew et al 1981: 235–236). Deer would have been fairly evenly distributed and therefore would generally have required a wide-ranging search and procurement strategy on the part of native hunters. Bison tended to be highly concentrated, but since the species is not territorial, it may have been unpredictable in terms of location, thus necessitating a mobile, dispersed, and perhaps prolonged hunting strategy. These large grazers would have predictably been found on the coastal prairies, away from the shoreline and the dense oak mottes of the littoral.

Different kinds of plant resources are available at different seasons.

Acorns and pecans are available in the fall, with acorns concentrated along the shoreline in the mottes on the Ingleside sands and pecans abundant on river floodplains. Nonbrackish floodplains provide various edible "greens," primarily marsh plants such as cattails. During the fall and winter, cattail roots are edible and provide an excellent source of starchy carbohydrate. Various plant foods are available on the upland prairies during spring and summer (e.g., prickly pear cactus pads in spring and fruits, or "tunas," during summer; granjeno and anacua berries during spring and summer; mesquite beans during summer).

Distributions, with the exception of the dense and extensive oak mottes, would have been characterized by a general mosaic of locally concentrated patches on floodplains and uplands, and prolonged exploitation would probably have required shifting utilization of a number of such localized patches. The distributional mosaic was probably fairly fine-grained, and numerous useful patches would have been available within viable distances of human encampments.

Based on the general availabilities of major resource categories, a hypothetical model of the seasonal scheduling of Karankawan resource procurement is presented in Figure 4. According to this model, major human caloric, protein, and fat requirements were met during fall, late winter, or early spring, primarily through fishing, in response to the predictable concentration and abundance of the largest of the common fish species, black drum and redfish. With the exception of fall gathering of nuts and fall-winter harvesting of cattail roots, important plant procurement activities would have focused on the spring-summer peaks of edible plant productivity. Shellfish gathering predictably would have accompanied fishing activities.

By spring the periods of major fish aggregation associated with spawning of the largest species would have passed. At the same time, there was a surge in available plant foods on floodplains and upland prairies. Along with the emergence of fresh plants would have been an increase in the fat content and body weight of the most important mammals, bison and white-tailed deer (see Speth 1985). Thus, a least-effort and least-risk economic strategy would have involved a significant shift of emphasis from estuarine resources to plant gathering and hunting of large terrestrial mammals, and this would have included a shift in camp locations away from shorelines to the riverine and prairie environments of the adjacent interior.

No doubt, there was a social dimension to the seasonal shifts in economic activities. Large social groups would have congregated

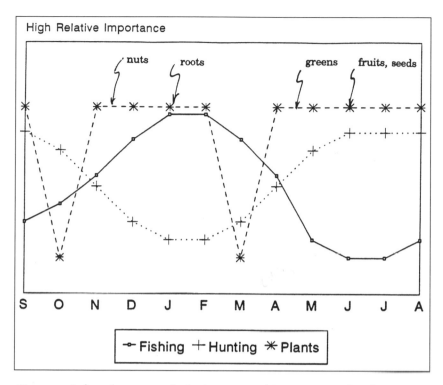

High Relative Importance

nuts  roots  greens  fruits, seeds

S O N D J F M A M J J A

─•─ Fishing  ─+─ Hunting  ✳ Plants

*Figure 4.* Inferred pattern of relative seasonal importance of major Karankawan subsistence activities.

during those times and at those locations where food resources were most predictable and most concentrated (Butzer 1982:240–243; Hassan 1981:180; Jochim 1981:148–163). During such times and in such places, small socioeconomic groupings, or "bands," would have aggregated into large groups of up to several hundred people when key resources were sufficiently abundant and localized to support a relatively large resident population. Such group aggregations as these would, in the long run, have been quite important because they could provide opportunities for establishment of mating networks as well as exchange of important information not available within otherwise semi-isolated small bands of people (Hassan 1981: 180–186; Lee and DeVore 1968; Wobst 1974:170). These times of coming together would also have provided indispensable opportunities for strengthening social and ideological ties beyond those of the small band grouping. In effect, population aggregations would have facilitated organizational integration and information flow at a scale impossible for small bands.

assume to be true

Given that the key resources postulated for spring and summer were more dispersed and/or spatially less predictable than those of the shoreline, a dispersed pattern of human settlement is predictable. Year-round large groupings may not have been feasible, given the reduced concentration of fish resources in the spring and summer and the need for a more spatially dispersed strategy for procuring the important spring-summer terrestrial resources. It can be inferred, therefore, that the overall adaptive strategy of the Karankawas would have been characterized by fall-winter aggregations at optimal bay/lagoon shoreline locales, with spring-summer dispersal into smaller groups that moved into the adjacent interior habitats to gain ready access to resources of the floodplains and upland prairies. Both the archaeological and historical information that follows is in line with this hypothetical reconstruction of the Karankawan lifeway.

# Chapter 3
# The Archaeological Exploration
# of Karankawan Adaptation

To reconstruct Karankawan life and culture prior to the recorded observations of Europeans, our inquiry must turn to the archaeological record. Although archaeological research cannot provide direct insight into many of the less tangible elements of extinct cultures, it does give access to important human-ecological aspects of past lifeways. Patterns of settlement are reflected in the way habitation sites are distributed across the landscape. The kinds of faunal bones, tools, and other refuse found on individual sites are important clues to the economic activities carried out at specific locations. Growth patterns on shells and fish otoliths indicate the season of death, allowing for determination of seasonal patterns of site occupation and resource use. The relative size of prehistoric encampments is reflected in the size of sites, so that, in a very general way, it is possible to determine in which environmental zones the largest groups tended to repeatedly congregate. Studies of animal bone debris show which kinds of faunal resources contributed to supporting groups of various sizes. When the data from various sites are placed in their larger environmental context, it is possible to reconstruct the seasonal movements of the Karankawa population and to determine a good deal about which economic resources were important at which times of the year. With these various lines of information, the basic human-ecological patterns of cultural adaptation—how the Karankawas arranged their lives to make a living within their environment—can be reconstructed.

Archaeological research has been carried out intermittently within the Karankawan area for over sixty years. Early amateur archaeologists made extensive collections of prehistoric stone and ceramic artifacts (Martin 1930, 1931; Potter 1930). In 1935 E. B. Sayles, a professional archaeologist, published *An Archeological Survey of Texas*, in which he described coastal artifact assemblages and made some initial attempts at placing them in chronological order. For the coast, Sayles defined two major periods of "Karankawan" culture. The earlier was a prepottery "Oso Phase," and the later was the "Rockport Phase," characterized by small thin arrowpoints and a native, sandy paste ceramic ware that was often decorated or coated with natural asphaltum.

During the 1930s and 1940s, several major archaeological sites near Corpus Christi were investigated by personnel from the University of Texas. Although the excavators did not publish their findings, summary reports were later prepared and published by T. N. Campbell of the Department of Anthropology at the University of Texas (Campbell 1947, 1952, 1956, 1958a, 1960). Through analyses of the materials from these sites, Campbell was able to substantially add to Sayles' work. The prepottery materials were assigned to an "Aransas Focus" of the Archaic Stage, which was characterized by a variety of stone dart point styles and by a suite of shell tools, mostly manufactured from large conch and whelk shells. The ceramic period was termed the "Rockport Focus" and was again defined on the basis of several arrowpoint types and sandy paste pottery that was decorated or coated with asphaltum. In the twenty-five or so years following Campbell's work, several surveys and excavations in the region added to the database and helped to refine chronology as well as to provide some information on economic patterns. The findings resulting from these efforts are incorporated into the various discussions that follow; suffice it to say at this point that, as of about 1985, cultural chronology in the region consisted of a generalized concept of a long-lived preceramic Archaic period (the Aransas Focus), followed after circa A.D. 1200 by a late prehistoric Rockport Focus, or as here termed, Rockport Phase (see Story 1968; Corbin 1974; Shafer and Bond 1985).

Our main archaeological focus here is the late prehistoric Rockport Phase, although the preceding Archaic period will be examined to some extent, as well. The Rockport Phase directly precedes the historic period, when the Karankawas were documented in Euro-American records, and so the patterns of human culture revealed archaeologically can be assumed to have still been operating at the time of early Euro-American contact. Early Historic European artifacts have been found at several Rockport Phase sites, leaving virtually no doubt that the archaeological materials represent, largely if not entirely, the Karankawas (Suhm et al. 1954; Campbell 1960; Newcomb 1983).

**Rockport Phase Material Culture**

A distinctive material culture assemblage, unique to the central coast region, marks the late prehistoric period. Archaeological sites producing this assemblage can be assigned to the Rockport Phase and thus can be linked to the Karankawas.

Stone tools include several arrowpoint types, small chert unifacial end scrapers, and tiny cylindrical, bifacially flaked chert perforators or drills. The predominant arrowpoint type is the contracting stem Perdiz point (Suhm and Jelks 1962; Corbin 1974; Turner and Hester 1993; Ricklis 1992a; see Figure 5, herein). As a result of the recent research described further on in this study, two other kinds of stone artifacts can be added to the list, namely, bifacially flaked knives and sandstone metates, or milling slabs. The knives are ovate in shape and of variable lengths. On sites where bison hunting was a significant subsistence base, some of the knives are of the alternately beveled form reported for contemporaneous sites in the interior of Texas, where they are associated with varying quantities of bison bone (e.g., Black 1986; Highley 1986; Johnson 1994; Ricklis and Collins 1995). The milling stones, which are not common, were probably used for grinding plant foods.

Shell tools were manufactured from conch and whelk and include adzes that were probably used in woodworking, edge-flaked sunray venus clamshell knives or scrapers, awls or perforators made from the central spires of whelk shells, whelk shells used as hammers, and perforated oyster shells that were probably used as net weights (Campbell 1958b). Ornaments made of shell include tubular and discoidal beads.

Tools and ornaments were also manufactured from bone. Perforators and flint-flaking tools were made from deer ulnas, and perforators, needles, and pins were fashioned from splinters of deer or bison bone. Beads were cut from bird long bone sections and often were highly polished.

The most distinctive artifact category is ceramics. Pottery is often quite abundant on Rockport Phase sites, though very few complete or restored vessels have been recovered. Judging by the curvatures of larger sherds and the few more or less complete vessels, pots were virtually always round-based and took the form of bowls, wide-mouthed jars, and narrow-mouthed ollas. The ollas were globular in form, sometimes with narrow necks, sometimes neckless. The pots were usually made from a sandy paste clay body, microscopically indistinguishable from the abundant sandy clays of the Beaumont

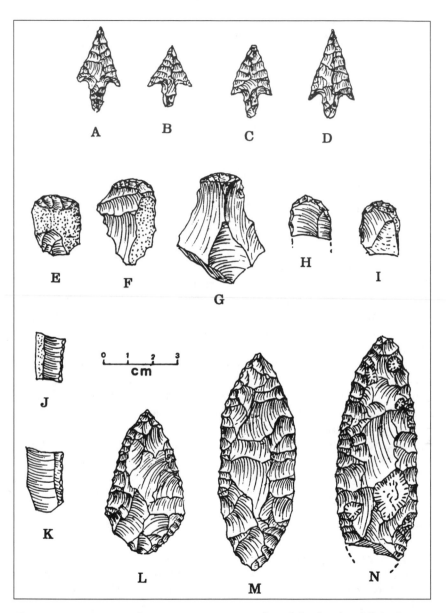

flintlike
form of
quartz

*Figure 5.* Drawings of representative examples of the kinds of flaked
chert artifacts most commonly found on Rockport Phase sites: A–D,
Perdiz arrowpoints; E–I, unifacial end scrapers; J, K, prismatic blade
fragments; L–N, bifacial knives (L and M are alternately beveled).

Formation. Most vessels were probably manufactured directly from raw Beaumont clay, with the naturally occurring fine sand particles acting as a natural tempering agent. Ceramic smoking pipes were also made and may have been quite common. They are of cylindrical shape and sometimes decorated with lines or dots of natural asphaltum. In shape, these pipes are similar to the preceramic tubular stone pipes of the interior and coastal Archaic (cf. Hester 1980; Highley 1980) and are probably a later ceramic counterpart.

Three specific pottery types have been defined within the Rockport ware ceramic series: Rockport Plain, Rockport Black-on-Gray, and Rockport Incised (Suhm and Jelks 1962). All were manufactured using a coiling technique. Construction coils were often obliterated by interior and exterior scoring of still-moist vessel surfaces with ribbed bivalve shells (Calhoun 1961). Rockport Plain is defined simply by the absence of decoration, though some examples of sherds with notched or crenelated rims are illustrated by Suhm and Jelks (1962). Rockport Incised is characterized by the presence of various geometric, sharply incised line motifs, confined to the sublip area of vessel exteriors. Rockport Black-on-Gray includes pottery bearing painted decorations and/or coating of asphaltum, a naturally occurring tar that washes up on beaches from petroleum seepages on the Gulf floor. As defined by Suhm and Jelks (1962), Rockport Black-on-Gray may bear interior and/or exterior asphaltum coating and decorations consisting of painted bands, squiggles, and dots, all or any of which were applied after vessels were fired.

Familiarity with Rockport ceramics gained from examination of samples from numerous sites led me to the conclusion that the original typology could be revised so as to better identify patterned stylistic variability. An analysis of the decorative and morphological attributes of 468 rim fragments, from four shoreline sites, resulted in a modification of the types proposed by Suhm and Jelks (1962). (The data and reasoning upon which my revisions may be found in detail is in Ricklis 1990.) Names of the three existing types— Rockport Plain, Rockport Black-on-Gray, and Rockport Incised—are retained, with some modifications, and one new type, Rockport Crenelated, is added. The Rockport Plain type is kept and includes vessels on which decoration of any kind is absent. Rockport Crenelated is distinguished from Rockport Plain on the basis of its notched rim decoration, to which is often added a painted band of asphaltum on the vessel lip. Rockport Incised, which remains unchanged, is characterized by various geometric incised designs that form a decorated zone just below the rim of the pot (see Figure 6). Rockport Black-on-Gray is divided into two demonstrably

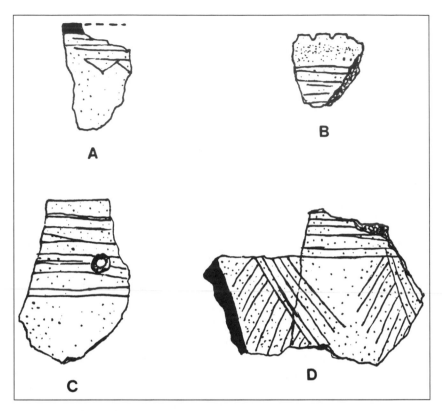

*Figure 6.* Examples of sherds of the Rockport Incised pottery type (all specimens from the Holmes Site [41SP120] on the northeastern shore of Corpus Christi Bay). Note the use of asphaltum paint on A and D.

different varieties. Rockport Black-on-Gray I (Figure 7.A–F) is defined as widemouthed bowls or jars with simple bands of asphaltum painted onto the lips. Rockport Black-on-Gray II (Figure 7.G–K) consists mainly of small-mouthed ollas, either neckless or with constricted, narrow necks, which have narrow lip bands of asphaltum and a series of vertical asphaltum squiggles or wavy lines extending from the lip to the bottom of the vessel. The basal portion of the pot is often coated with asphaltum. Rockport Black-on-Gray I vessel interiors are plain, whereas Rockport Black-on-Gray II interiors are nearly always coated with asphaltum.

Considering the narrow openings and the interior coating on the Rockport Black-on-Gray II, it seems likely that it served as a water jar, with the interior coating functioning to seal the vessel. Because the vertical wavy line motif is restricted to this vessel form, it is

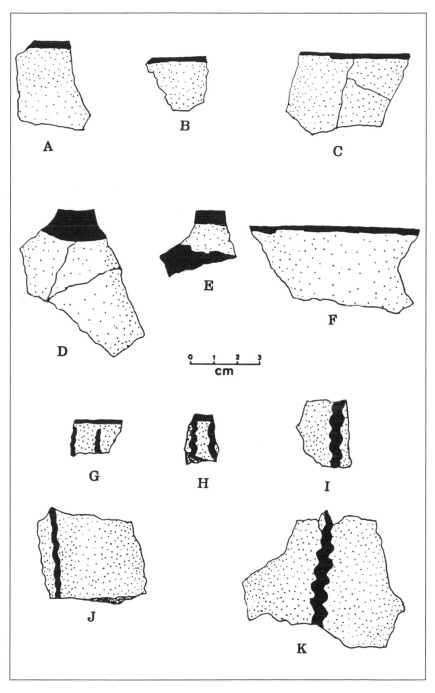

*Figure* 7. Examples of sherds of the Rockport Black-on-Gray I (A–F) and Rockport Black-on-Gray II (G–K) pottery types (A–H are rim fragments).

tempting to infer that this decorative element was associated with flowing water. This is, of course, speculative and will probably remain so. The openmouthed jars and bowls represented by the other types could have served, variously, as cooking, storage, and serving vessels. Judging by rim fragment curvatures, orifice diameters generally range between 15 and 30 centimeters, so that the deeper bowls or jars would have had capacities of up to 4 to 6 liters.

It is interesting, and probably significant for inferring functions of pots of different types, that the narrow-mouthed Rockport Black-on-Gray II variety rarely has added temper; the sole tempering agent was the fine sand natural to the Beaumont clay deposits. On the other hand, the other types, all of which are characteristically of widemouthed vessel forms, often contain intentionally added tempering agents, usually crushed bone. It can be inferred that these tempered vessels were used in cooking, with the added tempers acting to mitigate the effects of thermal shock from repeated heating and thus to prolong vessel use-life. Data on the mitigating effects of crushed bone are not available, but it is known that crushed calcite and crushed shell have a coefficient of expansion and contraction very similar to that of clay (Rice 1987:229). According to Rice, "The optimal solution in the manufacture of vessels intended for use with heat would be to have inclusions (temper) with coefficients similar to or less than that of the clay" (ibid.). Quartz sand, by contrast, has a much higher coefficient than does clay, so that untempered, sandy paste vessels such as Rockport Black-on-Gray II would tend to fare poorly if used in cooking. As Rice (1987:230) points out, ethnographic data does not always conform to these kinds of expectations. Nonetheless, when the attributes of vessel shape, presence/absence of added temper, and presence/absence of interior coating are considered in combination, such basic functional-typological correlations can at least be suggested for Rockport pottery.

Despite some variation in type percentages between sites, it is clear that we are dealing with recurrent, definable types in what was a fairly consistent ceramic tradition operating within definite spatial boundaries. The most common stylistic theme—asphaltum painting—is common within the confines of the Texas central coast area, yet rare in immediately adjoining areas. Neither of the Rockport Black-on-Gray types occur on the upper coast except rarely (e.g., Aten 1983a; Gadus and Howard 1990; Hole and Wilkinson 1973; Ricklis 1994; Fritz 1975), while analyses from the Matagorda Bay area indicate a marked geographical shift from Rockport Black-on-Gray to plain upper coast pottery in the eastern Matagorda Bay–Colorado River delta area. To the south, extensive surveys and

testing in Hidalgo and Willacy Counties have not produced specimens of these types (Mallouf et al. 1977; Day et al. 1981). In the very
extensive A. E. Anderson collection from the Rio Grande delta area,
housed at the Texas Archeological Research Laboratory, Rockport
ware is represented by only a single sherd of Rockport Black-on-
Gray II. Inland, to the west, only one or two sherds of Rockport
Black-on-Gray are reported from the Berclair Site (41GD4) (Hester
and Parker 1970), a component of the Toyah Phase or Horizon, a
late prehistoric archaeological complex contemporaneous with the
Rockport Phase but confined to the interior of South and Central
Texas (Hester 1980; Prewitt 1981; Johnson 1994; Highley 1986).
Similarly, at the Toyah Horizon Hinojosa Site (41JW8) in Jim Wells
County (Black 1986), Rockport ware is absent in a sample of nearly
800 sherds. Several vessel body sherds from this site do have asphaltum banding decoration. However, I have examined these, and they
do not bear typical Rockport motifs, since straight banding in
Rockport ware is confined to vessel lips, while vessel bodies exhibit
either overall coating or vertical painted squiggles. Thus, while
asphaltum was occasionally used for decorative purposes by Toyah
potters operating just inland from the coastal zone, designs did not
conform to the characteristic Rockport stylistic elements.

In sum, the Rockport Phase artifact assemblage, as a whole, is
readily distinguishable from contemporaneous assemblages in adjoining areas on the basis of a distinctive ceramic tradition. In other
categories of archaeological material culture, however, clear geographic distinctions fade. The stone artifacts are, for the most part,
similar in form and typology to materials from adjacent areas
(Ricklis 1992a), except to the south where a largely different set of
arrowpoint types predominates (see Mallouf et al. 1977; Turner and
Hester 1993). The common use of shells for tools, primarily conch
and sunray venus, was characteristic of the central coast since earlier Archaic times, and the common shell tool forms are not found
in any abundance on the upper Texas coast. This may, however, be
due simply to a lack of raw material, since the preferred species for
tool production require higher salinities than are generally present
in upper coast estuaries, where feeder streams have much higher
rates of freshwater discharge than those of the central coast (see discussion in Steele 1988). The bone assemblage has little if anything
to distinguish it from other areas; indeed, the simple awls and bird
bone beads that occur on Rockport sites have counterparts throughout aboriginal North America.

It is the distinctive ceramics, therefore, that stand as a regional
stylistic expression and that are the primary basis for defining the

Rockport Phase as a geographically discrete cultural phenomenon. That Rockport pottery was a stylistic marker of group identity and operational areas, and is therefore a suitable archaeological criterion for demarcating the limits of a distinct human ecosystem, is indicated by the correspondence of its distribution with sociocultural boundaries as evidenced in the ethnohistoric record (see discussion in Appendix A).

## Seasonality Indicators

While the geographical limits of the Rockport Phase can be defined according to the distributions of archaeological sites producing Rockport pottery, the seasonal use of different environmental zones is revealed through analyses of the remains of certain kinds of mollusks and fish. Three kinds of materials that are highly useful for seasonality studies on the central coast are marine fish otoliths, *Rangia cuneata* clamshells, and oyster (*Crassostrea virginica*) shells. Marine fish and oysters are readily available along bay and lagoon shorelines, while *Rangia cuneata* live in rivers sufficiently far inland that they were available to coastal people operating on the margins of the coastal prairie–savanna environment. Thus, with occasional exceptions, the seasonality of resource use and site occupation in all Karankawan habitats can be determined, permitting examination of annual patterns of population mobility.

All three methods involve observations of cyclical, annual growth patterns and estimation of season of death of the organism on the basis of the amount of new growth past an identifiable point of growth interruption associated with cold water temperatures during the winter. In the case of otoliths, which are small concretions of protein and calcium carbonate found in pairs in fish skulls, the annual growth cycles are visible in the cross-sectional profiles of the specimens under a 20X binocular microscope. The growth patterns on oyster shells are observable macroscopically and are interpreted according to methods initially used on archaeological shells from the eastern U.S. seaboard (Kent 1988; Lawrence 1988). Rangia clamshells are also placed in estimated seasonal categories by macroscopic observation, according to methods developed on the upper Texas coast by Lawrence Aten (1981). Each of the three methods is presented in more detail in Appendix B.

# Chapter 4
# Archaeological Evidence for Prehistoric Occupation of Shoreline Fishing Camps

Archaeological sites represent points on the landscape where focused human activity took place in the past, leaving behind recoverable traces in the forms of broken, discarded, and lost tools, food residues such as fragments of animal bone, and various kinds of features such as hearths, pits, and refuse piles. In cases of nonagricultural societies, occupation sites show characteristic residues according to on-site subsistence activities that were directly related to the kinds of resources available at, or within a viable distance from, any given locale.

Rockport Phase sites can be generally separated into two groups according to several key criteria: the size of the site, the density and thickness of cultural debris, and the kinds of predominant faunal remains present (Ricklis 1988:49–62, 1992b). One set of sites, termed here Group 1 sites for the sake of convenience and clarity, is restricted to the shoreline environment, while the other, Group 2 sites, is found mainly on upland margins of the inland prairies overlooking stream floodplains (Figure 8). The Group 1 shoreline sites are extensive, have thick midden deposits, and yield large quantities of estuarine fish and shellfish remains. In contrast, Group 2 sites along prairie margins, overlooking stream floodplains, are much smaller, contain only thin archaeological deposits with sparse cultural debris, and yield little in the way of estuarine fauna but, proportionately, a significant quantity of bones of large terrestrial game, mainly white-tailed deer and bison. Our examination of the archaeological record begins with recent findings at several Group 1 sites, where Karankawan subsistence activities centered around a seasonal exploitation of the rich fish resources of the coastal bays and lagoons.

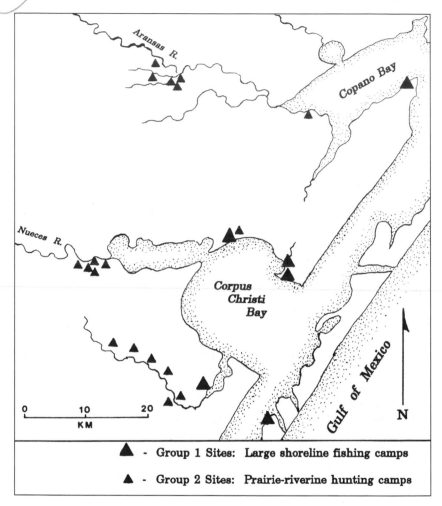

*Figure 8.* Map of the Corpus Christi Bay and Copano Bay area, showing locations of known large shoreline fishing camps (Group 1 sites) and smaller prairie-riverine camps (Group 2 sites).

## The Holmes Site (41SP120)

This important site lies on the edge of a bluff overlooking the shallow, quiet waters of Ingleside Cove, an extension of Corpus Christi Bay. At its southern margin, the cove is bounded by a spitlike formation that extends westward into Corpus Christi Bay and generally affords protection from relatively high-energy wave action. The cove's shallow, quiet waters and sandy bottom provide an ideal habitat for shellfish, as well as excellent conditions for fish feeding and nursery grounds. The wealth of estuarine resources surely accounts for intensive occupation of the cove shoreline, which is evidenced by thick stratified midden deposits.

In fact, the Holmes Site is only a small part of an extensive zone of prehistoric occupation that extends some 2 kilometers along the cove. Examination of the bluff indicates that the archaeological deposits along the cove have been partially eroded by wave action associated with major storm surges, and numerous prehistoric artifacts can be found in the shallow waters at the base of the bluff.

Excavations at this site yielded over 4,000 prehistoric artifacts, many thousands of fragments of vertebrate bone (mostly fish), and nearly 20,000 marine shells. The excavations were carried out in two areas, using exclusively small hand tools. All excavated soil was screened through 1/4- and/or 1/8-inch mesh hardware cloth, and soil matrix samples were water screened through 1/16-inch mesh in the laboratory. The first excavation area, the South Block (Figure 9, top), consisted of twelve contiguous 1-meter-square units, all of which were excavated in 10-centimeter arbitrary levels through stratified cultural deposits down to the surface of the Pleistocene sandy clay. The second area, the North Trench (Figure 9, bottom), excavated using the same procedure, was a 1 × 4-meter trench located some distance north of the first area. During excavation, all potentially species-diagnostic vertebrate faunal bones were saved for analysis. Shells were counted by excavation unit and level so that mollusk species could be accurately quantified in terms of their representation in the total faunal sample.

The upper 5 or so centimeters consisted of a loose sand containing humus debris and grass rootlets. Below the thin humus zone, the sandy soil was rather compact and laden with a profusion of small shell and fish bone fragments, as well as numerous Rockport Phase artifacts. The top 25 to 50 centimeters of the deposits yielded an abundance of cultural debris including ceramic, lithic, bone, and shell artifacts as well as faunal material.

At between 25 and 50 centimeters, depending on horizontal location, a discrete stratum of densely packed shell was encountered (see Figure 9). The contents of this shell-rich stratum proved to represent a late pre-Rockport occupation of the late-to-terminal Archaic (preceramic) period. The Archaic component was stratigraphically quite distinct from the overlying Rockport Phase deposit.

*Figure 9.* Two views of excavations at the Holmes Site (41SP120). Top photograph shows part of the South Block, with a late Archaic shell stratum exposed in the excavation wall. Bottom photograph shows the North Trench, with exposure of massive late Archaic shell deposit.

Immediately beneath the stratum of dense shell, additional cultural material was found within a dark brown sand matrix. At about 60 to 80 centimeters, the sand matrix graded to a lighter brown color, and the quantity of cultural debris dropped markedly. At between 100 and 150 centimeters, light tan Pleistocene clay, devoid of cultural material, was reached. Excavation by 10-centimeter levels was resumed below the dense shell stratum down to the basal clay, since, as in the upper 30 to 50 centimeters, there were no marked stratigraphic breaks in the deposits.

## Artifacts

The excavations at the Holmes Site produced an unusually large array of artifacts that reflects an intensive use of the locale over a long period of time. Stone artifacts of the Rockport Phase include 33 arrowpoints, mostly of the narrow-stemmed Perdiz type (see Figure 5), oblong flint knives, small flint scrapers, and small pinlike flint drills or perforators. Shell artifacts are abundantly represented and consist of forms previously noted for the central coast region (cf. Campbell 1947, 1952; Story 1968; Steele and Mokry 1985). The most numerous is the edge-flaked sunray venus clamshell knife, of which a total of 37 whole and fragmentary specimens was recovered (see illustrated examples from 41SP43 in Figure 15). Two whelk (*Busycon perversum*) adzes were recovered from the late Archaic shell stratum (Figure 10). Four roughed-out blanks for these tools were found in the shell stratum, and 1 was recovered from the 10–20 centimeter level in the Rockport Phase deposit (Figure 11.A). These represent adzes that were not finished, apparently because of breakage during the manufacturing process. Four lightning whelk hammers were found: 3 in the shell stratum and 1 just below that stratum (see examples from Site 41SP43, illustrated in Figure 16). Fourteen small whelk columellae (the central spire of the shell), pointed at both ends (see Figure 11.B), were found. These have been interpreted as awls or perforators by previous investigators (e.g., Campbell 1947; Steele and Mokry 1985). Four specimens were recovered from the Rockport Phase deposit, 1 from the late Archaic shell stratum, and 9 from the lower levels. A single triangular projectile point flaked from sunray venus shell (Figure 11.C), probably an arrowpoint, judging from its light weight, was found near the bottom of the Rockport Phase deposit. This tool form is uncommon north of Corpus Christi Bay but is fairly common to the south at sites along the shores of Oso Bay and Oso Creek (e.g., Steele and Mokry 1985; Headrick 1993).

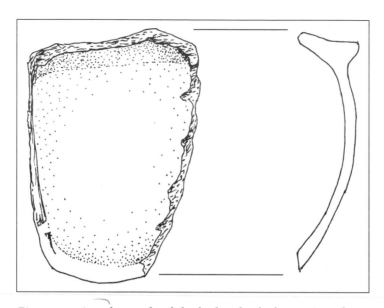

*kind of axe*

*Figure 10.* An adze made of the body whorl of a portion of
a large lightning whelk shell. From the late Archaic shell
stratum in the South Block, the Holmes Site (41SP120).

Two small discoidal beads (Figure 11.D) of whelk shell were recovered from the upper 20 centimeters. A whelk disk, perhaps a bead blank, and a cylindrical bead blank of *Busycon* columella were also found in these levels. These ornamental forms have been previously documented on the Texas coast (e.g., Janota 1980; Dreiss 1994).

The excavation produced a variety of bone artifacts (Figure 12), including deer long bone awls or perforators, modified deer ulnas, generally thought to have served as chert flaking tools (e.g., Hester 1980:121), beads cut from sections of bird long bone, fragments of grooved deer long bone (possibly by-products of the manufacture of large beads), an engraved hair(?)pin fragment, two polished deer long bone fragments of unknown function, antler tine flaking tools, and a bone projectile point. Also found was a fragment of fossil, bison-sized long bone, the end of which had been rounded by grinding. The engraved pin, from the late Archaic shell stratum, has similar counterparts from other sites in the region (Campbell 1952) and further inland on the Texas coastal plain (Hall 1989).

Asphaltum, a natural black tar that washes up on Gulf coast beaches, was a multipurpose material in aboriginal technology. During the Archaic Period, it was used to coat baskets (Campbell

1952; Cox and Smith 1988) and as a hafting mastic. During the late prehistoric, it served as a decorative paint and as a coating for ceramic vessels, as well as a hafting mastic for arrowpoints (two of the arrowpoints recovered show traces of asphaltum adhering to the basal, hafted portions). Small nodules of asphaltum, between 1 and 4 centimeters in diameter, were found in both the Rockport Phase and late Archaic deposits. These are round and smooth and appear to be the cooled, solidified state of droplets of molten asphaltum. Several fragments of basketry-impressed asphaltum were found in the densest excavated part of the late Archaic shell stratum. All appear to be fragments of a thick (1–1.5 centimeters) asphaltum

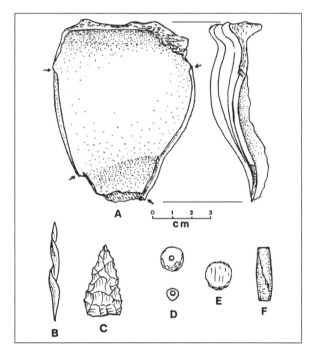

*Figure 11.* Various shell artifacts from the South Block, the Holmes Site (41SP120): A, blank for whelk shell adze (arrows delimit cut edges); B, bipointed columella or central spire of a small lightning whelk shell; C, arrowpoint flaked from sunray venus clamshell; D, discoidal beads of whelk shell; E, probable whelk shell bead blank; F, blank for cylindrical bead made of columella of lightning whelk.

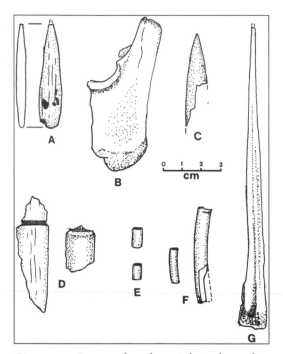

*Figure 12.* Bone and antler artifacts from the South Block, the Holmes Site: A, projectile point with asphaltum hafting mastic adhering to the base; B, deer ulna chert-flaking tool; C, antler projectile point; D, two fragments of grooved mammal (probably deer) bone; E, F, bird bone beads; G, awl made from a deer metapodial bone.

coating that had been applied to the outside of a basket made by twining twisted grass fibers.

The only metal artifact recovered (except for several obviously recent Anglo-American items mostly from the top 10 centimeters of the excavation) is a small (1.3 × 1.4 centimeters) rectangular fragment of crudely cut sheet copper from the 20–30-centimeter level. One edge is folded over. This specimen may be cut from a Colonial Period copper kettle, an item that was widely distributed among native groups throughout North America by French and British traders. If such is the case here, it represents the only trace of historic European-Indian contact material known from the site.

Ceramic artifacts consist of over 2,400 pottery fragments (see Figure 13), 18 fragments of smoking pipes, and a single ground potsherd disk. All of the pipe fragments were found in the Rockport Phase deposit. Most bear exterior asphaltum decoration in the form of bands or dots, as well as a dark brown, burned carbonaceous residue on their interior surfaces. A single specimen, consisting of 2 reassembled fragments, is plain but highly burnished on the exterior and contains moderately profuse crushed bone tempering.

The pottery has been studied in some detail because it is a marker of the spatial extent of the area used by coastal people and because it sheds light on the question of cultural continuity in the region. Analysis focused on those ceramic attributes that can be most readily used to distinguish Rockport ware from other contemporaneous ceramic traditions or to define internal stylistic and/or technological evolution within the central coast ceramic tradition. The ceramics are thus viewed in terms of attributes that are either spatially or temporally diagnostic.

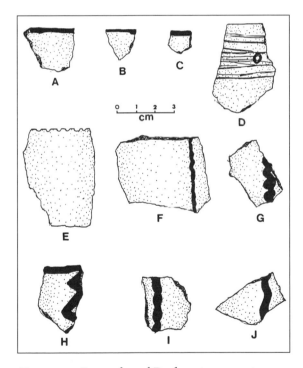

*Figure 13.* Examples of Rockport ware potsherds from the Holmes Site: A–C, Rockport Black-on-Gray I; D, Rockport Incised; E, Rockport Crenelated; F–J, Rockport Black-on-Gray II (A–E are rim fragments).

The results of these analyses are presented in detail in Appendix A. Summarized very briefly, they show that samples of Rockport Phase pottery fragments can be readily distinguished from those from sites representing interior (non-Karankawa) peoples. The separation is possible on the basis of significant differences in key attributes of the two different ceramic traditions. Late prehistoric pottery of the interior is usually undecorated, and the clay is tempered with considerable amounts of burned and crushed bone. In Rockport pottery, the clay more often than not had no intentionally added tempering agent; the naturally occurring fine sands in the Beaumont Formation clays were the sole tempering agent in the majority of pots. Also, the prolific use of painted asphaltum decorations and surface coating readily distinguishes samples of Rockport pottery from those at interior sites. The inland extent of Rockport pottery helps determine the inland territorial range of the pre-Colonial Karankawas, a key factor in defining patterns of settlement and resource use.

## Dating the Cultural Deposits at the Holmes Site

The ages of the stratified cultural deposits at the Holmes Site are determined on the basis of radiocarbon dates and the depths of various time-diagnostic artifact types. The richness of the stratified cultural deposits, combined with a rather large number of radiocarbon dates from different levels in the site, makes possible a reconstruction of several thousand years of cultural and ecological change at the site.

The earliest date at the site comes from a stratum of shell and other occupational debris at a depth of about 110 centimeters below the surface in the northern of our two excavation blocks. A "raw" radiocarbon age of 3560 ± 80 years B.P. (before present) was obtained on quahog shells by the University of Texas Radiocarbon Laboratory. This must be corrected for the ratio between two carbon isotopes, 13-C and 14-C, in order to arrive at an accurate age. This yields age of 3970 ± 80 years B.P. Further adjustment is required by calibrating the 13-C/14-C corrected age according to the dendrochronological (tree ring) time scale, which accounts for the variable atmospheric production of 14-C through time. This procedure produces a final age on the quahog shell sample of 4484 B.P. Factoring in the margin of error inherent in the radiocarbon assay, an age range of between 4553 and 4333 B.P. is obtained. The statistical probability is that the human occupation that produced this shell deposit took place within this time span.

This is a relatively early date and places the oldest known use of estuarine resources (shellfish) at the site at the late end of what is generally considered the early Archaic Period in Texas prehistory (see Prewitt 1981, 1985). Shell and other debris, as well as artifacts, are not abundant at this level, suggesting that the site was only occasionally used at this time, probably by relatively small groups of people.

Still, this was not the earliest occupation at the site. Beneath the dated shell stratum in the North Trench was evidence of a still earlier occupation in the form of a few worked chert tools and flakes and a scatter of deer bones. While no datable organic materials were present, the stratigraphic position and depth of these materials places them earlier than about 4,500 years ago. Interestingly, there is no definite evidence for estuarine resource use in this earlier period, perhaps because sea level was still low enough that the area was not yet inundated by postglacial-period sea level rise. Ingleside Cove would not yet have existed, and the site environs were still dry land. The economy of the people using the site at this early time most likely revolved largely around the hunting of deer and gathering of plant foods.

The next oldest radiocarbon-dated shell stratum is in the South Block (see Figure 9, top). After correction and calibration of a raw radiocarbon assay, the sample has an age range of 3157–2948 B.P. Shell species exploited at this time consist mainly of quahog clam, oyster, and lightning whelk. Fish remains are still not abundant, and artifacts and other debris are sparse, indicating that the site was not yet intensively occupied.

Use of the site intensified markedly by around 1,500 years ago, and this appears to have been related to a great increase in economic reliance on fishing. A series of nine radiocarbon dates on shell and wood charcoal, from several closely superimposed occupational strata, yield corrected and calibrated age ranges that fall between 1338 and 730 B.P. During this period, the exploitation of estuarine food resources became a relatively intensive economic focus at the site, as indicated by profusions of fish bones and thick and dense deposits of shell debris. A corresponding increase in the intensity of occupation compared to earlier times appears to be indicated by a much greater abundance of artifacts in the deposits.

The time-diagnostic artifacts during this period are assignable to the late Archaic Period. The bow and arrow had not yet been introduced, as shown by the fact that the heavier dart points, used on darts propelled by the atlatl, or spear thrower, are the only kind of projectile point found. Pottery is present by the end of the period but is uncommon. The bow and arrow seems to have appeared after about A.D. 1000–1100. Small, thin triangular points were found just above the terminal Archaic levels that date to circa A.D. 1000. In the North Trench, shells from a distinct debris stratum produced a corrected and calibrated age range of 928–738 years B.P., or A.D. 1022–1212. Associated with the stratum were several of the triangular arrowpoints. Pottery was present and appears to have been becoming increasingly abundant. Fishing and shellfish gathering continued as the economic mainstay.

The Rockport Phase, as defined by abundant pottery decorated or coated with asphaltum and later arrowpoint types, begins by around A.D. 1250–1300, judging by the predominance of the Perdiz arrowpoint, a type that appears over much of Texas at this time (e.g., Prewitt 1981; Mallouf 1987; Ricklis 1992a; Turner and Hester 1993; Johnson 1994). The upper level at the Holmes Site has yielded many Perdiz arrowpoints and thousands of fragments of Rockport pottery, along with profusions of fish remains. For reasons not yet well understood, shellfish gathering seems to have declined in importance at this time, though it was still being carried out in a relatively limited way.

The findings at the Holmes Site show important continuities in material culture, strongly suggesting that the Rockport Phase emerged from in situ cultural antecedents. The late Archaic deposits contained evidence for the use of asphaltum in coating baskets, in the form of thin fragments of hardened asphaltum bearing clear basketry imprints. The use of asphaltum for coating containers apparently shifted to pottery vessels in the Rockport Phase, when these doubtless became the most common kind of container. Key shell tool types—conch adzes, conch columella perforators, whelk hammers, and edge-flaked clamshells—are present in the Rockport Phase deposits and have abundant counterparts in the underlying late Archaic strata. Pottery, while not abundant until Rockport times, was present in small amounts in lower levels, and some indication exists for a local evolution in pottery technologies and styles beginning perhaps as early as A.D. 500 (see Appendix A).

Finally, as we shall see, the kinds of resources used in Rockport Phase times, and the seasonal patterns of exploitation, have direct antecedents in the late Archaic. All of this points to fundamental continuities in culture from the Archaic into the late prehistoric Rockport Phase, strongly suggesting that the Karankawas of early historic times had a regional ancestry of considerable time depth.

## Prehistoric Economy and Ecology

Judging by the abundance of shellfish and fish remains encountered throughout the late Archaic and Rockport Phase deposits at the Holmes Site, estuarine fauna clearly were of high economic importance. In order to determine with some degree of accuracy the relative significance of the various fauna, the contribution to the total meat diet of each faunal category must be quantified. The relative significance of faunal categories such as fish, shellfish, and mammals, and the relative importance of individual species within those categories, can be quantified on the basis of the minimum number of individuals (MNI) represented by bones from the excavated deposits and the meat weight of the total MNI, based on an estimation of the live meat weight of an average individual of a given species.

The MNI of any given species is here estimated on the basis of different criteria for different species. The numbers of bony fish represented can be readily estimated by dividing the numbers of otoliths of a particular species in half, since each fish has two otoliths. While this method cannot account for nonbony species such as rays and sharks, they were apparently not particularly important, given that only a few small shark teeth and stingray spines were found in the excavation. In the case of alligator gar, otoliths are not present, so a sporadic occurrence of gar scales is taken to represent a MNI of one.

An alternative method of estimating the relative significance of meat weight by species is based on estimations of biomass in relation to bone weight, according to known allometric formulas (Reitz et al. 1987). However, this method may be inaccurate when meat weights are retrodicted from incomplete skeletons (Jackson 1990; Russo 1991). The generally high degree of fragmentation of fish bone at the Holmes Site (and other fishing camps discussed here) makes assessment of bone weight for individual fish difficult. Furthermore, there is a significant, possibly culturally relevant, underrepresentation of postcranial fish bone elements at the site, which may reflect meat-processing techniques employed by the occupants. Thus cranial elements best reflect the total number of fish represented in the faunal bone sample. Since most cranial elements are, again, highly fragmented, the most useful indicator of numbers of individuals according to species is otoliths.

One exception to the use of otoliths as indicators of species MNI is in the case of sheepshead. Sheepshead otoliths were not recovered during our excavations, which is incongruent with the fairly large representation of sheepshead mandibles in the bone sample. The lack of otoliths of this species is not due to an absence of fish head representation in the sample, as is clear from the presence of the mandibles. Rather, it is inferable that sheepshead otoliths, which are very thin, are so highly fragmented as to be unidentifiable as such. Since sheepshead mandibles approximate the morphology, thickness, and durability of black drum mandibles, the MNI is estimated by comparing the number of fragments to black drum mandible fragments and then to the number of black drum otoliths as representative of drum MNI. This system provides only a very rough estimate of MNI for sheepshead, since it is based on the assumptions that the preservation of sheepshead mandibles is the same as black drum and that drum mandibles and otoliths both represent the same MNI (a proposition impossible to test with accuracy, considering the fragmentary condition of almost all mandibles). This approach can provide only a very gross approximation of reality, but it at least gives some idea of the proportional significance of sheepshead in terms of MNI.

For shellfish, MNI is derived by halving the number of whole valves or umbo fragments for a bivalve species and by an unadjusted count of whole shells and more or less complete columella sections in the case of whelk and other gastropods. Species represented by only 1 or a few shells are not included, since their meat weight representation among the thousands of shells recovered is negligible. Blue and rock crab claw fragments were present, but only a handful were found, indicating that crabs contributed little to the diet; crabs are therefore not included in the quantification of dietary patterns. Similarly, a few vertebrae of mullet fish were found, but again, this species was clearly of very minor significance and so is not included in the overall analyses. Mammal and bird MNI are calculated according to the commonly followed procedure of counting the most abundant skeletal element of a given species (e.g., White 1953; Klein and Cruz-Uribe 1984:26–29). For example, if 3 white-tailed deer right distal humeri were the most numerous single element of that species, the MNI of deer would be 3. Additionally, for skeletal elements with epiphyses, the state of fusion (fused or unfused) is considered. Thus 3 right distal deer humeri with fused (adult) epiphyses and 1 left distal deer humerus with unfused (juvenile) epiphysis would be considered as representing a MNI of 4.

It should be stressed that there are inherent problems in estimating actual species usage on the basis of MNI counts, as discussed by various authors (e.g., Grayson 1979; Binford 1980; Butzer 1982: 191–198; Klein and Cruz-Uribe 1984). The assumption that MNI reflects actual prehistoric dietary patterns may be questioned on the basis of (1) selective transport/deposition of different anatomical parts of species by prehistoric site occupants; (2) postdepositional disturbance of site deposits (e.g., removal of certain anatomical parts by scavengers); (3) bias due to inadequate sampling of archaeological deposits; or (4) the fact that MNI represents only the minimum number of individuals necessary to account for all identifiable bone and may in fact underrepresent a given taxon relative to all other taxa.

In the present case, postdepositional disturbance probably is not of great significance, as there is almost no indication of scavenging in the form of carnivore gnaw marks on bones. Sampling bias is probably of least significance as regards profuse fish and shellfish remains. Every 2 bivalve shells or umbos and each gastropod shell or columella can be taken to accurately represent one individual, as can every 2 otoliths in the case of fish. Thus problems of underrepresentation are minimal in these cases. Sampling bias is more likely to be of significance in the case of the less abundant mammalian and bird remains. However, the fact that bones of the most abundant (and, presumably, by far the most significant) of these taxa, white-tailed deer, are scattered throughout deposits along the bluff (at 41SP120 and in the various excavations at 41SP43, discussed further on) suggests that there is not a high degree of spatial clustering that would greatly bias their representation in a given excavation area.

It should be noted, however, that this is not so with bison remains. Contrary to the case of a small animal, a MNI of 1 bison can contribute significantly to the total meat weight estimate derived from an excavated bone sample. Very few bison bone fragments were found in the Holmes Site excavation, but none were found at the nearby Ingleside Cove Site (discussed further on). Bison remains, therefore, may not approximate an even distribution, and the presence of a few bones from a single individual in the excavation at the Holmes Site, counted as a MNI of 1, is probably a significant overrepresentation of bison significance in terms of meat weight, relative to all other species. In other words, if the bones of a single bison were scattered over, say, a 100-meter-square area, the proportional representation in that area of other, more evenly distributed taxa would be greater by many orders of magnitude. Since the densest part of the Rockport Phase midden area in which the excavation was conducted is estimated, on the basis of limited shovel testing, to cover an area of at least 160 square meters, roughly 5 percent of this part of the site was excavated. Assuming that the remains of 1 bison were scattered within this area, then 5 percent of the meat weight of that animal is represented by the bones from the excavation. This is admittedly a very arbitrary and crude calculation, but it is believed to better reflect the actual significance of bison than does adding several hundred kilograms to the total meat weight from the MNI of all species in the excavated bone sample. At the same time, a large animal such as bison is likely to have been butchered at inland kill sites, with the result that bones were not transported back to camp. In this case, bison could be underrepresented in shoreline midden deposits. Given these sorts of problems, dietary significance of various taxa is, at best, only an approximation of prehistoric economic reality. However, the results from the Holmes and Ingleside Cove Sites compare quite closely, both in the case of shell midden deposits and middens with relatively low shell content, suggesting that the deposits are sufficiently homogeneous for consistent analytical results and general inferences concerning diet.

The estimated usable meat weight for a given species is based on (1) the total estimated live weight of the animal, (2) the percentage of the total weight that is usable meat, and (3) a multiplication of usable meat weight per average individual by the MNI for that species. All of these various quantifications are presented in Table 2 for 10-centimeter levels 1–3 and for the shell stratum, which in combination are quite representative of the faunal data at the site.

Weights of the "average" individual of the various fish species are derived from various sources. For black drum and redfish, the average individual fish weighed between 3,500 and 3,600 grams, respectively. These figures were obtained through correlations of the average fish age, as determined by microscopic examination of randomly selected samples of cross-sectioned archaeological otoliths, with published data on the relationship between fish ages and weights. Using samples of 51 drum and 34 redfish otoliths, it was found that the average ages at the time of death were 4.9 and 3.1 years, respectively. Growth curve data for northern Gulf of Mexico black drum (Beckman et al. 1988a) and redfish (Beckman et al. 1988b) indicate the respective weights, given above, for fish of these ages. Weights for other species are general estimates for mature individuals and are derived from Becker (1964), Compton (1975), and Hoese and Moore (1977). While these would seem less reliable than the figures derived for drum and redfish, the potential margins of error are thought to be acceptable for the present purposes, since these species were clearly of far less significance in terms of their contribution to the prehistoric diet.

**Table 2.** *Holmes Site (41SP120): MNI and Meat Weight*

| | MNI | Est. Average Individual Weight | Est. Usable Wt./Individual | Est. Total Meat Wt./Species | All Meat Weight by % Level |
|---|---|---|---|---|---|
| **Levels 1–3** | | | | | |
| **Fish** | | | | | |
| Black drum | 103 | 3,500 | 1,925 | 200,850 | |
| Redfish | 52 | 3,600 | 1,980 | 102,960 | |
| Sheepshead | 103 | 1,450 | 800 | 82,400 | |
| Trout | 53 | 900 | 495 | 26,235 | |
| Croaker | 69 | 200 | 110 | 7,590 | |
| Marine catfish | 22 | 400 | 220 | 4,840 | |
| Gar | 1 | 8,000 | 4,400 | 4,400 | |
| Total | | | | 429,275 | 79.7 |
| **Mollusks** | | | | | |
| Scallop | 291 | | 10 | 2,910 | |
| Oyster | 262 | | 15 | 3,930 | |
| Lightning whelk | 44 | | 30 | 13,200 | |
| Shark eye | 56 | | 10 | 560 | |
| Quahog | 21 | | 20 | 420 | |
| C-barred venus | 44 | | 5 | 220 | |
| Banded tulip | 20 | | 10 | 200 | |
| Horse conch | 7 | | 20 | 140 | |
| Pear whelk | 6 | | 15 | 90 | |
| Ponderous ark | 5 | | 10 | 50 | |
| Total | | | | 21,720 | 4.0 |
| **Mammals** | | | | | |
| White-tailed deer | | | | | |
| Adult | 2 | 53,000 | 26,500 | 53,000 | |
| Juvenile | 1 | 20,000 | 10,000 | 10,000 | |
| Bison | .05[b] | 590,000 | 295,000 | 14,750 | |
| Bobcat | 1 | 12,000 | 6,000 | 6,000 | |
| Cottontail rabbit | 1 | 1,600 | 800 | 800 | |
| Total | | | | 84,550 | 15.7 |
| **Birds** | | | | | |
| Duck | 1 | 1,000 | 700 | 700 | |
| Great horned owl | 1 | 3,000 | 2,100 | 2,100 | |
| Total | | | | 2,800 | .5 |

**Table 2.** (Continued)

|  | MNI | Est. Average Individual Weight | Est. Usable Wt./Individual | Est. Total Meat Wt./Species | All Meat Weight by % Level |
|---|---|---|---|---|---|
| **Shell** |  |  |  |  |  |
| **Stratum** |  |  |  |  |  |
| **Fish** |  |  |  |  |  |
| Black drum | 35 | 3,500 | 1,925 | 67,375 |  |
| Redfish | 34 | 3,600 | 1,980 | 67,320 |  |
| Sheepshead | 35 | 1,450 | 800 | 28,000 |  |
| Trout | 16 | 900 | 495 | 7,920 |  |
| Croaker | 52 | 200 | 110 | 5,720 |  |
| Marine catfish | 8 | 400 | 220 | 1,760 |  |
| Gar | 1 | 8,000 | 4,400 | 4,400 |  |
| Total |  |  |  | 182,495 | 53.8 |
| **Mollusks** |  |  |  |  |  |
| Scallop | 1,572 |  | 10 | 15,720 |  |
| Oyster | 709 |  | 15 | 10,635 |  |
| Lightning whelk | 1,048 |  | 30 | 31,440 |  |
| Shark eye | 237 |  | 10 | 2,370 |  |
| Quahog | 96 |  | 20 | 1,920 |  |
| C-barred venus | 27 |  | 5 | 135 |  |
| Banded tulip | 54 |  | 10 | 640 |  |
| Horse conch | 27 |  | 20 | 540 |  |
| Pear whelk | 23 |  | 15 | 345 |  |
| Ponderous ark | 5 |  | 10 | 50 |  |
| Total |  |  |  | 63,795 | 18.8 |
| **Mammals** |  |  |  |  |  |
| **White-tailed deer** |  |  |  |  |  |
| Adult | 3 | 53,000 | 26,500 | 79,500 |  |
| Juvenile | 1 | 20,000 | 8,000 | 8,000 |  |
| Bobcat | 1 | 12,000 | 4,800 | 4,800 |  |
| Total |  |  |  | 92,300 | 27.2 |
| **Birds** |  |  |  |  |  |
| Duck | 1 | 1,000 | 700 | 700 |  |
| Total |  |  |  | 700 | .02 |

*Note*: [a]MNI, estimated average individual weight, usable meat weight, total usable weight by species (in grams), and percent of usable meat weight by species and excavation level groupings. All weights are in grams.

[b]MNI of one bison is divided by 20 for reasons discussed in text.

Shellfish weights are based solely on the live meat weight, exclusive of shell weight. These are derived directly from specimens, gathered within the present study area, of *Rangia cuneata* clam, oyster (*Crassostrea virginica*), and lightning whelk (*Busycon contrarium*). These were collected with an eye to obtaining individuals whose shell height or length approximated the average shell height or length of archaeologically excavated specimens (approximately 40 millimeters, 80 millimeters, and 100 millimeters for *Rangia cuneata*, oyster, and whelk, respectively). All meat was extracted from the shells and weighed in its raw state. The average weight of the several specimens of each species was determined and rounded to the nearest 5-gram increment (average weights for *Rangia cuneata* were 10.2 grams; for oyster, 14.3 grams; and for whelk, 28.6 grams). Rough estimates of raw meat weight of other bivalve and gastropod species are based on these figures and adjusted according to the average shell height/length of archaeologically derived specimens. Thus, for example, a quahog or scallop is assumed to have been of approximately the same live meat weight as a *Rangia cuneata* of about the same size, since all are bivalves and have similar anatomical structures. The same assumption is held in the case of the various gastropod species. Some degree of inaccuracy is inevitable in transferring the average weight of one bivalve species to another, or one gastropod species to another, but it is assumed that this is not sufficient to prevent useful general comparisons.

Average weights of individual mammals and birds are from White (1953), with the exception of white-tailed deer, which in general are smaller in South Texas than the more northern varieties that apparently formed the basis for White's estimate of 200 pounds (91 kilograms). Study of deer growth patterns on the Welder Wildlife Refuge, located along the Aransas River within the present study area, indicates average weights of 43 kilograms (94.6 pounds) and 63 kilograms (138 pounds) for mature does and bucks, respectively (Knowlton et al. 1978). The average of these two figures, 53 kilograms, is used here for deer represented by archaeological bones with fused epiphyses. In the case of juveniles (not including very young fawns), represented by bones with unfused epiphyses, an approximate average weight of 20 kilograms is extrapolated from data presented in Knowlton et al. (1978:Figure 6).

The percentage of total body weight that was usable meat is derived here, for mammals and birds, from White (1953). Usable meat for mammals was estimated by White at 50 percent of total body weight; for birds, the estimate was 70 percent. For fish, the percentage of usable meat is here estimated at 55 percent, after Geiger and Borgstrom (1962:31).

Minimum numbers of individuals and meat weights are calculated by clustered levels and strata. The shell stratum, on the basis of lithic typology and radiocarbon dates, can be considered a discrete occupational unit and is thus analyzed separately. Further, it represents a logical analytical breaking point between underlying and overlying midden materials, assignable to the Archaic and late prehistoric periods, respectively. The 50-centimeter-thick Rockport Phase midden above the shell stratum is represented by levels 1–3 (surface to 30-centimeter depth). Results of faunal analyses from both the late Archaic and Rockport Phase deposits represent several centuries of occupation and show basic similarities.

Table 2 shows the meat weight estimates by strata and clustered 10-centimeter levels and indicates percentages of each species, grouped and totaled for each stratigraphic unit by the appropriate class or phylum. It is immediately apparent that estuarine aquatic fauna were the overwhelming component in the meat diet throughout the several centuries of occupation represented by the late Archaic and Rockport Phase deposits. In levels 1–3, fish account for nearly 80 percent of total meat weight, while shellfish constitute only about 4 percent. Terrestrial mammals account for 16 percent in these levels, with white-tailed deer clearly predominant. Birds were consistently of little overall significance and were presumably procured on an opportunistic basis.

In the late Archaic shell stratum, shellfish were of considerable significance, though still of tertiary importance after fish and mammals. Fish represent about 54 percent of the total meat weight, and shellfish represent about 19 percent. Estuarine animals still account for about 70 percent of the total meat weight.

A fairly consistent picture emerges: though there is some variability, fish is by far the most important meat resource represented in the deposits pertaining to the late Archaic and Rockport occupations. Consistently of overwhelming significance were drum and redfish, species which together account for most of the fish meat weight in the various levels. Mammals, most importantly white-tailed deer, were invariably second in importance, while shellfish seem to have varied in significance, from a minor supplement to as much as almost a fifth of the total meat diet by weight. Despite the presumed abundance of waterfowl in this kind of shoreline setting, birds were of little dietary significance.

## Seasonality of Occupation

As mentioned earlier, seasonality of resource use and site occupation can be inferred in the Karankawa area based on analyses of fish otoliths, oyster shells, and *Rangia cuneata* clamshells. Rangia was virtually absent in the deposits at the Holmes Site, since the average salinity of Ingleside Cove and Corpus Christi Bay is too high to provide a suitable habitat for this low-salinity clam. Seasonality estimates were obtained using samples of fish otoliths and oyster shells.

The results of seasonality analyses of a sample of 79 marine fish otoliths from the Rockport Phase deposit broke down into seasonal categories as follows:

| | | |
|---|---|---|
| Fall | 15 | (19 percent) |
| Winter | 50 | (63 percent) |
| Spring | 4 | (5 percent) |
| Summer | 10 | (13 percent) |

In another sample of 36 otoliths taken from the late Archaic shell stratum, the breakdown is as follows:

| | | |
|---|---|---|
| Fall | 11 | (31 percent) |
| Winter | 12 | (33 percent) |
| Spring | 6 | (17 percent) |
| Summer | 7 | (19 percent) |

In both cases, a fall-winter emphasis on fishing is indicated. The Rockport Phase sample is probably the more representative of the long-term pattern of seasonal use of the site, since the late Archaic sample came from a discrete lens of densely packed shell in the South Block that almost certainly represents a much shorter occupational span (conceivably a single seasonal occupation). The higher incidence of spring and summer otoliths could reflect the expectable variation in lengths of seasonal occupations, which would have covaried with yearly variations in the timing of optimal fish abundance near the site.

Two samples of oyster shells were analyzed for seasonality. Both come from different parts of the late Archaic deposits. The seasonal breakdowns for these two samples are as follows:

Sample 1 (30 specimens)

| | | |
|---|---|---|
| Fall | 10 | (33 percent) |
| Winter | 12 | (40 percent) |
| Spring | 6 | (20 percent) |
| Summer | 2 | (7 percent) |

Sample 2 (20 specimens)
Fall          5    (25 percent)
Winter       13    (65 percent)
Spring        0    (0 percent)
Summer        2    (10 percent)

As with fishing, a fall-winter emphasis on oyster gathering is indicated.

### The Ingleside Cove Site (41SP43)

The Ingleside Cove Site is located only about 200 meters north of the Holmes Site. The two sites were originally part of one continuous archaeological zone that extended for several hundred meters along the cove shoreline. Modern residential construction has destroyed much of the original deposit and has artificially separated the two sites.

This site was tested by Dee Ann Story in the summer of 1967, and the results were promptly published (Story 1968). Her report represents the first modern, ecologically sensitive site analysis in the central coast region and has justifiably been cited in numerous later references to the regional archaeology. This work is notable on at least three counts: it was the first site report from the region to list faunal remains by species and to consider the ecological implications of those remains; it contained the first in-depth analysis of the technological variability in Rockport pottery in terms of paste constituents; and it presented the first radiocarbon dates for the central coast region.

During the summer of 1987, I directed additional excavation at the site with two goals in mind. The foremost of these was to obtain a marine fish otolith sample for seasonality analysis. The second major goal was to collect faunal materials in order to acquire quantitative data on economic patterns.

Story's 1967 investigations consisted of several narrow trenches excavated across the level top of the bluff, within an area about 50 feet square. A consistent site stratigraphy consisting of several superimposed zones was defined. Zone 1 was composed of the basal sandy clay of the Pleistocene Ingleside Strandplain, which was overlain by Zone 2a, a culturally sterile stratum of gray-brown sand. Over this was Zone 2b, a dense, moderately thick (40-centimeter) shell midden deposit consisting of estuarine shell species, primarily oyster, whelk, and scallop, in a dark sandy midden soil matrix. Zone 2c lay directly above the shell midden, was slightly more compact

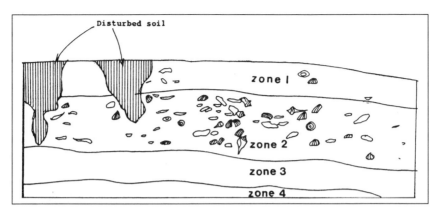

*Figure 14.* Excavation profile, 1987 investigations at the Ingleside Cove Site (41SP43). Profile is 2 meters wide.

and lighter in color than 2b, and contained considerably less shell (Story 1968:10). Zone 2d was a thin (2–3 foot thick) surficial layer of humus debris and loose sand (Story 1968:9–10).

Four radiocarbon dates were obtained on materials from the Zone 2b shell midden by the Radiocarbon Laboratory of the University of Texas at Austin. Three assays were run on scallop shell, and one on charcoal from a small hearth feature. The uncorrected results are as follows (Story 1968:40):

| | |
|---|---|
| Tx-520 (charcoal) | 780 ± 40 B.P. (A.D. 1170) |
| Tx-521 (shell) | 820 ± 50 B.P. (A.D. 1130) |
| Tx-522 (shell) | 710 ± 40 B.P. (A.D. 1240) |
| Tx-523 (shell) | 820 ± 50 B.P. (A.D. 1130) |

Artifacts were collected in 1967 from the surface at the base of the eroded bluff and from the trench excavations. A total of 968 potsherds was collected; in the excavations the overwhelming majority of sherds came from the upper cultural stratum, Zone 2c. Lithic artifacts were scarce in the excavated trenches. From the upper cultural stratum ( Zone 2c) came 1 square-stemmed (Alba-like) and 3 Perdiz type arrowpoints, 2 chert scrapers, and a chert biface fragment. From the lower shell midden stratum (Zone 2b), a Matamoros dart point, an untyped stemmed dart point, and 3 small triangular untyped points were recovered. Shell tools consisted of a modified conch fragment, thought to represent a container, and a perforated oyster shell. Both were from the lower shell midden cultural stratum. Bone artifacts consisted of a bone bead from the upper stratum

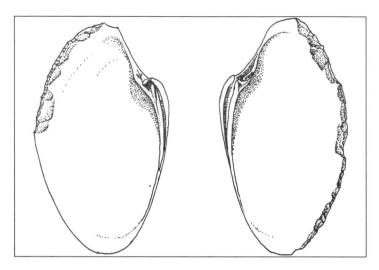

*Figure 15.* Two examples of edge-flaked sunray venus clam-shell knives or scrapers, from the Ingleside Cove Site (41SP43). Specimen on the left is 100 millimeters long.

and a total of 11 modified bone fragments from tools of indeterminate form from both strata (Story 1968).

Faunal materials found in 1967 included numerous fish and shellfish remains, with the latter more abundant in the lower of the two culturally relevant zones. Terrestrial fauna were most abundantly represented by bones of white-tailed deer, found in both zones. Small quantities of rodent, rabbit, reptile, and bird remains were found. Overall, the two most abundant vertebrate species were fish and white-tailed deer, and both appeared to have contributed significantly to the prehistoric diet (Story 1968:38). Though fish were only partially quantified in terms of species, elements of drum, gar, and skate or ray were identified. The most abundant shellfish species (oyster, scallop, and whelk) were inferred to have been collected from bayshore and lagoonal areas near the site (ibid.:42).

On the basis of these findings, Story concluded that the lower shell midden represented a late Archaic occupation. The upper stratum was assigned to the Rockport Focus on the basis of the Rockport ware pottery and the arrowpoints. The radiocarbon dates from the Archaic zone indicated a chronological position in the A.D. 1100–1200 range, suggesting that the regional Archaic persisted to perhaps as late as A.D. 1250, several centuries later than in the Central Texas region. On this basis, Story suggested the possibility of a "cultural lag" on the central coast (ibid.).

The 1987 excavation was in an area of level ground surface next to the bluff edge, very close to the locations of the 1967 trenches. This work revealed a stratigraphic profile (Figure 14) in no way different from that described by Story. The top 5 or so centimeters consisted of very loose sand mixed with humus, corresponding to Story's Zone 2d. This was underlain by 15 to 20 centimeters of dark brown sandy loam, designated in the field as Zone 1, which contained artifacts and faunal remains. Beneath this was a shell midden stratum, made up of a dark brown, organically rich sandy matrix about 30 centimeters thick. This was designated Zone 2. In addition to several thousand shells, this zone yielded fish and other faunal materials as well as a fairly large sample of artifacts. Underlying the shell midden was a light gray-brown sand stratum, designated Zone 3, which varied considerably in thickness, from as little as 5 to as much as 20 centimeters. There was a relative dearth of cultural debris in this zone, and the amount present probably reflects downward displacement of the abundant debris of Zone 2. Zone 4,

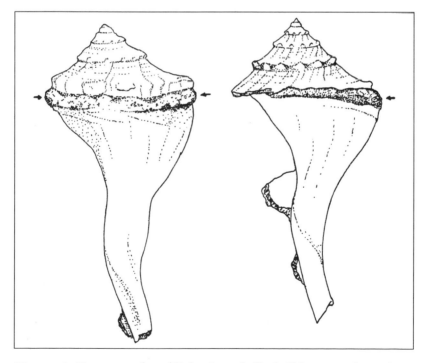

*Figure 16.* Two examples of lightning whelk shell hammers from the Ingleside Cove Site. Specimen on the right is 127 millimeters long.

reached at depths of between 50 and 70 centimeters below the ground surface, consisted of the light tan-colored sandy clay of the Pleistocene Ingleside Strandplain.

## Artifacts

A total of 443 prehistoric artifacts was recovered during the 1987 work. The collection of artifacts from Zone 1 can be readily placed within the late prehistoric Rockport Phase. The sample consists of 140 potsherds, 19 lithic artifacts, 2 shell artifacts, and 2 small lumps of asphaltum. The potsherds are all readily placed within the Rockport series. All are sandy paste: 40 percent have plain surfaces; 54 percent bear asphaltum coating on one or both surfaces; and 6 percent have asphaltum decoration. Of the decorated sherds, one is a rimsherd with asphaltum lip banding; the others are body sherds bearing exterior asphaltum squiggles and interior asphaltum coating. A single sherd with exterior asphaltum coating is probably a ceramic smoking pipe fragment similar to those found at the Holmes Site. Flaked stone artifacts from Zone 1 include 3 Perdiz arrowpoints, an edge-trimmed prismatic blade, a biface fragment resembling the distal end of an Olmos tool (a small gougelike tool; see Turner and Hester 1993), and 15 small pieces of chert debitage. Shell artifacts consist of a scallop shell with a rough perforation in the umbonal area and an adze made from whelk shell.

Zone 2 yielded 158 potsherds, 25 lithic artifacts, 29 shell artifacts, and 3 bone artifacts. Lithic artifacts are very few, consisting only of 24 pieces of chert debitage and a small unifacial chert end scraper. Potsherds were most abundant in the upper 10 centimeters of the zone, their abundance decreasing with depth. This strongly suggests that most of the pottery actually pertains to the Zone 1 Rockport Phase deposit and that much had become slightly displaced into the underlying Zone 2 by animal burrowing or root activity (both of which are significant factors at this site). On the other hand, 2 large sherds, both clearly from the same vessel, were found in the middle third of Zone 2 in what is confidently interpreted as undisturbed context. Both fragments were resting flat and were embedded in a matrix of tightly packed, undisturbed oyster shells that also were lying flat. Considering the size and inclination of these sherds, their position at the same level in the shell stratum, and their position within dense and undisturbed oyster shells, there is little doubt that they represent a late Archaic pot. The sherds are relatively thick (.6 centimeter average thickness), of sandy paste, and dark gray throughout. Surfaces are roughly smoothed, and the rimsherd lip is pointed in profile and somewhat unevenly modeled. The rim configuration represents a widemouthed jar or deep bowl.

Artifacts of shell were by far the most abundant category of material culture in Zone 2, next to ceramics. These consisted of 4 complete and 7 fragmentary edge-flaked sunray venus clamshell tools (Figure 15), 7 whelk hammers (Figure 16), 6 small conch columella "awls," 2 perforated oyster shells, 1 perforated scallop shell, a small (8 millimeters in diameter) conch shell disk bead, and a rectangular fragment of quahog shell with one smoothed edge, perhaps intended as a bead blank.

Bone artifacts are few, consisting of a deer metapodial awl, 2 flat, end-rounded ground and polished bone splinters that resemble the basal portion of the bone point from 41SP120, and the distal portion of a duck humerus that has been cut from the bone shank, probably a by-product of bone bead manufacture.

## Economic Patterns at the Ingleside Cove Site

The faunal remains recovered have been analyzed according to the same methods used for the Holmes Site materials. The results from the two sites are in close agreement.

In Zone 1, a minimum number of 17 marine fish are represented, based on otolith counts. These consist of 7 black drum, 3 redfish, 6 trout, and 1 catfish. Based on the estimated average weight of these species, an estimated total of 20,955 grams of meat is indicated, which makes up 40.6 percent of the total meat weight represented by the Zone 1 faunal materials. In terms of the quantities of food indicated, drum and redfish were clearly the overwhelmingly significant fish constituents.

Shellfish represent only a very minor dietary constituent in Zone 1. By halving the number of bivalve shells recovered and counting the central columellae of gastropods, it is apparent that 379 mollusks are represented, accounting for approximately 3,105 grams of raw meat, or only 6 percent of the Zone 1 meat weight. Mammals are represented only by a minimum of 1 white-tailed deer, which would have supplied the Late prehistoric site occupants with an estimated 27,500 grams of meat, or 53.3 percent of the Zone 1 total. Thus during the Rockport Phase occupation(s) represented by the Zone 1 remains, white-tailed deer and fish were the major animal food resources, while shellfish represented only a minor resource of supplementary food value.

The Zone 2 faunal remains indicate that aquatic estuarine resources provided the clear majority of dietary meat for the site's late Archaic occupants. Fish are represented by a minimum number of 81 individuals, accounting for an estimated 80,630 grams of usable meat and 47.2 percent of the total meat weight represented. Again, drum and redfish provided the overwhelming majority of fish meat, with trout a distant third in terms of dietary significance. Croaker and catfish are nearly negligible.

The Zone 2 molluscan remains indicate a far more significant shellfish contribution to overall diet than is the case for Zone 1. Shellfish provided an estimated 23 percent of the total meat consumed. Lightning whelk was by far the most significant of the shellfish, constituting an estimated 11 percent of the total Zone 2 meat weight. Scallop, oyster, and cross-barred venus made up 5.7 percent, 3.2 percent, and 1.5 percent of the total meat weight, respectively. Other species—quahog, shark eye, tulip, and ponderous ark—all constituted less than 1 percent each of the zone's total meat weight.

Mammals, most notably white-tailed deer, again provided a significant dietary contribution, though the significance, as compared with Zone 1, is offset by the relative importance of shellfish. Minimum numbers of 1 adult and 1 juvenile deer are represented, which combined accounted for an estimated 40,000 grams of meat, or a combined total of 23.5 percent of the total usable meat weight indicated for the zone. Additionally, a minimum number of 1 coyote or fairly large dog and a single cottontail rabbit added, respectively, 5,650 (3.3 percent) and 800 (0.5 percent) grams to the total zone meat weight.

As at the Holmes Site, birds seem to have been only a minor dietary component. Bird bones were relatively scarce, and identifiable remains represent only 1 little blue heron and 1 duck of unidentified species. The combined usable meat weight of these 2 individuals is estimated at 4,200 grams, or 2.4 percent of the zone's total.

Despite some differences, the faunal remains from both zones at the Ingleside Cove Site represent similar proportions of meat weight, in terms of the various species, to those found at the nearby Holmes Site. With the exception of Zone 1 at 41SP43, where a relatively small faunal sample probably has skewed analytical results, fish represent the single most important food category in terms of meat weight in the various identified stratigraphic zones at both sites. Among the fish species, drum and redfish, in that order, are of overwhelming significance. Other fish species represent markedly less important components of total meat weight, with trout considerably more significant than either croaker or catfish. Mammals, particularly white-tailed deer, invariably represent a significant component, second in total weight only to fish. Shellfish are consistently of less importance, though the various species—most importantly scallop, oyster, and lightning whelk—combine to represent about 20 percent of the meat weight in the Archaic shell middens at both sites, as compared with only between 4 and 6 percent in the Rockport Phase occupations.

## Seasonality of the Ingleside Cove Site

A total of 99 fish otoliths was analyzed in order to determine the seasonality of fishing at the Ingleside Cove Site. Twenty specimens were from Zone 1, and 79 were from Zone 2. The results are nearly identical for both zones. The seasonal breakdown for otoliths in Zone 1 was 25 percent fall, 60 percent winter, 5 percent spring, and 10 percent summer. In Zone 2, the breakdown was 25 percent fall, 56 percent winter, 4 percent spring, and 15 percent summer. A clear fall-winter emphasis on fishing is indicated.

These results fit very closely with those from the Holmes Site, particularly from that site's Rockport Phase occupation. Again, a fall through early spring emphasis on fishing is ecologically expectable, considering the fall and winter–early spring spawning peaks for the two overwhelmingly important species, redfish and black drum.

Because the methodology for oyster seasonality had not seen publication at the time of the 1987 excavations, oyster samples were not retained for seasonality analysis. However, in view of the general similarity in subsistence patterns to those from the Holmes Site, it seems quite likely that the winter oyster-gathering season suggested by the analyses on shells from that site was also the case at the Ingleside Cove Site.

## Radiocarbon Ages

Four samples of marine shell from Zone 2 were submitted for age determination to the Radiocarbon Laboratory of the University of Texas at Austin. Two samples, one consisting of scallop shell and the other of quahog, were recovered from the upper 10 centimeters of the zone. A third consisted of quahog shell from the middle part of the zone, while the fourth was of quahog shell from the lower 10 centimeters. The uncorrected sample ages (S. Valastro, pers. comm.) are as follows:

1180 ± 70 B.P. scallop, upper part of zone
1230 ± 60 B.P. quahog, middle part of zone

1260 ± 70 B.P. quahog, upper part of zone
1450 ± 60 B.P. quahog, lower part of zone

Corrected for the 13-C fraction and calibrated dendrochronologically, the age and age ranges of these assays are as follows:

1509 B.P. (1546–1395 B.P.)
1545 B.P. (1682–1514 B.P.)
1552 B.P. (1689–1515 B.P.)
1816 B.P. (1873–1711 B.P.)

## Summary of Findings at the Ingleside Cove Site

The data from the Ingleside Cove Site point to recurrent occupation from the late Archaic into the Rockport Phase. The earliest Archaic cultural remains were deposited about 1700–1900 B.P. The extensive Rockport Phase materials are consistently found overlying the combined Archaic deposits. The faunal and seasonality data indicate a recurrent emphasis on fall-winter occupation, with subsistence relying heavily on exploitation of fish resources and augmented significantly by procurement of white-tailed deer and, less importantly, by shellfish gathering.

Limited evidence suggests that the sandy paste pottery, generally considered diagnostic of the Rockport Phase, may have been present in prototypical form during the later years of Zone 2 shell midden deposition. Also considered diagnostic of Archaic as opposed to late prehistoric material culture are dart points, several of which were reported by Story from her Zone 2b shell midden stratum. If these were in use as late as A.D. 1100–1250, a very late technological shift from the Archaic dart and atlatl to the late prehistoric bow and arrow would be indicated. This would suggest, as noted by Story (1968), a significant time lag in technological developments between the central coast and interior Texas, where the bow and arrow was established by circa A.D. 700.

However, the assignment of the points reported by Story to a true Archaic occupation bears reexamination. Story reported a small sample of 5 projectile points from excavated contexts within the Zone 2b shell midden, all of which I have examined. Three of these are triangular, unstemmed specimens, rather crude but quite small and thin and falling within the size and weight range of arrowpoints (as is in fact indicated in the data presentation in Story's 1968 report), and not unlike the triangular arrowpoints of the period found at the Holmes Site. They may in fact represent initial arrowpoint production on the central coast. The 2 remaining points are clearly dart points. One is a good example of the small but thick triangular unstemmed Matamoros type; the other, an untyped stemmed specimen. The Matamoros point is quite distinguishable from other lithic materials from the shell stratum in that it bears a heavy surface patination not seen on the other lithics from either the 1967 or 1987 excavations. It may thus be an older Archaic artifact that had been exposed to surficial weathering and that was subsequently carried onto the site by the people responsible for the shell midden deposit. The stemmed point was found at the very bottom of the shell stratum at its interface with the underlying Zone 2a sand and may thus pertain to a context that predated formation of the shell stratum.

It is distinctly possible, therefore, that during the later years (circa A.D. 1100–1250) of shell stratum deposition at 41SP43, the occupants of the site were not operating with a definably Archaic technology. Ceramics seem to have been present, albeit not yet in abundance, and the shift to the bow and arrow may have already taken place. This postulation accords well with the data from Holmes Site, which indicate a very late Archaic deposit, dated to circa A.D. 1000, immediately underlying late prehistoric materials characterized by a developing ceramic technology and arrowpoints. These combined findings support Story's postulation of a lag effect between the coast and Central Texas but suggest that the lag time was not quite as long, nor the shift to the late prehistoric as sudden, as was originally postulated.

## The Kirchmeyer Site (41NU11)

One of the earliest-documented archaeological sites in Nueces County, the Kirchmeyer Site, has long been recognized as a source of abundant late prehistoric cultural material. The site is quite large, covering an area of about 10,000 square meters along the crest of a clay dune overlooking the southwest shore of Oso Bay, a secondary bay connected to the southern part of Corpus Christi Bay. Since the early decades of this century, numerous artifacts have been surface-collected from the site, and a large collection is now housed at the Texas Archeological Research Laboratory of the University of Texas at Austin. This collection has been thoroughly described and abundantly illustrated in a recent publication (Headrick 1993) and does not need to be described in detail here. Included are over 12,000 sherds of aboriginal pottery that exhibit the characteristic attributes of Rockport ware. Flaked stone artifacts include numerous arrowpoints of the Perdiz and Fresno types, as well as many small unifacial end scrapers. Shell tools are fairly abundant and include several dozen edge-flaked sunray venus knives or fragments thereof, as well as several whelk adzes.

Despite the abundant evidence of late prehistoric occupation, the site has never been extensively investigated. Subsurface testing conducted in 1969 by T. R. Hester and J. E. Corbin (field notes on file at the Texas Archeological Research Laboratory, University of Texas at Austin) recovered a range of faunal remains, including shellfish (whelk, oyster, sunray venus), fish (black drum), and mammal bones (deer, bison). This work was severely hampered by the very hard, blocky nature of the clay matrix (Hester and Corbin field notes; T. R. Hester, pers. comm.; see also Headrick 1993).

I investigated the site during the summer of 1987 and found that it had suffered from natural erosion as well as partial grading associated with residential construction. Cultural debris in the form of small potsherds, chert debitage, shell fragments, deer bone fragments, and fish otoliths were visible in eroded sections of the site. An attempt was made at subsurface testing, but the hard, dry clay matrix was so resistant to any known excavation technique that the hope of purposeful excavation was quickly abandoned.

One area did produce useful data for the present study, however. This was near the crest of the clay dune, where incipient sheet and rill erosion had recently exposed Rockport Phase materials along a 10-meter stretch of apparently intact clay matrix. Rockport ware potsherds, chert flakes, shell fragments, deer bone and marine fish vertebrae, and otoliths had been exposed. Fish otoliths, collected for seasonality analysis, consisted of 27 drum, 3 croaker, 2 redfish, and 2 trout. All but 11 of these were too small for reliable seasonal readings. The 11 readable specimens fall into seasonal categories as follows:

| | | |
|---|---|---|
| Fall | 1 | (9 percent) |
| Winter | 9 | (82 percent) |
| Spring | 1 | (9 percent) |
| Summer | 0 | (0 percent) |

Interpretation of this site is limited by the intractable nature of the clay dune sediments. However, it shows important characteristics that link it with other shoreline fishing campsites. It covers a large area and has produced an abundance of artifacts and other cultural debris. Fish remains are plentiful, suggesting a heavy economic reliance on estuarine fish species, particularly black drum.

Though the sample is small, the otoliths show a marked seasonality peak in the winter period, in keeping with the majority of otoliths from the sites on Ingleside Cove.

### The Mustang Lake Site (41CL3)

This site is located on Mustang Lake, a small lagoonal extension of San Antonio Bay and created by a sand spit deposited by currents circulating within the bay. The site, on the Aransas National Wildlife Refuge, is situated on the many stable sand dunes that border the western shore of San Antonio Bay. Dense oak mottes cover most of the shoreline dunes, though the site itself is primarily covered by various short and medium grasses with only a scattering of oaks. The dune surface slopes gently to the shore of Mustang Lake. Mustang Lake is shallow, contains an abundance of small shellfish species, and is a prime winter feeding ground for the whooping crane. Numerous oyster reefs are found in nearby San Antonio Bay, which remains a productive area for commercial oyster harvesting.

The site is very large, extending from the shoreline of Mustang Lake onto the crest of the dune and covering an area on the crest of the dune of some 30,000 square meters. Abundant shells, fish bones, and potsherds can be seen scattered on the surface, and hundreds of perforated oysters and other shell tools, chert flakes, and potsherds have been exposed by wave action along the shoreline. Based upon surface inspection, the site is virtually contiguous with Sites 41CL48 and 41CL84 to the south and north, respectively, so that cultural debris in the forms of shell midden, faunal bone, and artifacts extends along the Mustang Lake shoreline for a distance of at least 1.5 kilometers.

In December 1988, a 1-meter-square test unit was excavated in the central part of the site, under my direction, with the goals of obtaining samples of fish otoliths and oyster shells for seasonality analyses, as well as a sample of faunal materials. Excavation was controlled in 15-centimeter arbitrary levels and reached a depth of 60 centimeters. The top 5 or so centimeters consisted of a loose sand containing humic debris and numerous grass rootlets. At a depth of about 5 centimeters, densely packed shell was encountered within a matrix of dark brown, fine sandy soil. This shell midden characterized the deposit to the floor of the unit at 60 centimeters. The base of the shell midden had not been reached at that level when excavation was terminated because of time constraints. Artifacts consisted of fragments of Rockport ware pottery, chert flakes, and shell tools. Eighty-six sandy paste potsherds were recovered from between 5 and 15 centimeters. Many of these exhibit asphaltum surface coating, and 3 specimens, including 1 rimsherd, bear exterior incising in motifs typical of the Rockport Incised type. Ceramics were confined almost exclusively to the top 15 centimeters; the 15–30-centimeter level produced 4 sherds; and the 30–45-centimeter level yielded only 1. The 91 sherds were sorted into 35 groups on the basis of the criteria already discussed. Fifteen, or 43 percent, of the sherd groups were characterized by asphaltum coating.

Nonceramic artifacts from the 0–15-centimeter level include 2 utilized flakes, 3 pieces of nonutilized chert debitage, and a small nodule of asphaltum. The 15–30-centimeter level yielded 1 piece of chert debitage, a small, water-worn piece of pumice, a sunray venus knife, a perforated oyster shell, and 3 asphaltum nodules. From the 30–45-centimeter level were recovered 1 piece of debitage, a perforated oyster shell, and 4 asphaltum nodules. The 45–60-centimeter level produced 2 perforated oyster shells and two asphaltum nodules.

## Faunal Remains and Economy at Mustang Lake

Because the testing at the site was limited, the sample of faunal material is too small for detailed analysis of proportional meat weights by species. The few deer bone fragments scattered within the ceramic-bearing upper 15 centimeters, for instance, if taken to represent an MNI of 1, would probably be grossly overrepresented in terms of meat weight significance relative to fish and shellfish remains.

It is obvious, however, that estuarine fauna were of major significance at the site. While available time did not permit a precise field count of oyster shell specimens, estimates were made based on numbers of five-gallon bucketfuls from each level and the approximate number of shells required to fill a bucket, as determined in the field. The approximately 1,000 oysters from the 0–15-centimeter level, represented by the estimated 2,000 valves recovered, would account for about 15,000 grams of uncooked meat. This compares to 11,380 grams of fish meat, represented by the otoliths and gar scales in that level (using the estimated average individual weights for the various species discussed above). Adding a minimum of 1 deer, with an estimated usable meat weight of 26,500 grams, a total meat weight of 52,880 grams is represented. Of this total weight, 21.5 percent consisted of fish, 28.4 percent was oyster, and 50.1 percent was deer. As noted, deer was probably of considerably less actual significance, with the combined estuarine fish and shellfish making up most of the meat weight. The faunal data for the other levels indicate the same basic proportions of fish, shellfish, and deer.

It is interesting to note that, unlike the findings at Sites 41SP120 and 41SP43, shellfish predominates over fish in terms of represented meat weight. This may be an artifact of the limited sampling at 41CL3, since there may be much higher densities of fish remains elsewhere on the site. Alternatively, it may actually reflect a particularly strong emphasis on oyster procurement at this site. Variability in emphasis on major estuarine subsistence resources at Rockport Phase shoreline sites should be explored in future studies on the Texas central coast.

## Seasonality of Occupation at the Mustang Lake Site

Two samples of fish otoliths were analyzed for seasonality. The otoliths from the upper 15 centimeters were treated as a single sample, since they were from the ceramic-bearing Rockport Phase level. All other otoliths were lumped together and taken to represent the long-term seasonal pattern of fishing during a recurrent Archaic occupation of unknown duration. The results are as follows:

| Rockport Phase Sample | | | Archaic Sample | | |
|---|---|---|---|---|---|
| Fall | 2 | (15 percent) | Fall | 9 | (39 percent) |
| Winter | 9 | (70 percent) | Winter | 12 | (52 percent) |
| Spring | 2 | (15 percent) | Spring | 0 | (0 percent) |
| Summer | 0 | (0 percent) | Summer | 2 | (9 percent) |

The seasonal breakdowns in both samples indicate that greatest emphasis on fishing was during the winter period. This is more marked in the late prehistoric sample, which indicates a fall through early spring seasonality. A fall-winter emphasis on fishing is indicated by the Archaic sample.

Two oyster shell samples, the first from 0–15 centimeters and the second from 15–45 centimeters, were analyzed for seasonality. The results, which clearly indicate a winter emphasis on oyster harvesting, are as follows:

| 0–15 centimeters | | | 15–45 centimeters | | |
|---|---|---|---|---|---|
| Fall | 2 | (13 percent) | Fall | 3 | (11 percent) |
| Winter | 13 | (81 percent) | Winter | 20 | (77 percent) |
| Spring | 0 | (0 percent) | Spring | 2 | (8 percent) |
| Summer | 1 | (6 percent) | Summer | 1 | (4 percent) |

Finally, a sample of 41 *Rangia cuneata* valves was collected from the uppermost 15-centimeter level, where the species was most abundant. Analyzed according to Aten's (1981) method for seasonality determination, the growth category breakdown is as follows:

| | | |
|---|---|---|
| Interrupted | 13 | (32 percent) |
| Early | 6 | (14 percent) |
| Middle | 4 | (10 percent) |
| Late | 4 | (10 percent) |
| Indeterminate | 14 | (34 percent) |

These results are unusual in that the indeterminate category, at 34 percent, makes up an unexpectably high proportion of the sample. In all of Aten's modern clam histograms, this category constitutes between 6 and 19 percent of any given sample total, with variability fluctuating around a mean of 13 percent (Aten 1981:190). The difficulty in assigning many of the rangia shells from 41CL3 to categories other than indeterminate derives from the obscure growth patterns on a relatively high percentage of the shells. The cause of this is unknown but may be related to habitat conditions that were in some way marginal for rangia growth, since shells were generally smaller for their respective age classes than the ranges presented by Aten (ibid.:184) or those seen at other sites in the study area.

Despite the anomaly of such a high percentage of indeterminate shells, when this category is eliminated from consideration, the resulting percentage breakdown best approximates Aten's late winter–early spring histograms (i.e., end of February and the end of March; see Aten 1981:187). A late winter or very early spring emphasis on rangia gathering is indicated.

## Summary of Findings at Shoreline Sites

The data from the four shoreline sites discussed here reveal a set of common, basic characteristics. All are large sites and yield large numbers of artifacts, suggesting that these locales saw frequent use, potentially by relatively large groups of people. At the Holmes, Ingleside Cove, and Mustang Lake Sites, thick debris deposits accumulated over long periods of time, indicating numerous recurrent occupations. The radiocarbon data from the Holmes and Ingleside Cove Sites demonstrate that prehistoric people were exploiting estuarine resources as far back as around 4,500 years ago. There was apparently an increasingly intensive use of these food resources through time, so that by the late Archaic, fish and shellfish—particularly fish—were the dietary mainstay at shoreline sites. The largest economic fish species, black drum and redfish, seem to have generally contributed most to the meat diet. The seasonality data point to a fall through winter or early spring emphasis on shoreline resource procurement. The majority of analyzed fish otoliths, as well as oyster and rangia samples, fall into a winter or fall-winter seasonality. Spring-summer specimens are in the minority, suggesting a considerably reduced use of bay and lagoon shoreline locales during these seasons.

A heavy fall-winter reliance on estuarine resources makes good ecological sense in that the most economically important fish species, redfish and black drum, would have been most predictably concentrated during these seasons. As noted above, redfish spawn in the fall and aggregate in large numbers as they swim to areas near tidal passes, where spawning occurs. Black drum spawn in the winter and early spring and would be most concentrated during that time of year; modern commercial data on black drum fishing show marked winter through early spring peaks in the number and weight of catches.

It is apparent, then, that a key element in Karankawan subsistence economy was a major reliance on fishing during those times of year when the most important fish resources were most predictably concentrated. Such a strategy would minimize risk of inadequate food resources and indeed may have maximized the potential for relatively large groups to come together at optimal shoreline locations. Shellfish were also important at these locations, though more often than not they were less important in terms of meat weight and calories than were fish. Scattered bones of white-tailed deer at all the shoreline sites indicate that this species was consistently hunted. The estimated meat weights at the Holmes and Ingleside Cove Sites indicate that venison, though of some importance, was of less overall economic significance than fish. In short, the economy at shoreline locales was seasonally focused on a reliable abundance of fish and was significantly supplemented by shellfish gathering and deer hunting.

# Chapter 5
# Karankawan Occupation of the Coastal Prairie Environment

The archaeological information from Group 1 sites points to an aboriginal Karankawan economy involving an emphasis on fall-winter fishing, importantly supplemented with shellfish gathering and deer hunting. The relatively low proportions of spring-summer seasonality indicators suggest a significantly reduced use of shoreline campsites during these seasons. What then, was the main economic focus during the spring and summer?

A considerable body of data shows that in the spring the Karankawas shifted their economic focus away from the shoreline to the nearby coastal prairie. Fishing was accorded a reduced importance at this time of the year, when subsistence activities revolved around hunting of large terrestrial game animals, particularly bison and deer. Probably, various plant foods, abundant on the coastal prairie and river floodplains during the spring and summer, were also important. Twenty-nine Group 2 sites, located within or adjacent to the coastal prairie environment, have yielded one or more classes of important information on settlement and subsistence patterns during the Rockport Phase. These sites, while containing the same basic Rockport Phase artifact assemblage as the shoreline sites, show important differences. They are all of relatively small size, have low densities of artifacts and other cultural debris, and yield little in the way of estuarine faunal materials. Proportionately, terrestrial mammal bones represent the major component in the meat diet. Most of these sites are located away from shorelines, along the courses of streams feeding the coastal bay systems. They are virtually always situated on prairie uplands, usually overlooking river valley floodplains. A number of these prairie-riverine campsites have yielded several important classes of data, as outlined in the following summaries.

## The McKinzie Site (41NU221)

This important site is located on the edge of the dissected Pleistocene uplands overlooking the floodplain of the lower Nueces River, about 4 kilometers upstream from the mouth of the river. Rockport Phase cultural debris, in the form of pottery fragments and flaked stone tools and flaking debris is sparsely scattered along the crest of the hill on which the site is located, in a linear distribution that covers an estimated area of 600 to 800 square meters. Excavations here encountered a discrete lens of Rockport Phase materials at a consistent depth of between 5 and 10 centimeters below the modern, grass-covered surface (Ricklis 1986, 1988).

Artifacts within this narrow vertical zone consisted of 596 chert debitage flakes, 196 pottery fragments, a Perdiz type arrowpoint, a unifacial chert end scraper, an unfinished arrowpoint, an alternately beveled bifacially flaked tool (probably a knife) fragment, a sandstone grinding stone, 3 probable bone awl fragments, and 2 edge-utilized *Rangia cuneata* valves.

Nine pots are represented by the ceramic fragments. All but 1 are good examples of Rockport ware. The exception had moderate bone tempering and a burnished exterior surface and more nearly resembles the bone-tempered plainware ceramics of the southern Texas interior. The faunal remains clearly indicate that large game composed the bulk of the meat diet. A scattering of rangia clamshells represented a total of 668 clams, equivalent to, at most, about 6,600 grams of uncooked meat. Fish were represented by only 2 otoliths: 1 from a sea trout, the other from a catfish. Bison and deer bones represent a minimum of 1 individual each (with the bison a female), thus accounting for over 200 kilograms of usable meat.

Nearly all cultural debris was thinly distributed in a semicircular pattern around a central complex of three basin-shaped hearths or fire pits. Along the perimeter of the debris were located possible post molds and a small pit, presumably for short-term storage. Infrared color photographs of the excavation, taken in a lift bucket from directly overhead, showed four additional probable pits of similar dimensions that were not discernible using regular excavation techniques. Taken together, the semicircular debris pattern around the hearths and the alignment of the pits and possible post molds around the perimeter of the debris pattern strongly suggest the floor of a circular domicile 5.5 meters in diameter. Circular skin- or mat-covered huts with central hearths were the common house type of the historic Karankawas (Newcomb 1983:363).

The distributional pattern of *Rangia cuneata* shells was essentially the same as the pattern of artifact distribution (cf. Ricklis 1988: Figures 20, 26), indicating that seasonality analysis of rangia shells would probably define the seasonality of the occupation represented by the Rockport Phase debris. Assuming that *Rangia cuneata* clams were gathered at various times throughout the occupation in question, a seasonal residence from about the end of March through May was indicated by the rangia growth category percentages (interrupted, 22 percent; early, 35 percent; middle, 22 percent; late, 6 percent; indeterminate, 15 percent; see discussion in Ricklis 1988:30–33).

Considering the distribution of materials, the probability of a circular domicile with central hearths and apparently small storage facilities, and the *Rangia cuneata* analysis, it was concluded that a seasonal, residential camp of a small group of people was indicated. Given the size of the small domiciliary area, the group represented was probably a single nuclear or perhaps a small extended family. Data did not allow assessment as to whether similar scatters of late prehistoric debris, exposed by artificial disturbances elsewhere on the hilltop, represented concurrent use of the site by other such groups within a single band.

## Site 41NU193

Site 41NU193 is also on a hilltop a few kilometers west of the McKinzie Site, near the edge of the uplands overlooking the southern margin of the lower Nueces River floodplain. A light scatter of cultural debris, exposed by machine grading operations at a depth below modern ground surface of about 15 centimeters, consisted of *Rangia cuneata* shell and an apparently isomorphic spread of lithic debitage. The total area covered by this material cannot be determined due to partial destruction of the site, but the observed portion extended along the machinery cut for about 30 meters. Within the area of greatest concentration of chert flakes were found a Perdiz arrowpoint, a typical late prehistoric edge-beveled chert knife, 3 sherds of sandy paste Rockport ware pottery, and several deer long bone fragments.

A sample of 27 *Rangia cuneata* valves was gathered from within the area of artifact debris concentration for seasonality analysis. The growth category percentages indicate occupation at the end of May. Following Carlson's (1988) estimate of a 1.5-month range of clam gathering time for a clear histogram match, a mid-April to mid-June range is indicated.

## Site 41NU255

Site 41NU255 is also on the edge of the Pleistocene uplands over-looking the lower Nueces floodplain, about 1.5 kilometers east of the McKinzie Site. Nearly the entire site was exposed by mechanical brush removal operations, which had removed the top 10 to 15 centimeters of the fine sandy loam soil to clearly expose a discrete scatter of late prehistoric debris covering an elliptical area of approximately 600 square meters. Within this area was a scatter of rangia clamshells intermixed with a few oyster valves, sparse chert flakes, and Rockport ware potsherds. Also present were fragments of deer and bison bone, 2 fragments of turtle carapace, and 1 fragment each of *Busycon*, sunray venus, and Atlantic cockle shells.

A 1-meter-square test unit was excavated to a depth of 30 centimeters at the north end of the site, in an intact area just beyond the machine-bladed area. A light scatter of *Rangia cuneata* fragments, several small nodules of burned clay, and 3 small Rockport ware pottery fragments were found confined to a depth of 12 to 18 centimeters. Beneath this level, fewer shell fragments and no sherds or burned clay nodules were present, supporting the inference that the nearby mechanical blading had in fact barely exposed a late prehistoric occupational surface.

Cultural material recovered from the site includes 50 fragments of Rockport pottery, a probable sandy paste smoking pipe fragment similar to those from the Holmes Site, an expanding stem arrow-point, 3 small unifacial chert end scrapers, 2 exhausted chert cores, a crude chert cobble chopping tool, 132 pieces of chert debitage, and a sandstone grindstone fragment.

Animal bones represent bison and deer. Shellfish are present only as a scatter, and only 9 fish otoliths were recovered. A very minor role for estuarine resources is indicated. By weight, bison and deer represent the great preponderance of the meat diet, though the small size of the sample precludes meaningful precise quantification.

A sample of 34 *Rangia cuneata* valves was collected for seasonality analysis. The results indicate that rangia gathering was emphasized at this site during both the spring and the late summer. Of the 9 fish otoliths recovered, 6 were too small for seasonality analysis (i.e., too young, with too few annuli, for reliable assessment of the relative amount of growth since the final winter growth interruption annulus). Of the 3 readable specimens, season of death was spring for 1 drum and 1 redfish, and fall for a second drum. Obviously, the sample is too small for interpretive reliability. These readings are, however, more or less in agreement with the rangia analysis, since the single fall reading could easily represent a late summer death, given variable growth rates between individual fish.

## Site 41NU46

Site 41NU46 is situated on the crest of a large clay dune on Oso Creek, a few kilometers upstream from the head of Oso Bay. At present the intact dune deposits bearing Rockport Phase materials exist only as a remnant at the crest of the dune. A 1-meter-square test unit was excavated to a depth of 60 centimeters under my direction. This failed to produce diagnostic Rockport Phase artifacts, with the possible exception of a small unifacial chert end scraper. Other materials included a few small pieces of chert debitage and small bits of deer-sized bone.

Immediately adjacent to the dune surface remnant, where the test unit was excavated, is a fairly level area, 30 to 50 centimeters below the level of the intact modern surface, onto which erosion has deflated late prehistoric materials. Surface inspection of this area (covering approximately 200 square meters) revealed a scatter of late prehistoric debris, including 14 small sherds of Rockport ware pottery, a Perdiz arrowpoint, several dozen chert flakes, deer bone fragments, and 23 marine fish otoliths.

Sixteen of the 23 otoliths collected were large enough for seasonality readings. These fell into seasonal periods as follows:

| | | |
|---|---|---|
| Fall | 1 | (6 percent) |
| Winter | 0 | (0 percent) |
| Spring | 3 | (19 percent) |
| Summer | 12 | (75 percent) |

Since these otoliths were found resting on a deflated surface, it is likely that they represent the general seasonal emphasis on fish procurement during the late prehistoric. Spring and summer fishing is clearly indicated.

No rangia shells were present anywhere on the site, nor are they usually found on sites along Oso Creek or Oso Bay (see Steele and Mokry 1985). Rangia have likely never been present in the Oso Creek/Bay system, probably because the wide localized fluctuations in salinity levels that occur in such a small estuary system are beyond the tolerance range of this low-salinity bivalve.

Inferences concerning the relative proportions of different kinds of faunal remains at this site are limited. Deer bones are present, and this species was almost certainly of considerable dietary significance. Shellfish remains are scarce; those observed in the area of the deflated late prehistoric surface consisted of a few oyster, sunray venus, and *Busycon* fragments. Fish otoliths are more numerous than at other prairie sites, though this is in large part the result of their settling onto the deflated surface from which they were collected over a fairly wide area.

## Site 41SP159

Site 41SP159 is one of several important Rockport Phase sites along the south side of the Aransas River that were discovered during survey and subsurface testing that I conducted to further investigate the nature of Rockport Phase prairie-riverine campsites. The working hypothesis was that if the kind of site documented for the Nueces River and Oso Creek represented a significant part of human adaptation during the Rockport Phase, then similar sites would be found along other stream systems that empty into central coast bays. In general, the findings are in accord with those from the sites along the Nueces River, and the Aransas River sites add important information on use of the coastal prairie-riverine environment during the Rockport Phase. Small, short-term camps, occupied during the spring and summer, with primary economic reliance on terrestrial food resources, are again the rule.

Site 41SP159 is located on the edge of the prairie uplands overlooking the south bank of Moody Creek near its confluence with the Aransas River (see Figure 17). When discovered, parts of the site had been exposed by very shallow (10–15 centimeters deep) bulldozer blading that had apparently just barely cut into and exposed late prehistoric occupational surfaces. Limited subsurface testing confirmed that late prehistoric materials occurred at depths of between about 10 and 20 centimeters below the undisturbed ground surface. These and underlying, apparently preceramic, cultural materials were found below a thin humus layer, within the dark brown Willacy fine sandy loam that caps the Lissie Formation clayey sands and sandy clays of the uplands.

Rockport Phase materials were exposed in two areas. A roughly east-west swath had been cut by machinery through the brush on the hilltop near the center of the site, and the entire north end of the hilltop and the adjacent northern slope had been exposed. These two areas yielded cultural materials that are assigned to two separate occupational components.

The material found in the east-west swath in the center of the site may represent, at least in large part, a single short-term occupation.

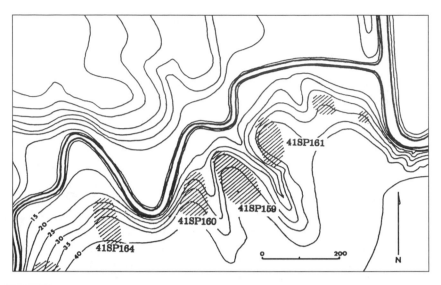

*Figure 17.* Map showing the locations of Sites 41SP159, 41SP160, and 41SP161 on upland margins overlooking Moody Creek near its confluence with the Aransas River.

A light scatter of *Rangia cuneata* shells and shell fragments, a few chert flakes, bison and deer bone fragments, and pottery fragments from no more than 4 vessels (see Figure 18.A–B) were found along only a 15-meter stretch of the machine cut. The inference of a single, short-term Rockport Phase occupation is drawn from the limited horizontal extent of this material, and the redundant findings within this area of fragments of the same 4 pottery vessels.

Twenty-one whole *Rangia cuneata* valves were gathered from the surface of the machine cut for seasonality analysis. The percentages of the various growth categories follow:

| | | |
|---|---|---|
| Interrupted | 0 | (0 percent) |
| Early | 2 | (19 percent) |
| Middle | 9 | (43 percent) |
| Late | 6 | (29 percent) |
| Indeterminate | 4 | (19 percent) |

This breakdown fits well with Aten's histogram for mid-July. If this is taken as the midpoint of a seasonality with the range of 1.5 months suggested by Carlson's (1988) analyses, the period from the beginning of June to the end of August is represented.

A subsurface test was conducted in this part of the site with the primary goals of identifying the depth range of late prehistoric materials and determining whether earlier (Archaic) occupation occurred in this part of the site. Located immediately to the south of the east-west machine cut, the test consisted of a 1-meter-square unit that was excavated with trowels to a depth of 40 centimeters. All excavated soil was screened through 1/4-inch mesh hardware cloth. Data were recorded according to three arbitrary levels: 0–15 centimeters, 15–30 centimeters, and 30–40 centimeters. A low density of cultural debris was found in all levels. The deposit was essentially homogeneous, consisting of the dark brown Willacy fine sandy loam. No vertical zonation of cultural material was discernible; sparse occupational debris was found throughout the 40-centimeter depth of the test. The cultural materials appear to have been sporadically deposited within the context of gradually accreting eolian sediments and soil formation.

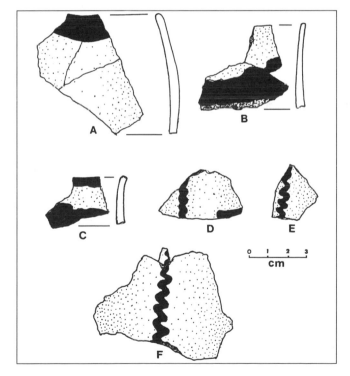

*Figure 18.* Examples of Rockport Black-on-Gray potsherds from Aransas River sites: A–D are from 41SP159; E and F are from 41SP167 (A–C are rim fragments).

The 0–15-centimeter level produced an edge-trimmed prismatic blade of brown chert and a rim fragment from the same small-mouthed, neckless globular vessel described above. This sherd exhibited a rather wide asphaltum band on the lip and interior asphaltum coating. Faunal material from this level included bones of deer (1 left humerus, 1 rib fragment, and 1 long bone fragment) and bison (4 rib fragments, 1 long bone fragment). Thirty-four *Rangia cuneata* (complete valves or umbo fragments) were found. Twenty-one whole valves were analyzed for seasonality, with the following breakdown into growth categories:

| | | |
|---|---|---|
| Interrupted | 3 | (13 percent) |
| Early | 10 | (48 percent) |
| Middle | 4 | (19 percent) |
| Late | 2 | (10 percent) |
| Indeterminate | 2 | (10 percent) |

These results conform closely to Aten's end of April rangia histogram. Following Carlson (1988), this could indicate either a short 2-week period or the averaging of a 3-month spring period of clam gathering, from mid-March through mid-May.

The 15–30-centimeter level produced the following evidence of prehistoric occupation: 1 utilized chert flake, 1 nodule of burned caliche, 1 burned clay nodule, deer bones (2 metapodial shank fragments, 1 radius fragment, 1 phalange, 1 distal tibia, 1 long bone fragment), 34 small unidentifiable bone splinters, and 55 *Rangia cuneata* valves and umbo fragments.

Thirty-three whole rangia valves from the 15–30-centimeter level were analyzed for seasonality, with the following results:

| | | |
|---|---|---|
| Interrupted | 2 | (6 percent) |
| Early | 8 | (24 percent) |
| Middle | 13 | (39 percent) |
| Late | 4 | (12 percent) |
| Indeterminate | 6 | (18 percent) |

The best fit with Aten's histograms is end of May, which represents the midpoint of a potential 3-month range from the beginning of April to the middle of June.

The 30–40-centimeter level produced a single chert flake and faunal materials consisting of deer bones (1 left distal humerus, 7 vertebra fragments, 3 rib fragments, 1 proximal tibia fragment, and

4 long bone fragments), 8 very small unidentifiable bone fragments, and 29 *Rangia cuneata* valves and umbo fragments.

Only 17 whole *Rangia cuneata* shells were recovered from 30–40 centimeters, less than the minimum number of 20 shells that Aten (1981) considers minimal for a reliable seasonality assessment. The growth category breakdown of this sample produces a rather unclear pattern, probably due to inadequate sample size. A late winter through early summer seasonality is suggested:

| | | |
|---|---|---|
| Interrupted | 4 | (24 percent) |
| Early | 5 | (29 percent) |
| Middle | 4 | (24 percent) |
| Late | 1 | (6 percent) |
| Indeterminate | 3 | (17 percent) |

Most of the exposed area at the north end of the site was on ground that sloped too steeply to be suitable for actual habitation. Along with a somewhat greater variety of cultural debris, this suggests that this part of the site was used for general debris disposal, perhaps during a number of recurrent occupations. About 10 man-hours of meticulous surface inspection of the exposed slope resulted in the recovery of a small sample of lithic and ceramic artifacts. Lithics consist of 24 chert flakes, a Perdiz type arrowpoint, an unfinished arrowpoint fragment, a small chert end scraper, and a rather small (length 44 millimeters) ovate bifacial tool, possibly a knife. Ceramics include 15 fragments representing 8 Rockport ware vessels (see Figure 18.C–D).

The scant faunal materials collected from the exposed surface of the north slope consist of bones of white-tailed deer (1 vertebra, 1 phalange, 1 long bone fragment) and bison (2 incisors, 1 proximal femur fragment, 1 proximal radius fragment, 1 phalange, and 6 long bone fragments). Shellfish remains consist of a scatter of *Rangia cuneata*, 1 oyster shell fragment, and 1 sunray venus clamshell fragment. A single marine fish otolith, from a sea trout is too small (young) for seasonality determination.

A sample of 50 *Rangia cuneata* shells was collected from the north slope for seasonality analysis. The results indicate growth category percentages that do not fit well with any of Aten's modern 2-week-period histograms:

| | | |
|---|---|---|
| Interrupted | 9 | (18 percent) |
| Early | 8 | (16 percent) |

| Middle | 16 | (32 percent) |
| Late | 9 | (18 percent) |
| Indeterminate | 8 | (16 percent) |

The middle category is best represented and indicates an emphasis on summer clam gathering. The approximately equal representation of the other growth categories produces an overall breakdown that is best interpreted as indicating March through midsummer gathering (see Aten's biweekly percentages, Aten 1981:Table 3).

A 1-meter-square test unit was excavated at about midslope to test for the presence of intact late prehistoric material beneath the 10 centimeters or so removed by bulldozer brush removal. Immediately beneath the surface of the machine cut was a cluster of bison bones that also contained 3 complete valves of *Rangia cuneata*.

### Site 41SP160

This small site is located some 100 meters west of 41SP159, on another hilltop that is also part of the dissected upland overlooking the Moody Creek floodplain (see Figure 17). The site was initially recognizable as a scatter of prehistoric debris recently exposed by the same mechanical brush removal as seen at 41SP159. The machine blading was no more than about 10 centimeters deep, judging from inspection of the edges of the bladed area. From the distributions of cultural debris within the bladed area at the northern end of the hilltop, as well as limited subsurface testing, a single small late prehistoric component appears to be indicated.

Most cultural debris was sparsely scattered over the hilltop, with the exception of a relatively dense spread of *Rangia cuneata* shells on the northwest slope. Also in this area was a concentration of deer bone that apparently represented a single animal. Artifacts were not similarly concentrated in this area but were found sporadically over the exposed area of the site.

Artifacts found on the freshly exposed surface consist of 2 Perdiz type arrowpoints, 2 small unifacial end scrapers, 2 prismatic blades, 2 chert cores, 40 pieces of chert debitage, an edge-utilized fragment of sunray venus clamshell, a whelk shell adze, and 1 fragment of Rockport pottery.

Mammal bones include the deer bones found on the northwest slope (1 skull fragment, 2 mandible fragments, 1 rib fragment, 2 scapulae, 2 femur fragments, 1 tibia fragment, 1 tarsal, and 1 long bone fragment) as well as 2 bison long bone fragments, both from near the center of the site on the hilltop. Shell debris, other than

*Rangia cuneata*, includes 3 oyster, 1 whelk columella fragment, a sunray venus fragment, and an Atlantic cockle fragment. No fish remains were found.

A sample of 31 rangia was gathered from both the hilltop and the northwest slope for seasonality analysis. The results indicate clam gathering in late May. In terms of potential time range of clam gathering, the period from mid-April to mid-July is indicated.

A 1-meter-square test unit, located on the crest of the hill near the center of the debris scatter, was excavated to a depth of 40 centimeters. The purpose was to test for the presence of late prehistoric debris below the level exposed by machine blading, as well as to determine the presence/absence of deeper cultural material. Excavation was accomplished using trowels and hand shovels; all soil was put through 1/4-inch hardware cloth.

This work yielded very little cultural debris. Several *Rangia cuneata* valves and 2 fragments of deer long bone were found in the upper 15 centimeters of the test. Below that level, only a single rangia valve and a burned clay nodule (at 40 centimeters) were found. No artifacts were found in the test unit.

The fact that most of the rangia, as well as the deer bone fragments, were found in the top 15 centimeters suggests an association with the scatter of debris exposed on the bladed surface. The dearth of deeper material, in combination with the discrete horizontal distribution of the exposed debris, suggests that most if not all surface material can in fact be attributed to a single late prehistoric component.

## Site 41SP161

Located on another hilltop at the upland margin, just east of 41SP159 (Figure 17), Site 41SP161 lies within an area of rather dense mesquite and acacia brush at the crest of the hill. Judging by the extent of a surface scatter of *Rangia cuneata*, the maximum size of the area of occupation is about 1,000 square meters. No significant artificial disturbances were seen on the site, except at the extreme northern edge, where fresh bulldozer blading had exposed a very light scatter of rangia and several fragments of bison long bone.

In order to test for evidence of late prehistoric occupation, 2 complete and 1 partial adjoining 1-meter-square units were excavated in the area of brush cover, at a locus where rangia shells were relatively abundant on the surface (though still only a scatter). This resulted in the identification of a vertically discrete zone of late prehistoric Rockport Phase debris confined to a uniform depth of between 6 and

10 centimeters. The excavation procedure involved exposure of the materials with trowels and brushes and recording of precise vertical and horizontal positions of all artifacts and faunal materials. The tight vertical distribution of cultural debris should be emphasized; troweling below the 10-centimeter level in all units failed to expose additional artifacts or bone fragments and only a scant quantity of rangia fragments. In terms of rangia, whole and relatively numerous shells were confined to the 6–10-centimeter zone that contained artifacts and bone fragments. A discrete short-term occupational surface, very much like that identified at the McKinzie Site, appears to be indicated.

Artifacts consist of 28 fragments of Rockport pottery representing 7 vessels, 15 pieces of chert debitage, and 1 small end scraper. Faunal bones include several identifiable deer bone fragments (1 rib, 1 metacarpal, 1 tibia, 1 tarsal, 1 astragalus, and 1 long bone fragment), 1 probable bison long bone fragment, 37 small splinters of unidentifiable mammal bone, a small fish vertebra (species unidentified), and 21 whole and several hundred fragmentary *Rangia cuneata* shells.

The sample of 21 whole *Rangia cuneata* valves was analyzed for seasonality. Mid-June clam gathering is indicated, with a potential seasonality range encompassing the period from the beginning of May to the end of July.

### Site 41SP167

Site 41SP167 is located on the northern edge of the upland margin, just south of the channel of the North Fork of Moody Creek (Figure 19). At this point in its course, Moody Creek flows only intermittently in a narrow and shallow channel. Though a narrow strip of arboreal vegetation is supported by moisture associated with the creek, the stream at this point is too small in scale to have an associated floodplain. The site is situated some 5 to 6 meters above the creek bed on level ground, within a fine sandy loam soil. The topography slopes gently down to the creek channel.

When the site was first discovered, the large open area in which it is situated had been freshly plowed. According to Steve Atzenhoffer, foreman of the ranch on which the site is located, this was the first time the area had ever been cultivated. This is confirmed by the fact that many of the numerous animal bone fragments associated with prehistoric occupation were large in size, clearly having undergone little or no breakage through plowing. The recent plowing, while unfortunately destroying the integrity of the upper 25 centimeters

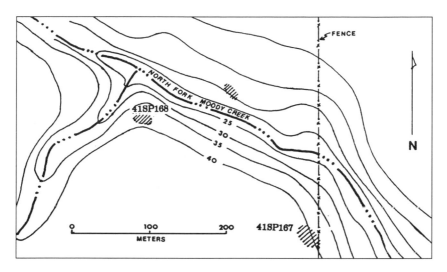

*Figure 19.* Map showing the locations of Sites 41SP167 and 41SP168 on the upland margins overlooking the North Fork of Moody Creek.

of site deposit, had clearly revealed the horizontal extent of the site. It was readily determined that Rockport Phase debris was distributed over a very discrete, elliptical area covering about 600 square meters.

Our investigation of this site involved meticulous surface inspection, including collection of all exposed artifacts and identifiable bone fragments, as well as the excavation of a 2-meter square to below the base of the plow zone. Because of the total horizontal exposure of the site, an unusually complete representation of artifacts was obtained for a Group 2 site. Lithics include stone projectile points, scrapers, knife fragments, 2 medial biface fragments, a cobble chopping tool similar to the specimen from 41NU255, 3 prismatic blades (1 with edge trimming), 214 pieces of chert flakes, and what may be a reworked mano fragment. The projectile points include 3 Perdiz and 2 expanded-stem arrowpoints, as well as 3 dart points (1 Catan, 1 Matamoros, 1 unstemmed specimen of no established type; see type definitions in Turner and Hester 1993). The end scrapers, 11 in number, are all of the small unifacial variety. Of the 3 thin bifaces categorized here as knives, 1 exhibits the alternate edge beveling commonly found on late prehistoric Texas knives associated with bison processing (Turner and Hester 1985; Johnson 1994; Prewitt 1981).

Shell artifacts consist of 3 fragments of edge-flaked sunray venus clamshell tools and 2 whelk (*Busycon perversum*) body whorl adzes.

Three bone artifacts were recovered: a deer ulna flaking tool; the end of a flattened, ground, and polished bone tool that may have been used for weaving mats; and a finely made needle, complete with basal perforation, or eye.

The 87 recovered potsherds may represent as many as 21 vessels. The sample is typical of Rockport ware. Ten sherd groups (48 percent) are characterized by some form of asphaltum surface treatment. Five of these bear interior coating; 5 have exterior coating. Two vessels of Rockport Black-on-Gray II are represented (see Figure 18.E–F). Judging by a rimsherd and body sherds in one group, a vessel that can be confidently assigned to the Rockport Plain type is present. Another group of sherds, including a rimsherd, represents a widemouthed vessel with exterior asphaltum coating on the vessel lip and exterior. The rimsherd in this group exhibits two parallel horizontal incised lines just below the lip, which places this group in the Rockport Incised type.

Bones collected at 41SP167 constitute the largest sample of faunal material from a Group 2 site in the study area. A complete listing of all identifiable elements from the various represented species, including those already mentioned from the plow zone of the test unit, is presented in Table 4. In terms of minimum numbers of individuals, identifiable bone elements represent 4 bison (2 adult females, 1 adult male, 1 juvenile male), 3 adult deer, 1 cottontail rabbit, and 8 fish (5 trout, 1 black drum, 2 redfish). The estimated meat weight of these animals, and their proportional percentage by species of total meat weight represented at the site, can be seen in Table 5. It is clear from the data presented in Table 5 that the overwhelmingly predominant meat food represented at the site is bison, which represents an estimated 90.9 percent of all meat weight. Deer, representing an estimated 7.7 percent of the total, is a distant second in terms of meat significance.

The percentage figure for *Rangia cuneata* meat weight (1.1 percent) is based on a gross estimate of 11,775 clams at the site, each containing an estimated 10 grams of raw meat. The number of clams is based on the multiple of the number of whole valves and umbo fragments found in the plow zone of the test unit ($N = 157$) by 150 (the 4 square meters of the test unit represent 1/150 of the total approximate area of the site), divided by two (each clam having 2 valves). This is considered a generally valid procedure because the density of rangia shells observable on the surface appeared to vary little across the site. Rangia was apparently an occasionally gathered minor supplement to the meat diet.

Fish were clearly of very little significance in the overall diet at the site. The 1 drum and 5 trout account for only an estimated 0.3 percent of the total meat weight. Most likely, fish were caught in the Aransas River estuary and brought back to camp on an opportunistic basis.

Data on seasonality at this site are available from both *Rangia cuneata* and marine fish otolith analyses. Two samples of rangia shells found in apparent association with Rockport Phase artifacts were analyzed. One, consisting of 43 shells, was collected from the surface across the entire site. The second (39 shells) represents a localized sample and comes from the plow zone in the excavated test unit. The results of the analyses, in terms of percentages of the seasonal growth categories, are as follows:

Sample 1 (site surface)
| | | |
|---|---|---|
| Interrupted | 3 | (7 percent) |
| Early | 14 | (32 percent) |
| Middle | 15 | (35 percent) |
| Late | 6 | (14 percent) |
| Indeterminate | 5 | (12 percent) |

Sample 2 (plow zone, test unit)
| | | |
|---|---|---|
| Interrupted | 4 | (10 percent) |
| Early | 12 | (31 percent) |
| Middle | 12 | (31 percent) |
| Late | 6 | (15 percent) |
| Indeterminate | 5 | (13 percent) |

The results on both samples are in close agreement, as both best approximate Aten's end of May rangia histogram. A 3-month range, approximating the period from the beginning of April through midsummer, is indicated.

Six of the 8 marine fish otoliths found at the site are large enough for seasonality analysis. Three trout and 1 black drum otolith are from either the surface or the plow zone in the test unit; 2 redfish otoliths are from the 25–45-centimeter level in the test unit. All 6 otoliths read as summer fish deaths and are thus in basic agreement with the rangia seasonality.

### Site 41SP170

Site 41SP170 is one several late prehistoric sites on the upland margins overlooking Hughes Lake, a small pond on the fossil floodplain of the Aransas River (see Figure 20). The pond, in a topographic low point, is fed by a small intermittent stream entering from the northeast that channels runoff from surrounding higher ground. The marshy margins of the pond support extensive stands of cattails. A winter habitat for migrating waterfowl, the pond was also doubtless a source of fresh water during late prehistoric times, since it contained standing water during a recent drought when other ponds on the fossil floodplain had dried up.

The Rockport Phase is represented by a small, roughly circular area of debris with a diameter of about only 5 meters. Over the surface of this area, scattered deer and bison bone fragments, small fragments of Rockport pottery, and chert flakes were found. A 1-meter-square test unit was excavated in the approximate center of the area. The unit was dug to a depth of 30 centimeters, which was sufficient to define the base of the Rockport Phase debris deposit.

Excavated artifacts of the Rockport Phase consist of 28 pottery fragments representing as many as 13 vessels, 19 chert flakes, a small quadrilaterally flaked chert scraperlike tool, a small (length 21 millimeters) prismatic blade, a unifacial end scraper, a chert biface fragment, a small chert core, a grooved and snapped proximal deer radius section, and an edge-flaked sunray venus clamshell tool fragment.

Animal bones consist of bone fragments of deer (1 proximal radius, 1 metapodial, 1 phalange, 7 long bone fragments) and bison (1 lower premolar, 1 carpal, 4 long bone fragments). Shellfish remains consist of 58 *Rangia cuneata* valves and umbo fragments, 1 oyster fragment, 1 Atlantic cockle fragment, and 1 sunray venus fragment. Hard-shell turtle is represented by 1 carapace fragment. Fish remains consist of 2 otoliths of sea trout (of different sizes and thus representing 2 fish) and 1 alligator gar scale.

The 22 whole *Rangia cuneata* valves were analyzed for seasonality. The results conform well with Aten's growth histogram for mid-June. In terms of a 3-month seasonal range, the period from the beginning of May to the end of July is indicated. The 2 trout otoliths from the 0–20-centimeter level were suitable for seasonality readings; both specimens indicate summer fish deaths.

### Summary of Findings at Group 2 Campsites

The sites reviewed in this chapter share several basic characteristics. The most important is that all sites can be attributed to the coastal Rockport Phase. All have yielded most or all of the key

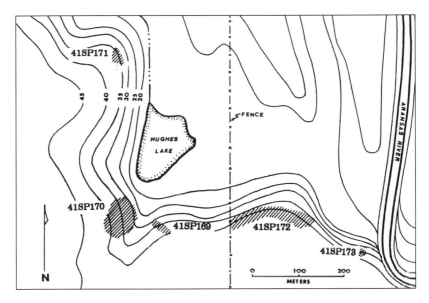

*Figure 20.* Map showing the locations of several sites on the upland margin overlooking Hughes Lake and the Aransas River floodplain. Sites 41SP169, 41SP170, and 41SP171 yielded data pertinent to this study.

artifact traits that define this archaeological manifestation, namely, arrowpoints (most commonly Perdiz, but also expanded-stem and unstemmed triangular Fresno points), small unifacial end scrapers, prismatic blades, and, most diagnostically, Rockport ware pottery (Table 3).

The seasonality data are remarkably consistent in indicating spring-summer occupations. For the most part, these data derive from analyses of *Rangia cuneata* samples. The rangia seasonalities, when expressed in terms of previously discussed 3-month ranges, place the range of occupations at prairie-riverine locales from late March through August.

It is significant that the 25 fish otoliths found at several of these sites (41NU46, 41NU255, 41SP167, and 41SP170) strongly support the rangia seasonality. Expressed graphically in Figure 21, the seasonal percentage breakdown of the composite otolith sample from these sites shows an overwhelming preponderance of summer fish catches, with a secondary representation of spring. Only a single fall otolith (from 41NU255) is present, and no specimens represent the winter season. This is clearly the reverse of the otolith seasonality

**Table 3.** *Artifacts by Material Categories, Group 2 Rockport Phase Sites*

| | NU 37 | NU 193 | NU 221 | NU 255 | SP 103 | SP 159 | SP 160 | SP 161 | SP 167 | SP 170 | Totals |
|---|---|---|---|---|---|---|---|---|---|---|---|
| **Lithic** | | | | | | | | | | | |
| Arrowpoints | | | | | | | | | | | |
| Perdiz | | 1 | 2 | | 2 | 1 | 1 | | 3 | | 10 |
| Prob. Perdiz | 1 | | | | | | 1 | | | | 2 |
| Fresno | 2 | | | | | | | | | | 2 |
| Scallorn | | | | 1 | | | | | 1 | | 2 |
| Edwards | | | | | | | | | 1 | | 1 |
| Unident. frag. | | | 1 | | | | | | 2 | | 3 |
| Preforms | | | 1 | | | | | | | | 1 |
| Dart points | | | | | | | | | | | |
| Catan | | | | 1 | | | | | 1 | | 2 |
| Matamoros | | | | | | 1 | | | 1 | | 2 |
| Untyped | | | | | | | | | 1 | | 1 |
| Drills | 1 | | | | | | | | | | 1 |
| Knife fragments | | | | | | | | | 2 | | 2 |
| Beveled knives | | 1 | 1 | | | | | | 1 | | 3 |
| End-side scraper | | | | | | | | | | 1 | 1 |
| End scrapers | | | 1 | 2 | 4 | | 2 | 1 | 11 | | 21 |
| Biface fragments | | | 1 | | | | | | 5 | 1 | 7 |
| Cores | | | 1 | 2 | | | 2 | | | | 5 |
| Chert debitage | 25 | 96 | 596 | 132 | 387 | 26 | 42 | 16 | 215 | 19 | 1,554 |
| Mano | | | | | | | | | 1 | | 1 |
| Milling slab | | | 2 | 1 | | | | | | | 3 |
| **Shell** | | | | | | | | | | | |
| Edge-flaked sunray | 1 | | | | | | 1 | | 2 | 1 | 5 |
| Whelk adzes | 2 | | | | | | 1 | | 2 | | 5 |
| **Bone** | | | | | | | | | | | |
| Awl fragments | | | 3 | | | | | | | | 3 |
| Deer ulna flaker | | | | | | | | | 1 | | 2 |
| Needle | | | | | | | | | 1 | | 2 |
| Weaving tool | | | | | | | | | 1 | | 2 |
| Grooved bone | | | | | | | | | | 1 | 1 |
| **Ceramics** | | | | | | | | | | | |
| Potsherds | 107 | 3 | 195 | 50 | 103 | 49 | 1 | 28 | 87 | 28 | 651 |
| Smoking pipe fragments | | | 1 | 1 | | | | | | | 2 |

at the large shoreline sites and is particularly important because it strongly suggests that the rangia analyses reflect seasonality of actual prairie-riverine occupations, rather than merely a seasonal preference in clam gathering. A clear seasonal dichotomy in occupation between Group 1 and Group 2 sites is apparent.

The animal bones from Group 2 sites (Table 4) are consistent in showing an overwhelming economic emphasis on terrestrial resources. In terms of the meat diet, there was a primary reliance on large game, namely bison and white-tailed deer. Fish remains are few, and some prairie-riverine sites have yielded none at all. This contrasts dramatically with the situation at the shoreline sites: all of the investigations at Group 2 sites have yielded less than a handful of fish bones and a total of only 34 fish otoliths, as compared to a total number of 2,009 otoliths from the excavations carried out at Group 1 sites (41SP120, 41SP43, and 41CL3).

Probably the most representative prairie-riverine faunal samples come from the McKinzic Site (41NU221), where a discrete living surface was extensively excavated, and from Site 41SP167, where extensive and fresh exposure permitted collection of faunal materials from across virtually the entire site. Table 5 shows the quantities of

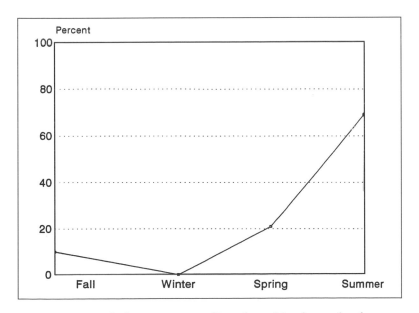

*Figure 21.* Graph showing seasonality of combined sample of 25 fish otoliths from Group 2 sites, according to the percentage of the sample falling into each seasonal grouping.

**Table 4.** *Faunal Remains from Group 2 Rockport Phase Sites*

| Taxa | NU 37 | NU 221 | NU 255 | SP 103 | SP 159 | SP 160 | SP 161 | SP 167 | SP 170 | Totals |
|---|---|---|---|---|---|---|---|---|---|---|
| **Fish** | | | | | | | | | | |
| Otoliths | | | | | | | | | | |
| Black drum | | 1 | 1 | | | | | 1 | | 2 |
| Sea trout | | 1 | 1 | | | | | 4 | 2 | 6 |
| Redfish | | | 1 | | | | | | | 1 |
| Catfish | 1 | | | | | | | | | 1 |
| Bone elements | | | 1 | 1 | | | 1 | 2 | 1 | 5 |
| Gar scales | | | | | | | | | 1 | 1 |
| **Shellfish** | | | | | | | | | | |
| *Rangia cuneata* | | X | X | | X | X | X | X | X | |
| Oyster | | | X | X | 2 | 3 | | 6 | 1 | |
| *Busycon perversum* | | | 1 | | | 1 | | | | 2 |
| Sunray venus | | | 1 | | 1 | 1 | | 5 | 1 | 9 |
| Atlantic cockle | | | 1 | | | | | | 1 | 2 |
| *Ischadium* | | | | | | | | | 1 | 1 |
| *Unio sp.* | | | | | | | | | 1 | 1 |
| **Mammals** | | | | | | | | | | |
| Deer | | | | | | | | | | |
| Skull frag. | | | | | | 1 | | 1 | | 2 |
| Mandible | | | | | | 2 | | 1 | | 3 |
| Molar | | | 1 | | | | | 1 | | 2 |
| Molar | | | 1 | | | | | 1 | | 2 |
| Vertebra | | | | | 1 | | | 5 | | 6 |
| Rib frag. | | 4 | | | 1 | 1 | 1 | | | 7 |
| Scapula frag. | | | | | | 2 | | 1 | | 3 |
| Humerus | | | 1 | | 1 | | | 3 | | 5 |
| Radius | | | 1 | | | | | 3 | 1 | 5 |
| Ulna | | | | | 1 | | | 2 | | 3 |
| Metacarpal | | | | | | | 1 | 2 | | 3 |
| Pelvic frag. | | 2 | | | | | | 2 | | 2 |
| Sacrum | | | | | | | | 1 | | 1 |
| Femur | | | | | | 2 | | 1 | | 3 |
| Calcaneus | | | | 1 | | 1 | | | | 2 |
| Tibia | | | 1 | | | | 1 | 1 | | 3 |
| Tarsal | | | 1 | | | | 1 | | | 2 |
| Astragalus | | | | | | 1 | | 3 | | 4 |
| Metatarsal | | | | | | | | 2 | | 2 |
| Metapodial | | | | | 1 | | | | 1 | 2 |
| Phalange | | | 1 | 1 | 1 | 1 | | 5 | 2 | 11 |
| Long bone frag. | 6 | | 4 | 17 | 9 | | 1 | 19 | 7 | 73 |

**Table 4.** (Continued)

| Taxa | NU 37 | NU 221 | NU 255 | SP 103 | SP 159 | SP 160 | SP 161 | SP 167 | SP 170 | Totals |
|---|---|---|---|---|---|---|---|---|---|---|
| Bison | | | | | | | | | | |
| Incisor | | | | | | 1 | | | | 1 |
| Premolar | | | | | | 1 | | | 1 | 2 |
| Molar | | | 1 | | | | | 6 | | 7 |
| Vertebra | | | | | | | | 5 | | 5 |
| Caudal bone | | | | | 7 | | | 1 | | 8 |
| Scapula frag. | | | | | | | | 1 | | 1 |
| Rib frag. | 1 | 9 | 4 | 1 | 21 | | | 21 | | 57 |
| Costal cart. | | | | | 13 | | | | | 13 |
| Humerus | | | | | | | | 2 | | 2 |
| Radius | | 1 | | | 1 | | | 4 | | 6 |
| Ulna | | | | | | | | 3 | | 3 |
| Carpal | | | | | 1 | | | 4 | | 5 |
| Femur | | | | | | | | 2 | | 2 |
| Patella | | | | | 1 | | | | | 1 |
| Tibia | | | | | | | | 3 | | 3 |
| Tarsal | | | | | 1 | | | 1 | | 2 |
| Metapodial | | | | | | | | 1 | | 1 |
| Metatarsal | | | | | 1 | | | | | 1 |
| Astragalus | | | | | | | | 3 | | 3 |
| Phalange | | | | | 2 | | | 3 | | 5 |
| Long bone frag. | 5 | 9 | 2 | 3 | 8 | 2 | 1 | 22 | 5 | 57 |
| Cottontail rabbit mandible | | | | | 1 | | | 1 | | 2 |
| Reptile | | | | | | | | | | |
| Turtle (carapace/ plastron frag.) | | 22 | 2 | | 1 | | 4 | 2 | 1 | 32 |

*Note*: X indicates scatter of shellfish remains.

faunal materials at these two sites as expressed in terms of minimum numbers of individuals and derivative estimates of represented meat weights. A glance at these data will show that the percentages of meat weight by species, as a fraction of the total weight represented, are very similar at both sites. Bison is of overwhelming significance, followed by white-tailed deer. All other meat foods combined account for less than 3 percent of the total estimated weight. Though faunal data are limited from other prairie-riverine

**Table 5.** **MNI at Group 2 Rockport Phase Sites 41NU221 and 41SP167**

| Site and Species | MNI | Estimated Meat Weight (kg) | Meat Weight % |
|---|---|---|---|
| 41NU221 | | | |
| Bison | 1 female | 182 | 84.7 |
| White-tailed deer | 1 | 27 | 12.5 |
| *Rangia cuneata* | 440 | 4.4 | 2.0 |
| *Rangia flexuosa* | 228 | 1.1 | .5 |
| Sea trout | 1 | .2 | .1 |
| Catfish | 1 | .2 | .1 |
| | | Total meat weight, 214.9 kg | |
| 41SP167 | | | |
| Bison | 2 females | 364 | |
| | 1 male | 409 | |
| | 1 juvenile male | 200 | 90.9 |
| White-tailed deer | 3 | 82 | 7.6 |
| *Rangia cuneata* | 11,775 (estimated) | 11.8 | 1.1 |
| Black drum | 1 | 1.9 | .2 |
| Sea trout | 2 | .9 | .1 |
| | | Total meat weight, 1,069.6 kg | |

sites, the consistent presence of bison and deer bones, the scattered nature of rangia, and the dearth of fish remains all combine to indicate essentially the same sort of dietary pattern.

As previously noted, the McKinzie Site is the only prairie-riverine location from which there is high-resolution excavated data on horizontal intrasite patterns. It seems reasonable to infer, however, that a similar range of residential activities was carried out at other prairie-riverine sites, since these locations in general have produced the same kinds of artifacts and faunal remains. Artifacts include arrowpoints and scraping and cutting tools, as well as chert flakes representing manufacturing and/or tool maintenance activities. All prairie-riverine sites have produced at least some pottery, suggesting cooking and possibly storage. Also, most sites have yielded *Rangia cuneata*, which suggests that some part of the population residing at these camps was engaged in forays to estuarine areas and return trips to camp with gathered clams. Such activities would have served to supplement the main focus on hunting and may have involved a simple kind of division of labor within resident groups.

Further contrasts between the Group 2 prairie-riverine and the Group 1 shoreline sites are the very different ranges in site size and the marked differences in the density of cultural deposits. Shoreline locations range in size from about 10,000 to 30,000 or more square meters in area. The prairie-riverine sites are much smaller, ranging from the extremely small debris area at 41SP170 (25–30 square meters) to about 2,500 square meters at 41SP159. As already discussed, the upper range at 41SP159 appears to represent multiple episodes of small-scale occupation. Intermediate sizes seem to be represented at other sites such as McKinzie, 41NU255, 41NU240 (Ricklis 1988), 41SP160, and 41SP167, which covered about 800, 600, 250, 200, and 600 square meters, respectively. Where discrete components can be spatially delineated, small resident groups of people are indicated.

In terms of density of cultural debris, there is some variability in the prairie-riverine sites. However, artifacts and/or faunal remains are never found in profusion and are usually quite sparse. The extensive excavations at McKinzie, and the subsurface testing at other locations, invariably failed to yield the quantities of debris per unit area documented for shoreline sites. Likewise, in sites where extensive exposure justified meticulous surface examination, only relatively small samples of cultural material could be collected.

In summary, the two kinds of sites are consistently contrasted in terms of faunal remains, artifact densities, size, seasonality, and environmental context. Given that all sites contain essentially the same material culture assemblage and that the two site groups show complementary seasonality, it is apparent that each group represents a different aspect of a single cultural system. Each of these aspects came into play, on a seasonally oscillating basis, within correspondingly different segments of the ecological niche represented by the combined shoreline and coastal prairie environments.

### Life on the Inland Margin of Karankawan Territory

During the course of our investigations of Rockport Phase occupation of the prairie-riverine environment, a body of data was collected that permits remarkably precise identification of the inland boundary of the Karankawan adaptive system and that sheds light on the nature of that boundary. This evidence, important to understanding later historical processes, is only summarized here (the interested reader may find more detailed presentation in Ricklis 1990).

Several sites were discovered along the Aransas River—in the same area as the Rockport Phase campsites discussed above—that appear to represent short-term seasonal encampments of inland non-Karankawan groups. In many ways, these sites are very much like the nearby Rockport Phase locations. They are small, covering only a few hundred square meters, and show only light scatters of cultural debris. Like the Rockport Phase sites, they contain thin scatters of rangia clamshells and scant artifacts consisting of arrow-points, knife fragments, end scrapers, prismatic chert blades and chert flakes, occasional bone or shell tools, and pottery fragments.

These sites differ significantly from Rockport Phase Group 2 sites in two key ways. First, the pottery is not Rockport ware but pertains to the contemporaneous but distinct bone-tempered plainware ceramic tradition of the Toyah Horizon of inland Texas (see Hester 1980; Black 1986; Highley 1986). This pottery is characterized by more or less abundant quantities of crushed bone temper and by simple shapes such as bowls, jars, and ollas with plain, smoothed, and often burnished exterior surfaces. While vessels were occasionally decorated with asphaltum designs (e.g., Hester and Parker 1970; Black 1986), this was uncommon and did not include the lip banding and vertical painted squiggles so typical of coastal Rockport pottery. Since most of the commonly found artifacts of the Rockport Phase and the inland late prehistoric, particularly stone artifacts, are virtually indistinguishable from those of the Toyah Horizon (Ricklis 1992), it is the ceramics that show a clear dichotomy between sites occupied by coastal versus inland peoples.

The presence of Toyah or Toyah-like sites in the Aransas River survey area indicates that the subsistence patterns of inland people brought them as close as 40 kilometers from the mainland coast-line. This must represent a major cultural boundary, since all known contemporaneous sites documented further inland pertain to the Toyah Horizon (e.g., Hester and Parker 1970; Black 1986; Highley 1986; Hall et al. 1986). It is probably highly significant that during the early nineteenth century, the Mexican government considered creating a Karankawan reserve with an inland boundary 10 leagues (40 kilometers) from the coast (Smithwick 1900:13). Archaeology and history thus both point to a single basic territorial boundary, one that apparently was in place for several centuries, if not longer.

The second important difference between the Aransas River Toyah and Rockport sites is seasonality. While rangia analyses from the Rockport sites invariably show spring-summer seasonalities, the seasonal ranges of the Toyah sites are within the fall-winter period (Ricklis 1990). The two groups of sites thus show exactly complementary seasonal ranges. This fact is not likely to be an accident of sampling, considering the number of combined Rockport and Toyah sites for which we have seasonality data. Rather, a seasonal complementarity in boundary zone use by coastal and inland peoples is strongly suggested. The coastal Rockport Phase people returned to their shoreline fishing stations in the fall, in effect creating an occupational void that was filled by inland folk who moved into the boundary zone.

A second significant aspect of life on the inland margin of Karankawan territory is elucidated by findings at the Melon Site (41RF21) near Refugio, Texas. Again located about 40 kilometers from the mainland shoreline, this site appears to represent an encampment shared by coastal and inland peoples for the purpose of hunting and processing bison and deer. The site is rather small, encompassing an elliptical area of about 1,500 square meters atop a low knoll near a branch of Copano Creek. Extensive testing and several small block excavations here (Ricklis 1989, 1990) exposed dense clusters of bison and deer bones (Figure 22), as well as late prehistoric artifacts.

The artifacts include numerous arrowpoints (mostly of the Perdiz type), flaked chert knives, end scrapers, chert drills or perforators, a few bone tools, and several hundred pottery fragments representing as many as 64 vessels. The distribution of the pottery is particularly significant because the vessels represented in the north half of the site conform, as a group, to expectations for the inland Toyah Phase. The great majority (86 percent) of vessels were bone tempered, and only a small minority (14 percent) showed asphaltum surface treatment, as do other known coastal plain Toyah locations (Black 1986; Hester and Parker 1970). The ceramics from the south half of the site present a marked contrast, since the vessels represented conform well to Rockport ware. The majority (55 percent) had no bone temper, and none showed the profuse amount of bone commonly found in Toyah pottery. About half (54 percent) of the vessels had asphaltum coating or decoration, the same proportion found at most Rockport Phase sites (see data presented in Appendix A).

Although excavations were limited, the materials were recovered from test pits and excavation blocks distributed across the site. The findings strongly suggest that the northern half of the site was used by inland people, while coastal Rockport Phase people occupied the southern half. The distributional shift between the two kinds of pottery occurred at nearly the precise center of the site at the highest point on the small rise, with very little overlap. The highly discrete separation of the Rockport and the Toyah materials at least

*Figure 22.* Two views of excavations at the Melon Site (41RF21) in Refugio County. Top: dense cluster of bison and deer bone in the south part of the site. Bottom: exposed living surface in the north part of the site, with exposed deer and bison bone fragments, chert tools, and fragments of bone-tempered pottery.

suggests simultaneous use of the location by people of both cultural traditions; had the occupations been sequential, it is likely that the two kinds of ceramics would have had considerable overlap on the top of the knoll. Also suggesting contemporaneity of the two groups is the fact that all the late prehistoric materials were found in a thin but continuous stratum across the site. Furthermore, radiocarbon dates from the north and south parts of the site are nearly identical: three from the south half (Rockport component) are A.D. 1250 ± 70, 1270 ± 100, and 1265 ± 130; one from the north half (Toyah component) is A.D. 1275 ± 190. Although the margins of error on these dates are quite large, the consistent agreement of the midpoints at least suggests contemporaneity.

Though not conclusively demonstrable, the aggregate data suggest that the Melon Site was a hunting camp shared by coastal Karankawas and inland people. The faunal material clearly indicates that the most important meat source at the site was bison (a minimum of 5 bison were represented; had more extensive excavation been possible, the number would doubtless have been higher). An intensive focus on bison hunting seems to have brought people to this site, and a cooperative hunting venture may have facilitated the procurement of such a large and potentially aggressive prey.

In sum, the presently available information suggests that life along the inland Karankawan boundary zone was characterized by practices that were mutually beneficial to both coastal and inland peoples. The Aransas River sites point to a seasonal complementarity in boundary zone use, and the data from the Melon Site suggest at least occasional joint hunting ventures. These two modes of boundary zone dynamics are presented schematically in Figure 23.

Mutually beneficial, or at least noncompetitive, interactions are also suggested by sixteenth-century observations made by Cabeza de Vaca, as synthesized and characterized by Campbell and Campbell (1981:13):

No hostilities between shoreline and inland groups are mentioned. There is indication of friendly contacts between inland groups and shoreline groups, with the inland groups (Anegados and Avavares) apparently visiting the coastal groups. Trade between Camoles [a coastal group] and Anegados is implied. These contacts suggest that the groups involved may have had adjoining territories.

If the Campbells' (1981:12) placement of Cabeza de Vaca's Camoles in the Corpus Christi Bay area is correct, then the kind of

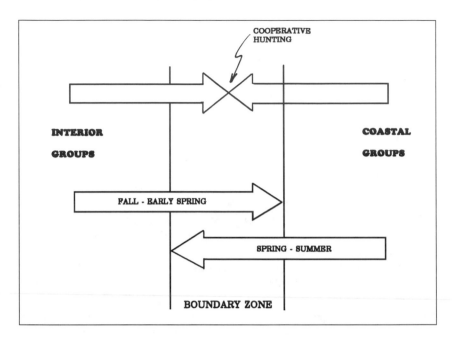

*Figure 23.* Schematic diagram showing modes of interaction between coastal and interior peoples, as suggested by archaeological data discussed in the text.

interaction described was taking place quite near the areas from which is derived our archaeological information. Certainly this placement of the Camoles puts the group within the area of the Rockport Phase and the inland groups within the southern range of the Toyah Horizon.

# Chapter 6
# Reconstructing Prehistoric
# Karankawan Adaptive Patterns

The archaeological evidence indicates that the late prehistoric Karankawas operated within a narrow strip of territory along the central coast of what is now Texas, with the inland margin of their operational area only about 40 kilometers from the mainland shoreline. Despite their tight adherence to the coastal zone, the Karankawas developed an adaptive strategy that took optimal advantage of resources in both the coastal estuarine and adjacent prairie-riverine environments. The seasonality data indicate that the fall and winter seasons were spent at recurrently occupied shoreline locations, all of which were in proximity to shallow and generally quiet bay or lagoonal waters. At these localities, subsistence economy was based upon a heavy reliance on fish, most importantly the largest species, black drum and redfish. Also important were large game animals, mainly white-tailed deer, and a variety of shellfish species that probably were of supplemental significance.

By spring, people began leaving the shoreline to establish camps along the rivers and creeks that empty into the coastal bays. Campsites on the upland prairie margins overlooking stream floodplains provided ready access both to the inland prairies and the riverine and floodplain environments. By this time of year, plant growth was well under way, and a variety of greens and, by summer, fruits and seeds could have been gathered on the uplands and along the floodplains. At the same time, bison and deer were reaching their peak condition, attaining maximum weights and highest yields of important subcutaneous and bone marrow fats. The seasonality data for both Groups 1 and 2 sites are summarized and contrasted graphically in Figure 24.

While the Group 1 fishing campsites are much larger and were clearly more intensively and repetitively utilized than the Group 2, they are also far less numerous. In the Corpus Christi Bay area, for example, six Group 1 sites have been documented (see map,

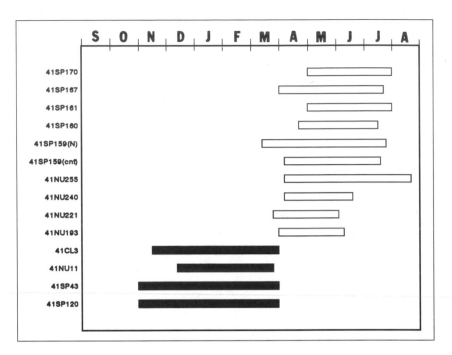

*Figure 24.* Graph showing seasonality estimates for Group 1 shoreline and Group 2 prairie-riverine sites, based on combined analyses of fish otoliths, oyster shells, and *Rangia cuneata* shells.

Figure 8), while a total of twenty-two Group 2 sites has been identified along the Nueces River and Oso Creek (Ricklis 1988; see also Figure 8 above). Considering the low archaeological visibility of Group 2, their actual number relative to that of shoreline Group 1 sites is almost certainly much greater. Given these contrasts in site size and numbers, it is likely that the shoreline locations represent relatively large population aggregates made possible by more or less predictable and concentrated fish resources. By contrast, the small but far more numerous prairie-riverine sites probably represent seasonal fissioning and dispersal of these larger groups.

As we noted earlier, the greatest abundance of black drum and redfish can be expected in central coast bays during fall and winter, a phenomenon probably linked to the spawning seasons of these species. Such a concentrated and predictable fish biomass would have permitted the large population aggregates inferred for shoreline locales with a minimal risk of subsistence failure. With the spring breakup of concentrated black drum populations, the least-risk human response would have been the pattern of dispersal indicated by the small, numerous, and lightly occupied prairie-riverine camp-sites. Dispersed settlement and subsistence would have again represented a least-risk strategy, since subsistence was oriented toward procurement of mobile bison and spatially dispersed white-tailed deer—resources that could not necessarily be counted on to provide adequate sustenance for large groups congregated at any one location.

The overall settlement and subsistence strategy of the late prehistoric Karankawas was thus predicated upon maximizing resource procurement while minimizing economic risk, within two major environmental zones in which greatest biotic productivity shifted in seasonally sequential phases. The system was marked by seasonal

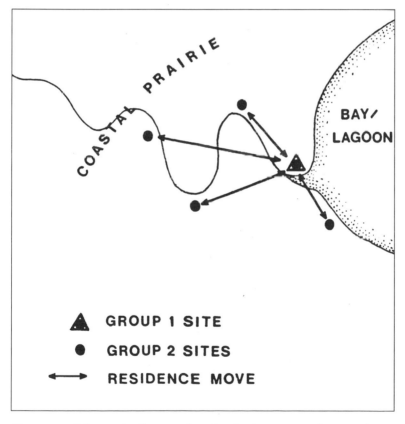

*Figure 25.* Schematic diagram showing basic pattern of seasonal settlement and subsistence patterns for the Rockport Phase, based on archaeological data discussed in text.

oscillations between use of concentrated and predictable shoreline resources (aggregated fish and shellfish beds), on the one hand, and mobile or dispersed terrestrial game located on the inland prairies and riverine environments, on the other, represented schematically in Figure 25. A social corollary to this economic pattern was seasonal aggregation at the large shoreline sites, in contrast to spring-summer dispersal into small and presumably closer kin groups at the prairie-riverine camps.

This seasonally oscillating pattern of population aggregation and dispersal need not be viewed in rigid terms. There is, at all the investigated shoreline sites, a small percentage of spring-summer fish otoliths. These may reflect a reduced use of these locations during the spring and summer, although they could just as well be indicative of variable rates in fish growth and a slight skewing of fall-winter otolith samples. It should also be pointed out that there are some small Rockport Phase sites on bay shores, although the presently available information suggests that they are not very numerous. Site 41SP103 (Ricklis 1988) on Corpus Christi Bay and perhaps a Rockport Phase occupation at Site 41AS16 on Copano Bay (see Prewitt and Paine 1988) may represent small and short-term occupations by Rockport people during spring-summer. Bison and deer bones have been found at both sites, and both sites are adjacent to upland prairie environments, despite their shoreline locations. On the other hand, such sites could represent specialized hunting camps associated with, and in relative proximity to, the large fishing camps. It must also be acknowledged that the present database may not permit identification of the complete range of site types for the Rockport Phase. For example, preliminary findings at a site on the lower Lavaca River suggest rather intensive occupation involving both fishing and extensive use of terrestrial resources in a particularly broad and biotically rich floodplain environmental setting (see data presented in Weinstein 1994); future research may provide insights into how this kind of resource use fit into the overall adaptive system of the Karankawas.

Despite the need for additional work, the data presented here are clear in pointing to a basic dichotomy in resource use between shoreline zone and inland areas, and that this involved seasonal emphases and a significant degree of residential relocation. Questions concerning the details of variability within the basic adaptive pattern need clarification through further identification of, and seasonality studies at, such sites.

It is unfortunate that preserved floral remains have not been found that give a better understanding of the role of plant foods in the Rockport Phase system. Plants must certainly have played an important role in the diet. The archaeological data indicate a meat diet at shoreline sites in which the overwhelming preponderance of caloric intake would have been in the form of protein. This would have had to be balanced by foods rich in fats or carbohydrates, as well as in fiber.

The sources of energy in human diets are proteins, fats, and carbohydrates (Wing and Brown 1980). The values of these nutrients per 100 grams of raw meat for major components of the Rockport Phase meat diet are indicated in Table 6. The relevant fish and shellfish species, as well as lean venison, consist mainly of protein. Extrapolating from these nutrient values, and exclusive of moisture content, venison consists of about 87 percent protein and 13 percent fat and contains no carbohydrates. Similarly, the various fish species combined yield 85 percent protein, about 15 percent fat, and only 0.2 percent carbohydrates. The combined shellfish species consist of about 77 percent protein, 9 percent fat, and 14 percent carbohydrates.

At the Holmes Site, the faunal data indicate that fish, mammals, and shellfish constituted, respectively, an estimated 80 percent, 16 percent, and 4 percent of the meat diet. The small balance of 1 percent came from birds. Leaving aside the very minor contribution from birds, the meat diet provided a caloric intake made up of approximately 85 percent proteins, 14 percent fats, and 1 percent carbohydrates. The actual fat content was probably proportionately somewhat higher, since the nutrient data for venison are based on lean meat and do not include subcutaneous or bone marrow fats. Despite this, and despite the fact that we are only dealing with general estimates of meat weights, it seems that the constraining factor in the Rockport Phase diet was not likely to have been a lack of protein. The essential dietary constituents of proteins—various amino acids, sulfur, and nitrogen—were probably not in short supply in the Rockport Phase diet.

Rather, a crucial requirement in the dietary strategy would have been foods with sufficiently high fat and/or carbohydrate contents to balance the high protein intake. Generally, various human diets worldwide involve only about 10–25 percent protein intake, and most modern diets are made up largely of carbohydrates from which the majority of energy needs are derived (McClellan and Dubois 1930; McGilvery 1983). Indeed, it is probable that the human organism cannot survive on a sustained diet consisting of over 40–50 percent protein, since this would result in "protein poisoning" from excess nitrogen production in the form of urea excreted by the

**Table 6.** *Selected Nutritional Values for Major Rockport Phase Meats*

|  | Kcal | Protein (grams) | Fat (grams) | Carbohydrates (grams) |
|---|---|---|---|---|
| Mammal |  |  |  |  |
| Venison | 126 | 26.0 | 4.0 | 0 |
| Fish |  |  |  |  |
| Black drum | 78 | 18.4 | 0.5 | 0 |
| Redfish | 85 | 19.0 | 1.0 | 0 |
| Sea trout | 88 | 17.3 | 6.0 | 0 |
| Sea catfish | 120 | 16.4 | 6.0 | 0.2 |
| Croaker | 96 | 17.8 | 2.2 | 0 |
| Mollusks |  |  |  |  |
| Scallop | 81 | 15.3 | 0.2 | 3.3 |
| Oyster | 66 | 8.4 | 1.8 | 3.4 |
| Whelk | 102 | 17.7 | 2.3 | 0 |
| Clam | 63 | 9.7 | 1.6 | 2.4 |
| Bird |  |  |  |  |
| Wild duck | 233 | 21.1 | 15.8 | 0 |

*Note*: All values are per 100 grams of raw meat weight (from Watt and Merrill 1975).

kidneys (Noli and Avery 1988; also see discussion in Speth 1983 of the deleterious effects of sustained lean meat diets).

At the prairie-riverine camps, high protein intake may have been offset to some degree by a relatively abundant supply of bone marrow and subcutaneous fats from bison and deer, which would have been at optimal levels from spring through fall (as suggested by data on deer fat contents from the Welder Wildlife Refuge on the Aransas River; Kie et al. 1983). Fruits of plant species such as mustang grape, prickly pear, Texas persimmon, anacua, and hackberry, as well as mesquite pods, all available on floodplains and the surrounding uplands, would have provided carbohydrate intake in the form of fructose or starch.

At winter fishing camps, with a high consumption of low-fat fish and shellfish, carbohydrate intake may have provided the most significant balancing factor in an otherwise high-protein diet. Despite the present lack of archaeological information concerning plant use at shoreline locations, an early sixteenth-century observation by the Spaniard Cabeza de Vaca, probably made on the upper Texas coast, provides relevant insight:

From October through February every year, which is the season these Indians live on the Island, they subsist on the roots I have mentioned, which the women get from under the water in November and December. Only in these two months, too, do they take fish in the cane weirs. When the fish is consumed, the roots furnish the staple. At the end of February, the islanders go to other parts to seek sustenance, for the root is beginning to grow and is not edible. (Covey 1983:61)

The precise location on the Texas coast of Cabeza de Vaca's "islanders" is uncertain. Newcomb (1983) places it just south of Galveston Bay, to the north of the present study area. Nonetheless, it is apparent that Cabeza de Vaca described a seasonal focus on shoreline occupation similar to that indicated for the central coast by the archaeological data outlined here. The said roots were an important dietary component, since they were perceived by Cabeza de Vaca as a staple food. The roots may in fact have been derived from cattails (*Typhus* sp.), certain species of which are salt tolerant and still grow in extensive stands in shallow bay and lagoonal areas along the Texas coast. Cattail roots, except for their fiber content, consist almost entirely of carbohydrate in the form of starch and, like Cabeza de Vaca's roots, are edible until midwinter (Tull 1987).

Another potentially important source of dietary carbohydrates and fats would have been acorns. The coastal fringe of the Ingleside sands supports dense stands of oak, primarily live oak (*Quercus virginiana*), which have relatively low tannic acid content and which produce acorns each autumn. Except for water and trace element contents, acorns are about 72 percent carbohydrates, 19 percent fats, and 9 percent protein (Erlandson 1988). They also are high in calories, providing 254 kcal per 100 grams (ibid.). An acorn dietary component would have contributed significantly to daily energy needs without adding substantially to the already high protein intake.

In sum, the available archaeological and environmental information can be synthesized into a coherent picture of the late prehistoric human adaptation to the central coast environment. During fall and winter, human groups aggregated at optimal shoreline loci in response to particularly abundant fish resources. Shellfish were gathered, and although they probably varied in importance from time to time and place to place, they did make up a significant component in the diet. Mammals were hunted, primarily white-tailed deer, providing a limited amount of much needed dietary fat. Bison do not seem to have been of great importance at this time of the year, although the bone samples from shoreline sites may be somewhat misleading in this regard, since these large animals may have been completely butchered during hunting expeditions at inland prairie kill sites, with few bones transported back to shoreline base camps. It must be inferred that nuts and roots, available along the coast during the fall and winter, represented an essential dietary component.

During the spring and summer, populations dispersed in small groups, in response to both reduced fish concentrations and new plant growth and improved condition of game. While some part of the population may have continued to reside around bay shores, particularly in back-bay areas in proximity to upland prairie and riverine floodplain environments, many, if not most, people traveled upstream to establish camps along the prairie's edge, overlooking stream floodplains. Terrestrial game and presumably greens, fruits, and seeds were now the seasonal dietary mainstay. The available data suggest that this basic adaptive pattern is rooted far back in prehistory, at least as early as the late Archaic. The Kent-Crane Site (41AS3) on Copano Bay, for example, is a massive Archaic Period shell midden deposit that extends along the shoreline for nearly a kilometer. Prior to severe erosion during recent decades, this very dense midden deposit was up to 1.5 meters thick (Campbell 1952; Duffen, field note). The most abundant shell species at this site— oyster, scallop, lightning whelk, and sunray venus—are the same as those found at the Holmes and Ingleside Cove Sites, implying similar estuarine environments.

The 1941 excavations at Kent-Crane revealed two major stratigraphic zones within the shell deposit (Campbell 1952; Duffen, field notes). Both zones produced essentially the same suite of shell tools (edge-flaked sunray venus clamshell tools, *Busycon* adzes, perforated oyster shells, whelk columella "awls," and conch columella "gouges"). Most lithic dart points were of two kinds: a rather crude, stemmed form and well-made side-notched forms. The former has been generally subsumed under the Kent type (Suhm and Jelks 1962; Turner and Hester 1985), while the latter pertains primarily to the very late Archaic Ensor type, placed at circa A.D. 200–550 in Central Texas (Prewitt 1985). Both forms were found in both of the gross strata within the midden, although seriation analysis by Corbin (1974) showed that the Ensor points became increasingly significant toward the upper part of the deposit. These points place the occupation of Kent-Crane within the late Archaic, in the early half of the first millennium A.D. The fact that the stemmed Kent points were relatively more significant toward the bottom of the deposit suggests that initial occupation of the site may have been somewhat earlier. The Kent type cannot be cross-dated with the Central Texas chronology but is assigned to a mainly late Archaic period on the upper Texas coast (cf. Ensor 1987:99; Gadus and Howard 1990). A recently obtained radiocarbon age of 2210 ± 60 B.P. (uncorrected), obtained on a sample of quahog shell from the base of the midden (Cox and Smith 1988:31), supports a general placement of initial occupation at Kent-Crane not long before the appearance of Ensor points in the Central Texas chronology. Fish otoliths recovered during testing by Cox and Smith provide the only seasonality data from Kent-Crane. A small sample of 9 analyzed otoliths from the Archaic shell midden all appeared to represent "late fall or winter" fish kills (Cox and Smith 1988:36).

The data from Archaic levels at the Holmes, Ingleside Cove, and Mustang Lake Sites, already mentioned, indicate late Archaic components immediately underlying late prehistoric deposits. The shell midden at Ingleside Cove probably overlaps chronologically with Kent-Crane, with the earliest evidence of intensive occupation dated to circa A.D. 100–200. The terminal Archaic shell stratum in the South Block at the Holmes Site, which directly underlies late prehistoric material, dates to about A.D. 1000. The latter component produced an artifact assemblage very similar to that from Kent-Crane, including most of the same shell tool forms, basketry-impressed asphaltum, bird bone beads, and an engraved bone pin virtually identical to Kent-Crane specimens. At all three sites, seasonality of fish otoliths points to the same basic pattern of fall-winter fishing inferred for the late prehistoric occupations.

In addition to the information from these various shoreline locations, there are also data from what are probably late Archaic campsites that were analogous to the Rockport Phase prairie-riverine occupations. These are the preceramic levels in test units at several of the sites along the Aransas River (41SP159, 41SP167, and 41SP170). As with the Rockport Phase deposits, artifact densities are low; fish remains are extremely scant; and rangia analyses consistently show spring-summer seasonalities. Data are limited, but deer bones are present, suggesting that by weight, terrestrial game constituted the bulk of the meat diet (Ricklis 1990).

The available data suggest, then, that patterns of seasonal subsistence and mobility were essentially the same during the late Archaic and late prehistoric Rockport Phase. A fundamental continuity of the spatial and seasonal structures of a single basic adaptive system appears to be indicated. Changes took place but within the framework of a basic pattern that was in place by perhaps 2,000 years ago. The information on seasonality and camp locations for the late prehistoric indicates no fundamental structural changes in the system. This does not mean that there was a static, unchanging lifeway over many centuries nor that the adaptive system was free from short-term oscillations or even ecological crises arising from occasional environmental perturbations (e.g., red tides or prolonged or unusually severe winter freezes). Nor does it suggest a culturally or demographically closed system from Archaic to Early Historic times. As the archaeological database is expanded through future research, it may become apparent that the emergence and maintenance of the adaptive strategies defined for the central coast included as yet indiscernible demographic and/or cultural exchanges with other regions. Indeed, considering that no living complex system is closed, these kinds of variables should probably be expected. The information presented here does, however, provide a picture that is broadly characterized by long-term continuity, rather than by rapid or dramatic change, and by adherence to traditional patterns rather than to major innovations or dramatic reformulations of lifeways.

# Chapter 7
# Karankawan Adaptive Patterns during the Colonial Era

The recorded accounts of contemporary European observers of native lifeways, both published and unpublished, offer direct insight into Karankawan adaptive patterns during the Colonial era. Gleaned from records left by Frenchmen and Spaniards, these observations form, in the aggregate, a coherent picture that both complements and augments the archaeological record. The historical documents support the basic patterns of Karankawan economy and land use modeled on the basis of the archaeological data and provide an important record of continuity and change in Karankawan lifeways.

The earliest recorded contact between Europeans and natives on the Texas coast took place in the fall of 1528, when members of the Spanish expedition of Pánfilo de Narváez were washed ashore while attempting to reach Mexico on improvised barges. The location of this landfall is uncertain but may have been Galveston Island or Follett's Island just to the southwest (Newcomb 1983:359). Cabeza de Vaca lived with one or more groups inhabiting the island for about a year, then moved to the mainland, and ultimately spent several years among the Mariames, an inland group that probably lived around the lower Guadalupe River (Campbell and Campbell 1981:13). We cannot be certain that Cabeza de Vaca's island peoples (the Capoques and Hans) were Karankawas. However, his observations on the subsistence and settlement patterns of these people accords in large part with archaeological data for the central coast and appears to describe an adaptation not unlike that recorded by the archaeological data presented here.

As already mentioned, Cabeza de Vaca noted that these people resided on the island from October through the end of February and then "went to other parts to seek sustenance" (Covey 1983:61). During their stay on the island, fish and some sort of root were the dietary mainstays. By spring they had moved to the mainland. Subsistence on the mainland for several months was derived from oysters, berries, and various fauna (Davenport 1924:230). It is interesting to speculate on the use of "oysters" as a generic term for bivalves, since archaeology indicates that *Rangia cuneata* clams were heavily gathered along the upper coast during the spring and summer (e.g., Aten 1983; Carlson 1988; Hamilton 1988). Significantly, when the Spaniards made landfall, these people were able to muster a group of one hundred men with bows and arrows within a short period of time (Covey 1983), suggesting that a large group of several hundred people were congregated on the island during the fall season.

Also mentioned were groups down the coast who were almost certainly Karankawas. Unfortunately, there are no explicit statements concerning settlement or subsistence patterns. It is observed only that these people frequented the shoreline, and the statement that they ate "nothing in all the year but a little fish" (Davenport 1924:278) is dubious.

The contact between the coastal groups and members of the Narváez expedition was a short-lived and episodic event. More or less sustained contact began only with the exploration and settlement in the Matagorda Bay area led by La Salle in 1685. During February of that year, the La Salle expedition encountered a large native group of some four hundred people, camped in fifty *"cabanes"* on the shoreline in the Matagorda Bay area (Joutel 1713:77; Minet 1987:109). Minet's (1987:107) map of the area clearly indicates that this camp was located at the north end of Matagorda Island, on the shore of the tidal pass separating the island from the peninsula of the same name.

Germane to the question of seasonal locations of Karankawan camps are two observations in the diary of Enrique Barroto, who was commissioned to explore the coastline in 1687 (Barroto 1987). Sailing north along the coast from New Spain, Barroto met, at 27°46' north latitude (the location of Aransas Pass near Corpus Christi Bay), a friendly group of Indians who "came to the beach to play games around the galley." This was on March 22. Fishing was clearly being carried out by the natives, since they offered the Spaniards gifts of fish (ibid.:167). The Indians abandoned their shoreline camp while Barroto was anchored at the spot. He continued to sail north and reached the entrance to Matagorda Bay (28°23' north latitude) on April 3. Interestingly, six days of reconnoitering of Matagorda Bay failed to find any native people, although Barroto and his crew certainly passed through the same area where La Salle had encountered the camp of four hundred people in February 1685.

Apparently the bay shoreline was abandoned by April, a situation that is also recorded two years later by the De León expedition.

The De León expedition of 1689, formed by the authorities of New Spain to locate the site of La Salle's Fort Saint Louis, set out from Coahuila in the early spring and arrived in the Matagorda Bay area in the latter part of April (West 1905). Slightly inland, along present-day Garcitas Creek, the expedition encountered several rancherías (camps) of Indians. That these were some of the same Karankawas responsible for the recent sacking of Fort Saint Louis in 1688 is indicated by De León's observation that

> . . . in the rancherías through which we had just passed before our arrival at the settlement [the remnants of Fort Saint Louis], we had found in the possession of the Indians some French books in very good condition, with other articles of very little value. . . . They must have carried these off. (West 1905:217)

That these rancherías were relatively small encampments is suggested by the fact that there were several of them scattered along the creek, and also by De León's failure to give population estimates, which he had previously done upon sighting large camps in the interior. The placement of the rancherías and the date of their sighting (April 17) locate the Karankawas in a near-coastal riverine environment in mid-April.

The De León party explored the entire southern shoreline of La Bahía del Espíritu Santo (Matagorda Bay), from near the mouth of Garcitas Creek to the outer edge of the mainland (a distance of "eight long leagues"), and saw no Indians along the bay. The only traces of native occupation noted were the remnants of a camp that "had been abandoned for some time" (West 1905:220). The route of this exploratory tour is clearly indicated on the contemporary map of the expedition (ibid.). Again, De León's observations suggest that during the spring season the Karankawas of the Matagorda Bay area were living away from the bay shore in scattered riverine camps.

An important record of a relatively early European visit to the central coast region was by the French navigator Jean Beranger, who sailed from Louisiana in 1720 and reached present Aransas Pass in late October. Beranger's report documents a large shoreline camp at Aransas Pass, near Corpus Christi Bay, apparently similar to that seen by La Salle:

> I was surprised, since I least expected to see in a moment a large market town built of these kinds of houses [hide-covered huts]

and five hundred persons, at least, well sheltered. (Carroll 1983:22)

A word list compiled by Beranger leaves no doubt that this group was Karankawan, since it shows close linguistic similarity with the word list recorded for the early nineteenth-century Matagorda Bay Karankawas by Gatschet (see Troike 1987).

Apparently associated with this large camp was a major storage facility for fish:

> Five leagues north of here, where I was anchored, they have a small permanent village of about a dozen large, quite round huts. That is where they put the supply for the winter that consists of fish that they dry without salt and where worms prevail in large numbers. They took my cook into this village, and after welcoming him and making him eat what they had they brought him back after five days. (Carroll 1983:22)

Beranger made some interesting notes on native diet at the shoreline camp that accord with archaeological indicators for shoreline sites:

> Although they do not cultivate the soil, they eat bread . . . [that] they make with acorns, ashes and hemp well crushed and pounded together and cook it over live coals. I ate some of it solely to oblige, but it is nasty eating, according to my way of thinking. The rest of their food is fish that they eat half raw, a great deal of hemp, and oysters. As for meat, it is not plentiful among them. (Carroll 1983:22)

The use of "hemp" (*chanvre*) is interesting. Frank Wagner, the annotator of Carroll's translation of the report suggests that, since hemp is not native to the Americas, Beranger may have actually been referring to crabs. Wagner (in Carroll 1983:21) points out that the *Dictionnaire de la Langue Français* (Emile Littre), under the entry for "crabe," contains the statement that "chancre de mer dit en français crabe." Wagner suggests that Beranger may have inadvertently used the French *chanvre* (meaning hemp) instead of *chancre*. This interpretation seems a bit far-fetched, considering that it relies on the assumption that Beranger not only misspelled *chancre* but also employed an uncommon term for crab, rather than the usual *crabe*. The context makes it far more likely that he was simply using the French for hemp, *chanvre*, to refer to some other fibrous plant that he saw being processed but could not identify. Cattail roots, for instance, are highly fibrous, and in order to extract the edible starch, the roots must be pounded so as to separate the fiber. Once this is accomplished, the resultant pulp can be grilled to make a pancakelike bread (Tull 1987). Mixed with drier substances (such as Beranger's ash and pounded acorns), a mix suitable for cooking over live coals could be obtained. This interpretation is also indirectly supported by the fact that Beranger states that a great deal of the hemp was consumed. If this actually refers to fibrous roots, it is in accord with Cabeza de Vaca's observation that roots were a staple item among his coastal group. Finally, crab remains are not abundant in the archaeological deposits, strongly suggesting that they could not have constituted a major part of the diet at shoreline camps.

In any event, Beranger's observations are important in that they indicate a large shoreline encampment occupied during the fall season. Fish were clearly an important dietary staple; shellfish were gathered; and red meat was of apparently supplemental significance.

Another source of relevant information from the same period is the "Relation of Simars de Bellisle." De Bellisle's account provides a graphic firsthand description of the annual cycle of native life on the Texas coast, one that accords remarkably well with the seasonal subsistence and mobility indicated by archaeology. The location of the events described in his "Relation" is generally considered to have been in the vicinity of Galveston Bay on the upper coast (Folmer 1940; Hale and Freeman 1978). Nonetheless, de Bellisle's account portrays an adaptive system quite similar to that of the central coast and is thus appropriately discussed here.

Marooned on the Texas coast with several of his French compatriots, de Bellisle, the sole survivor, lived for over a year with a native group during 1719–1720. De Bellisle first encountered native people on a coastal island during the spring. At that time, the Indians were busy gathering bird eggs along the beach, a specific kind of subsistence activity not yet documented in the archaeological record. By summer, a dispersed terrestrial subsistence is indicated:

> I passed the entire summer in this country with them in going everywhere in search of food because they possess no cabins or fields. That is why they travel in this manner the entire summer. The men kill a few deer and a few buffaloes and the women search for wild potatoes. (Folmer 1940:216)

Also relevant to summer subsistence patterns is the observation that deer in riverine areas "were very frightened by the Indians who come here in the summer" (ibid.:211).

By winter the dispersed summer subsistence activities apparently gave way to a coastal focus when de Bellisle's group aggregated within a related group on the bay shore:

> When the beginning of the winter came we all left to join a band of their people who were waiting for us at the end of the bay. We arrived there at the end of seven or eight days. (Folmer 1940:217)

Hunting was also carried out during the winter. However, this was not within the context of the entire socioeconomic band, as seems to be implied for the summer season. Rather, it was carried out by male hunting parties that set out with the goal of procuring game and transporting meat back to what must have been a base camp:

> After a few days had passed, they told me that all the men were going to hunt buffaloes and were going to war against their enemies, and that I should keep myself ready to go with them the next day and that I should carry part of their baggage on my back. . . . I walked for two days under these conditions, and the third we arrived at a prairie which seemed endless in every direction and where numerous buffaloes were grazing. We halted there to hunt. . . . That morning they killed fifteen or sixteen buffaloes. . . . They decided the next morning to return to the place where they had left their wives. We left accordingly at daybreak. They went very fast. All I could do was follow them, running as fast as I could. In addition, they had given me my portion of the buffalo meat to carry. (Folmer 1940:218–220)

De Bellisle makes it clear that this hunting expedition was facilitated by the use of horses, though he himself had to travel on foot. Apparently, as early as 1720, coastal groups in the Galveston Bay area had at least limited access to these animals, which were perhaps taken from feral herds descended from strays from the early East Texas missions or perhaps from horses left behind by the De León expeditions of 1689–1690. However, while the winter hunting party used horses and went "very fast because they have good horses" (Folmer 1940:218), it seems likely that travel during the summer season was mainly on foot, since the group moved at the modest pace of "but three or four leagues a day" (ibid.:217). On the coast, de Bellisles's Indians traveled in the traditional dugout canoe (ibid.:216).

In sum, early historic documentation presents a picture of aboriginal adaptation that essentially agrees with the archaeological data. The accounts of Cabeza de Vaca, Joutel/Minet, and Beranger all document large groups of people at shoreline camps during the fall or winter seasons, and it is clear from both Cabeza de Vaca and Beranger that fishing was important at this time of year. Cabeza de Vaca mentions roots as a significant dietary component during the fall-winter, and Beranger refers to oysters, acorns, a minor amount of red meat, and possibly the same or similar roots. These accounts offer strong support for the interpretations of the archaeological findings made at shoreline sites, which are large, evidence an important economic reliance on fish, and were occupied primarily if not exclusively during the fall and winter. Significantly, both the Barroto diary of 1687 and the De León account of 1689 make no mention of Indian groups living on the shoreline of Matagorda Bay during the spring season, suggesting movement of population away from the shore during that time of the year. In close agreement is De León's observation of scattered rancherías of coastal Karankawas along Garcitas Creek, a feeder stream of Matagorda Bay, in mid-April. De Bellisle's remarkable account indicates that his coastal people spent the entire summer as a socioeconomic group exploiting terrestrial resources, importantly bison and deer, but merged with another, related group on the bay shore during the winter, the pattern of seasonal dispersal and aggregation indicated by archaeology for the central coast. Though winter hunting was carried out, it did not involve a residential relocation of the entire group but only a short-term foray made solely by men, who brought meat back to the larger group immediately following a rather large bison kill.

Later historical references to settlement and subsistence patterns come mainly from various letters and reports associated with the Spanish missions near the central coast. Although the first of these enterprises, the mission of Nuestra Señora del Espíritu Santo, was established near the site of Fort Saint Louis in 1722, the earliest documented eyewitness accounts of native group size and locational patterns date to the latter part of the eighteenth century. At this time, a concerted effort was made by Franciscan missionaries to convert the Karankawas. This involved various trips to the coast that resulted in documentation of Indian camps and their locations and group sizes.

Such firsthand accounts represent the only reliable sources for the times and places of native settlement because Spanish knowledge of coastal geography was generally poor, even at the end of the eighteenth century. As late as 1791, most of the Spaniards associated with the missions at La Bahía were largely ignorant of the configurations of the coastline, as indicated by this comment by Father Manuel de Silva:

> It would not profit the Indians to rebel under Treviño [a sergeant at Presidio de La Bahía], since [under his guidance] the Spaniards could enter [Karankawan territory] and travel by water or by land, which has not been possible so far due to their ignorance of the passages along the coast, which only the Indians have known, and which fact has allowed them to make war for the past twelve years, thus mocking the Spaniards who have been unable to follow them to the islands. (Silva to Muñoz April 26, 1791, author's translation)

It would seem that the Spaniards felt much more comfortable with the inland prairie environment than with the topographical maze of the coastal littoral, an environment that was very difficult to chart with the technology of the time (cf. 1771 map by La Fora, in Kinnaird 1958). Both the mission of Espíritu Santo and that of Nuestra Señora del Refugio were originally founded on or close to bay shores, and both were moved inland within a short time. Espíritu Santo, originally located in 1722 on Garcitas Creek just a few kilometers upstream from Lavaca Bay, was moved in 1726 to a place on the Guadalupe River over 30 kilometers farther inland. This relocation was probably in large part a response to the failure of the mission to establish viable relations with the Karankawas of the area. A similar move was involved in the early years of the Refugio mission, first located in 1791 near the mouth of the Guadalupe River. There was ultimately a degree of successful continuity in relations with the coastal Indians at this mission, and it was in part the Spaniards' inability to acclimatize to the coastal environment that resulted in its move further inland to the banks of the Mission River in 1795 (Oberste 1942).

Contemporary statements concerning movements and locations of native groups should, therefore, be treated with caution when attempting to determine patterns of settlement and subsistence. Only those references that specifically record locations or subsistence activities are used here.

The earliest available eyewitness account of the location and size of a coastal group during the latter part of the century comes from an Indian "spy" reporting to the commander at Presidio de La Bahía, Francisco de Továr. Továr writes to Hugo Oconor, governor of the Province of Tejas, regarding the demise of Spanish shipwreck victims at the hands of Carancahuase (Karankawa proper) Indians at Port Matagorda (the tidal pass between Matagorda Island and Matagorda Peninsula) in March 1768:

> The mentioned Indian said he had seen this place [at the northern end of Toboso or Matagorda Island]. . . . After convincing this Indian to take me to this place he said he would, and he did, but he warned me it would be necessary to take plenty of men since there were great numbers of Indians there. (Továr to Oconor June 6, 1768)

Apparently the Indian guide had seen a sizable group of Karankawas camped in the area of the same tidal pass at which a large group was noted by the La Salle expedition eighty-three years earlier. This would seem to have been a perennially favored fishing spot. That the group that killed the Spaniards was engaged in fishing is indicated by the Indian spy's statement that the shipwreck victims were feasted by the Indians on fish before they were killed (ibid.). A date in the latter part of March is suggested for these events, since Továr, writing on June 6, refers to the incident as having occurred "more than two months ago" (ibid.).

Several specific references to group sizes and locations come from letters associated with the founding of Refugio mission. In 1791 Father Manuel de Silva, superior of the College of Our Lady of Guadalupe at Zacatecas, was instructed to explore the possibility of establishing a Zacatecan mission for the coastal tribes. Accompanied by Father José Mariano Garza, Silva visited native camps in the central coast area, from Matagorda Bay to Copano Bay, to determine whether the Indians were responsive to the idea. Some interesting observations will be made later concerning the Indians' replies to Silva's inquiries, but for now the locations and sizes of the groups visited are of primary interest.

Setting out on foot, and heading northeast from Espíritu Santo mission, then located at present-day Goliad on the San Antonio River, Silva and Garza first encountered Karankawan groups in the Matagorda Bay area. Silva described the encounter as follows:

> Following our route, we came on this day [April 12, 1791], at about 8:30 in the evening, to Garcitas Creek. The third day [April 13], we proceeded on to San Miguel [Lavaca] Bay, which we crossed on rafts made by the same Indians. From there we went to their ranchería, at which we arrived about two in the afternoon. There we found 86 infidels, including adults and

children. We stayed with them for two days. On one of these days, we set out in the Indians' canoes with the same infidels, on what has been called Arroyo de la Vaca, which is a river of heavy flow. We traveled for over a quarter of a league to where this river divides into two arms, neither of which has a fording place. Here we disembarked, and went on foot, seeing with enjoyment the best and most beautiful of lands held by the King, and which, according to Treviño, who is the most knowledgeable person concerning this coast, has never been claimed by any Spaniard. There was another ranchería there of the companions of the people of La Vaca, which since it was very far, and since I needed to be going, I could not see. (Silva to Muñoz April 26, 1791, author's translation)

Silva here describes the upper end of Lavaca Bay, the lower Lavaca River, and the confluence of the Lavaca and Navidad Rivers. Apparently, the ranchería at which the party stayed for two days was on the lower Lavaca River, about 1 kilometer (quarter of a league) downstream from its confluence with the Navidad. Beyond the fork in the river, an unspecified distance, was another camp of related Indians.

The party then went south and after a 5-day walk reached, on about April 23, a place called Los Copanos, where Silva found:

a ranchería of 69 people, including adults and children. Some were infidels, who in past years had fled from the missions and the mission of Rosario. They were situated on the shore of a beautiful lagoon that, it was said, has a width of three leagues and then joins the sea. We did not attempt to embark on it and see something of it because of furious winds the day and a half we were with these Indians, and the risk to the canoes and anyone who was in them. (Silva to Muñoz April 26, 1791, author's translation)

The location of this camp was probably on the northwestern shore of Copano Bay. This is suggested by the name Los Copanos, by the direction from which the party had come, and by the fact that the body of water was said to be 3 leagues (12 kilometers) wide, just about the width of Copano Bay.

Father Silva returned to Espíritu Santo, but before leaving he commissioned Garza,

who was resting a bit, to stay on there a few days and to repeat visits to the two rancherías we had visited, and in which we had established good relations, and to visit the three other rancherías of which we had heard, and still others which, according to the testimony of the same Indians, are very numerous, and to visit all the Carancaguases. (Silva to Muñoz April 26, 1791, author's translation)

In a letter to Governor Muñoz, dated June 27, 1791, Garza reported visiting, on June 15, an Indian camp on San Miguel Creek. The location of the creek is uncertain, but it must have been in the Matagorda Bay area, since Garza had to cross the Guadalupe River to reach it. At this camp, which was associated with the "chief" Frasada Pinta, Garza counted a total of 41 Indians, including 10 men, 12 women, and 19 children (cited in Oberste 1942:32).

By the following fall, the group associated with Frasada Pinta had relocated to a place suggestively called Las Conchitas (the "little shells"). This camp was visited by Father Garza and Captain Juan Cortes, commander of the presidio at La Bahía, at the end of October. A relatively large group of 111 people was congregated there, consisting of 38 men, 28 women, and 45 children. A significant increase in population since the previous spring is represented, indicating aggregation similar to that implied in the de Bellisle account and by the archaeological record. A shoreline location is suggested by the place name and further indicated by the location of the place 9 or 10 leagues east of the mouth of the Guadalupe River (Silva to the Viceroy March 10, 1792, cited in Oberste 1942:36–37). This distance and direction would place Las Conchitas at or near the southeastern shore of Matagorda Bay, close to the main tidal pass between that bay and the open Gulf.

The largest group sizes for which late eighteenth-century documentation has been found can be located around the head of San Antonio Bay. Garza reported a group of 186 Indians congregated at the mouth of the Guadalupe River on December 12, 1791 (Garza to Muñoz December 15, 1791). About a year later, on January 14, 1793, Garza again reported a relatively large group of 161 Indians at the same location, residing in two camps within close proximity to one another. Among this group, Garza counted 80 men and women and 81 children (Garza to Muñoz January 18, 1793).

Prior to Garza's arrival, this encampment had been still larger, consisting of 208 individuals. Forty-seven Indians had left the main group, "motivated by the search for food" (ibid.). This is an interesting observation in that it (1) seems to show fluidity in larger group memberships, (2) suggests the splintering off from an aggregate group of a smaller socioeconomic unit similar in size to those seen by Silva and Garza during the spring, and (3) indicates that shoreline locations could not always be counted on to provide adequate sustenance for aggregate groups.

These fragments of information from the early 1790s are of significance on several counts. The locations and sizes of the documented groups are basically in accord with earlier historical observations and with the patterns of settlement inferred from the archaeological evidence. Groups observed between April and June were mostly located in riverine camps. The exception is the group seen by Silva and Garza at Los Copanos, probably on the west shore of Copano Bay. However, this would be an inland bay margin adjacent to a broad prairie environment. The location would have been similar to those for the small archaeological sites such as 41SP103 and 41AS16, both located in upland prairie environments on Corpus Christi and Copano Bays, respectively. Significantly, the sizes of these groups were relatively small: the camp visited by Silva and Garza on the lower Lavaca River contained 86 people; that at Los Copanos consisted of 69 people; and the ranchería on San Miguel Creek, associated with the chief Frasada Pinta, was made up of 41 people.

The information for fall-winter camps contrasts with that for the spring camps. Group sizes are larger, and camps are located on bay shores. Particularly significant is the camp at Las Conchitas. Associated with Frasada Pinta, this fall camp had 111 residents, as compared to the 41 people, associated with the same Frasada Pinta, observed on San Miguel Creek the previous June. A fall aggregation of people at a shoreline location is implied. The large camps reported by Garza at the mouth of the Guadalupe River (i.e., San Antonio Bay) in the late fall of 1791 and winter of early 1793 also appear to represent relatively large fall-winter groupings. That a gathering of smaller groups is represented is strongly suggested by the fissioning off of what was probably a component socioeconomic band of 47 people.

These two large groups were, at least in the perception of Father Garza, congregated in anticipation of the founding of Refugio mission. Given the other historical and archaeological data, however, such groupings during the fall and winter were part of the traditional pattern of settlement and subsistence. Indeed, this location for the mission was, as will be shown below, chosen by the Indians themselves, and not by the missionaries, and must therefore have been an economically productive and traditionally favored residential location. In this regard, it is probably not coincidental that

**Table 7.** *Historically Documented Karankawan Encampments by Size and Environmental Location*

| Group Size | Environment | | Season | | Source |
| | Shoreline | Riverine | F-W | S-S | |
|---|---|---|---|---|---|
| 400 | X | | X | | Cabeza de Vaca |
| 400–500 | X | | X | | Joutel/Minet |
| 500 | X | | X | | Beranger |
| "Numerous" | X | | X | | Croix |
| 208 | X | | X | | Garza |
| 186 | X | | X | | Garza |
| 111 | X | | X | | Oberste/Silva |
| Probably large | X | | X | | Kuykendall |
| Small rancherías | | X | | X | De León |
| 86 | | X | | X | Silva |
| 69 | X | | | X | Silva |
| 41 | | X | | X | Oberste/Garza |
| 30 | X | | | X | Croix |

41CL2, a major Rockport Phase site, highly productive of cultural debris, is situated in this same area, on the north shore of Guadalupe Bay just over a kilometer from the Guadalupe River delta (notes and artifacts on file at the Texas Archeological Research Laboratory, Austin; see also Weinstein 1992).

Documentation specifically relevant to settlement patterns is very scarce for the early nineteenth century. However, one brief reference is worth mentioning because it suggests that winter camps were still placed in shoreline locations. During the 1820s, relations between the Karankawas and the growing number of Anglo-American settlers became overtly hostile, and a company of the settlers attacked a Karankawan camp on the shoreline of East Matagorda Bay in the winter of 1826 (Kuykendall 1903:250). Although the Indians fled into the surrounding oak mottes, about 30 were killed. Assuming that only a fraction of the fleeing Karankawas was shot by the settlers, it is likely that the resident group was fairly sizable. A relatively large shoreline winter encampment is, probably, once again indicated.

Taken together, the historical records from the early contact period and the later, mainly eighteenth-century, observations concerning group locations, sizes, and subsistence patterns are congruent with the archaeological data on settlement and subsistence patterns. This information is collated and summarized in Table 7, which shows that larger groups resided at fall-winter shoreline camps, whereas smaller groups were dispersed inland from the shore along river courses during spring-summer. Furthermore, the consistency in the variables of camp size, location, and seasonality between the earlier and later documents warrants the conclusion that there was a fundamental continuity in these basic cultural-ecological patterns from late prehistory through most, if not all, of the Colonial Period.

# Chapter 8
# The Impacts of European Colonization: Continuity and Change in Karankawan Lifeways

From the time of La Salle's first entry into the Matagorda Bay area to the period of Anglo-American settlement, the Karankawas found themselves on the margins of Euro-American frontier settlement. La Salle's Fort Saint Louis, destroyed for uncertain reasons by Karankawas near the end of 1688, was a short-lived venture. From that year until the founding of the first coastal Spanish mission in 1722, contacts with Europeans must have been sporadic but perhaps not infrequent. We have, for the early decades of contact, several documentations, beginning in the late 1680s with the De León and Barroto expeditions. We know that in 1691 Domingo Terán and a military contingent traversed Texas to establish a small garrison and several missionaries in East Texas (Gerhard 1978:337). Although undocumented, late seventeenth- and early eighteenth-century Karankawan contacts with French and Spanish are a distinct possibility, if not a probability. In the early eighteenth century, French traders were operating in East Texas, and these activities may have involved some contact with Karankawan groups. By midcentury, French traders were doing a brisk fur-trading business in East Texas and the Galveston Bay area that involved at least one Karankawan group, the Cocos (Bexar Archives, Report from Nacogdoches, September 20, 1754). Despite the seemingly limited opportunities for contact between Karankawas and Spaniards prior to the mission period, the French navigator Beranger made the following suggestive observations when visiting a Karankawan group in 1720:

> They have a certain word in their mouths that they call *captenne* that comes, from the best of my belief, from the Spaniards, whom I take to be not far from them in the direction of the kingdom of León. I found among them, also, Flemish knives blunted at the tip in the same way as those carried by Indians who are tributaries of the King of Spain. (Carroll 1983:22)

Also of interest in Beranger's Karankawan word list is _cousila_, meaning knife, that has an intriguing similarity to the Spanish _cuchillo_.

Starting as early as 1690, the Spaniards, motivated in large part by a desire to secure the northern border of New Spain from French incursions, had begun to establish a string of missions in Texas, first in East Texas and later in the San Antonio River valley (Bolton 1915; Castañeda 1936). Between 1719 and 1722, the Marqués de San Miguel de Aguayo led an expedition into Texas from Coahuila in response to the request of the Franciscan missionaries to establish a mission for the coastal tribes (Buckley 1911).

In 1721–1722 the mission of Nuestra Señora del Espíritu Santo and its attendant Presidio de Nuestra Señora de Loreto, or La Bahía, were established on Garcitas Creek, just a few kilometers upstream from Lavaca Bay at the site of La Salle's Fort Saint Louis (O'Connor 1966:10; Gilmore 1984). Initially, the mission attracted Indians of four Karankawan groups, the "Cocos, Cujanes, Guapites, Talan-caguaches [Carancaguases]" (Ciprian 1979:20). "The mission had little effect on these tribes, who returned to their savage ways" (ibid.), and in 1726 it was reestablished, along with Presidio La Bahía, further inland on the lower Guadalupe River. This mission and presidio were moved again in 1749 to their final locations on the San Antonio River at modern Goliad. At both the Guadalupe and San Antonio Rivers locations, Espíritu Santo mission was devoted to conversion of inland coastal prairie groups, notably the Jaranames and Tamiques. A fresh attempt was made in the 1750s to convert the coastal tribes through the establishment, near La Bahía and Espíritu Santo, of a new mission, Nuestra Señora del Rosario. In part, the motivation underlying this venture was to strengthen Spanish control over the coastal zone (Bolton 1906:120). The new mission was expressly intended for the Karankawan groups and was, accordingly, sometimes referred to as Nuestra Señora del Rosario de los Cujanes (the generic term for the various Karankawan groups in the mid-eighteenth century was Cujanes or Coxanes). The mission had minimal success in converting the Karankawas (see Bolton 1906), and by the 1780s it had been completely abandoned by the Indians (López 1940).

The establishment of Nuestra Señora del Refugio mission in the early 1790s was the final effort to convert and acculturate the Karankawas. This enterprise did meet with some measure of success, for various reasons discussed further on.

## European Diseases and Historic Karankawan Demography

Initial and ongoing European contacts in the New World were attended by the introduction of European diseases, which had severe impacts on native populations. Research of recent decades has made increasingly clear that various Old World epidemic diseases, for which aboriginal groups had little or no immunity, reduced native populations drastically (e.g., Dobyns 1966, 1983; Cook 1973, 1976; Denevan 1976). Pathogens such as smallpox and measles were so virulent, and their effects so devastating, that it has become increasingly evident that historical estimates of native group sizes usually document populations already impacted by disease and the resulting high mortality rates. Whether severe depopulation preceded initial native and European contact as the result of pandemics, or rather resulted only from more regional or localized epidemics involving direct (though perhaps undocumented) contact, remains a subject of debate (cf. Ramenofsky 1987; Snow and Lamphear 1988). However, while the timing and severity of initial population declines have yet to be established to general satisfaction, there is a consensus that aboriginal populations were virtually always higher than many long-cited estimates (e.g., Mooney 1928; Swanton 1952).

A number of contemporary accounts are available with which to chart Karankawan population decline during historic times. The earliest evidence of mortality through the introduction of European diseases on the Texas coast is documented by Cabeza de Vaca for the year 1528. During the first winter among his island Indians, Cabeza de Vaca saw about one-half the natives die of some form of stomach ailment. The Indians quickly blamed their Spanish guests for this pestilence and refrained from killing them only because the Spaniards were also suffering from illness (Covey 1983). The disease, which remains unidentified, seems to have run its course during that winter on the island, since there are no further references to high mortalities from illness in the accounts.

The lack of subsequent documentation concerning the coastal tribes of Texas up to 1685 makes impossible any definitive assessment as to whether these groups were severely affected by disease prior to the beginning of continuous, direct contact with Europeans. About all that can be said is that large groups were observed by La Salle in 1685 and by Beranger in 1720 and that these groups of 400 or 500 individuals represent about the maximum size of population aggregate ethnographically expectable for mobile hunter-gatherers (see Lee and DeVore 1968; Birdsell 1953). If the Karankawas had suffered from epidemic disease prior to late seventeenth-century contact, it had not resulted in their inability to congregate in numbers considered maximal within the economic and sociopolitical contexts of mobile nonagricultural peoples. Whatever the Karankawan population in 1685, it can probably be taken as a baseline for subsequent decline during the eighteenth and nineteenth centuries, a demographic trajectory that is definable.

In 1928 the anthropologist James Mooney (1928) estimated the precontact Karankawan population at 2,800. Newcomb has suggested that Mooney's figure was too low and estimates a total population of 3,600 (Newcomb 1983:365). This figure is based on three working assumptions: (1) the aggregate group of about 400 seen by La Salle represented the total population of a single major grouping (i.e., the Clamcoehs, or Karankawas proper); (2) based on Cabeza de Vaca's list of coastal groups, there were nine such groups of Karankawan affiliation; (3) these nine groups were all about the same size.

Aten (1983a), in a discussion of population levels of various upper coast groups, in which he includes at least some Karankawas, somewhat arbitrarily estimates the preepidemic population for the larger sociocultural entity at between 4,000 and 6,000 individuals. While recognizing that population around the year 1800 was about 2,000 and that declines in the first century of contact could have been as high as 85 to 90 percent, Aten seems uncomfortable with a higher estimate of total population (ibid.).

Contemporary observers usually estimated native populations in terms of the numbers of warriors in any given group. Since in relatively simple societies, which did not involve occupational specialization, virtually all able-bodied men were "warriors," historical observations are taken to refer to a group's adult male population. Therefore, to reliably determine the total population, it is necessary to multiply such numbers by a factor that reflects the ratio of men to total population. In the case of the Karankawas, this factor can be estimated at four. Table 8 presents eighteenth-century demographic data, both from within and outside of the Spanish missions, which show ratios between adult men and total numbers for particular documented groups. Although there is variation between the groups, the average ratio of men to the total number of people is about 1:4. A multiple of four is thus used throughout the following discussion of Karankawan population during historic times.

It can be argued that the estimates of both Newcomb and Aten are somewhat too low. The earliest recorded estimate of Karankawan population comes to us through the French historian P. Margry,

**Table 8. *Historical Data on Ratios of Karankawan Men to Total Group Population***

| Men | Women | Boys | Girls | All | Men:All | Date | Source |
|-----|-------|------|-------|-----|---------|------|--------|
| 1 | 1 | 2 | | | 1:4 | 1779 | Croix |
| 10 | 12 | | | 19 | 1:4.1 | 1791 | Oberste 1942:32 |
| 38 | 28 | | | 45 | 1:2.9 | 1791 | Oberste 1942:36 |
| 18 | 25 | 29 | 20 | | 1:5.1 | 1794 | Rosario census (Jaudenes 9/26/1794) |
| 10 | 10 | | | 36 | 1:5.6 | 1795 | Refugio census (Cortes 10/23/1795) |
| 19 | 16 | 35 | 16 | | 1:4.3 | 1795 | Refugio census (ibid.) |
| 20 | 15 | 9 | 8 | | 1:2.6 | 1797 | Refugio census (Elquezabal 7/3/1797) |
| 17 | 12 | 7 | 11 | | 1:2.8 | 1797 | Refugio census (ibid.) |
| 13 | 16 | 35 | 12 | | 1:5.8 | 1797 | Refugio census (ibid.) |

*Note*: Average ratio of men to total population: 1:4.13.

who cites a 1699 French estimate of the Quelancouchis (i.e., the Clamcochs, Talancaguaches, Carancaguases, or Karankawas proper) as having had 400 warriors in the late seventeenth century (Margry 1886:IV:316). Thus the earliest estimate for the population of the Quelancouchis, or Karankawas proper, should be in the neighborhood of 1,600 people. This could, of course, be taken to represent the greater Karankawan population, including the Karankawas proper and the several other named groups. This is, in fact, the conclusion at which Bolton arrived (Bolton 1906:115).

However, this figure is considerably lower than later eighteenth- and early nineteenth-century estimates for the larger Karankawan grouping, which makes little sense in view of the fact that the later figures surely reflect significant population loss from epidemic disease.

On the other hand, taking the estimate of 1,600 at face value, that is, accepting it as a figure for just the Quelancouchis or Carancaguases group only, this inconsistency in historical arithmetic is avoided. It is then necessary only to multiply the estimate for this single group by the number of major groupings in order to arrive at a population estimate for the greater Karankawan entity. A total of nine groups for the Karankawas, as suggested by Newcomb, may be too high. The assumption of nine groupings is derived from the inclusion of several of Cabeza de Vaca's groups that were probably located between Galveston Bay and the Colorado River. For reasons alluded to in Chapter 1, these should not necessarily be assumed to have been Karankawas. The northernmost of the eighteenth-century Karankawan groups, the Cocos, was, as previously noted, centered further down the coast, around the lower Colorado River and eastern Matagorda Bay. As also pointed out, the number of groups mentioned by Cabeza de Vaca that can be located along the central coast, from the Colorado River southward to the Corpus Christi Bay area, is five. This is the same number of groups known in the eighteenth century as Karankawas, suggesting that five major groups resided in the larger Karankawan area from at least the early sixteenth century through the late eighteenth century. Cabeza de Vaca's more northerly groups may have been related to the upper coast Akokisas, for which eighteenth-century correlations cannot be made or, at least, have not been made. However, even if these earlier groups were related to the later Karankawas, the apparent consistency through time in the presence of five groups on the central coast suggests that a population estimate for those groups alone will provide a useful baseline for assessing the severity of depopulation after about 1685.

Assuming that the Karankawas proper had a population of 1,600 and, with due caution, that the other four groups were of roughly comparable size, a tentative and rough estimate of 8,000 people is derived for all the groups in the late 1600s. At the present time, there are no independent data with which to directly test this figure. It is, however, consistent with (1) expectations derived from ethnographic data for coastal hunter-gatherer population densities and (2) a preepidemic population size expectable in view of later Karankawan population estimates, taking into account estimated rates of postcontact population decline for other North American groups.

Hassan (1981:8) lists population densities for ten temperate and arctic coastal hunter-gatherer groups. Excluding an unusually high density figure for the Northwest Coast Haidas, the range in density for these groups is between .4 and 3.9 persons per square kilometer; average density is 1.1 persons per square kilometer. Considering the Karankawan area to include all of the mainland from the lower Colorado River delta area to and including the Corpus Christi Bay area, and from the mainland shore to 40 kilometers inland, plus the barrier islands, an area of roughly 8,200 square kilometers is represented. With a population of 8,000, the Karankawan area would have had a population density of just under 1 person per square kilometer.

By 1751 the four groups of the Carancaguases, Cojanes, Guapites, and Copanes were estimated to have had, together, 500 warriors (Piczina to the Viceroy December 26, 1751). This estimate implies a total population of about 2,000, with an average of 500 individuals in each group, again assuming groupings of roughly equal size. Counting the Cocos (again assuming a population of 500), a total population of 2,500 is suggested, a figure also suggested by Aten (1983a) for this period. Tentatively accepting a population of 8,000 in 1685, 2,500 in 1751 reflects a 69 percent decrease in population during the first sixty-six years of repeated contact. This rate of decline is in line with estimates for other North American groups, for which population declines of between about 75 and 95 percent in the first one hundred years of contact have been suggested (Dobyns 1966, 1983; Cook 1973; Jennings 1976). Specific episodes of smallpox epidemics are estimated to have triggered mortality rates as high as 50 to 75 percent (Heidenreich 1971; Crosby 1972; Milner 1980).

Table 9 presents a chronological list, drawn from various sources, of documented epidemics in the Texas area during the late seventeenth through early nineteenth centuries. At least five epidemics were recorded in Texas prior to 1751, any of which could have reached the Karankawas. Leaving aside Cabeza de Vaca's apparently isolated gastrointestinal epidemic, the first of these involved smallpox that broke out at Fort Saint Louis, within the Karankawan territory, in late 1688 (West 1905). While not certain that this disease spread to the Indians, it is entirely possible that it did if even very limited interaction took place between settlers and Indians. The typhus epidemic of 1739, really a pandemic, began in central Mexico in 1736, spread northward into Texas (Gerhard 1978:26), and could well have reached the coastal Indians through direct or indirect contact with individuals frequenting the missions at San Antonio or La Bahía. Certainly the smallpox or measles epidemic of 1749 did reach the coast, since the Karankawa Cocos were affected (Morfi 1935:307).

By 1767 the Karankawas had been greatly reduced from the numbers recalled by living memory. In his *Autos y Diligéncias*, reporting an exploratory expedition along the Texas coast, Coronel Diego Ortiz Parilla reports a discussion with an informant familiar with the region:

And asked if on the said island [Isla de las Culebras, probably San Jose/Matagorda Islands] he had seen either political

**Table 9.** *List of Protohistoric and Early Historic Period Epidemics*

| Date | Disease | Locus, Affected Groups | Source |
|---|---|---|---|
| 1528 | ? | "Isla del Malhado" (Cabeza de Vaca) | Covey 1983 |
| 1688–1689 | Smallpox | Fort Saint Louis, Karankawas(?) | West 1905 |
| 1691 | Smallpox, measles | Caddoan tribes | Ewers 1973, Gerhard 1978 |
| 1718 | ? | Caddoan tribes | Ewers 1973 |
| 1739 | Typhus, smallpox | San Antonio missions | Ewers 1973 |
| 1746 | Smallpox, measles | Atakapan groups, Tonkawas | Ewers 1973 |
| 1749 | Smallpox, measles | Cocos (Karankawas) | Morfi 1935: 307 |
| 1750 | Smallpox | Atakapan groups, Tonkawas | Ewers 1973 |
| 1750–1751 | Smallpox | San Antonio area | Ewers 1973 |
| 1753 | ? | Atakapan groups | Gerhard 1978 |
| 1759 | Smallpox | Nacogdoches | Ewers 1973 |
| 1759 | Measles | Caddoan tribes | Ewers 1973 |
| 1763 | ? | San Antonio area | Ewers 1973 |
| 1764 | Smallpox | Presidio La Bahía | Ewers 1973 |
| 1766 | ? | Karankawan groups | Ewers 1973 |
| 1777–1778 | Bubonic plague(?) | Caddos, Atakapas, Tonkawas | Ewers 1973 |
| 1778 | Smallpox, measles | Karankawan groups | Ewers 1973 |
| 1780s | Smallpox | Provincia de Tejas | Gerhard 1978 |
| 1789 | ? | Presidio La Bahía | Espadas, letter of 1789 |
| 1793 | ? | Refugio mission | Rodrigues, letter of 1793 |
| 1801–1802 | Smallpox | Caddoan tribes | Ewers 1973 |
| 1803 | Measles | Caddos | Ewers 1973 |
| 1816 | Smallpox | Caddos, Comanches | Ewers 1973 |
| 1820s | Smallpox | Refugio mission | Oberste 1942 |
| 1839–1840 | Smallpox | Comanches | Ewers 1973 |

*Note:* Epidemics are reported for eastern part of Texas, with location of reported outbreaks, groups known to have been affected, and bibliographic sources. Two or more reports of a single disease, closely spaced in time, may reflect different observations of the same epidemic.

[European] peoples or populations of Indians, he declared that on the said Culebra Island he had seen in times past habitations of Copanes, Piguiques, and Carancaguases Indians in the vicinity of Santo Domingo [Copano] Bay, but that few are left because they have succumbed to the diseases of measles smallpox. (Parilla 1767:29, author's translation)

Later contemporary estimates of Karankawan population suggest that the rate of decline after the mid-eighteenth century had slowed, or even that the population had stabilized. Fray Juan Agustín Morfi (1935:79–80) in 1780 estimated the Carancaguases to have at most 150 fighting men, which suggests a population of about 600. Since later estimates for the greater Karankawan entity are considerably higher than this, it is reasonable to conclude that Morfi's estimate is for the Carancaguases (Karankawas proper) group only. This is also supported by the fact that he considered the Cocos separately (Morfi's only estimate for the Cocos appears to refer to a single band of about 50 individuals that had fled the mission). If the other groups were of comparable size, a total population for the five groups would have been as much as 3,000. This seems high, considering that several epidemics are documented for the greater Texas region during the third quarter of the eighteenth century, including that of smallpox or measles that in 1778 affected the Karankawas directly (Table 9). However, Morfi's figure is roughly in keeping with two later estimates for the Karankawan population. William Bollaert (1850) estimated the number of fighting men in 1800 to have been 600, which indicates a population of about 2,400. John Sibley (1807:45) estimated a total of 500 fighting men in 1805, for a total population of 2,000, or an inferred average of 400 persons per major grouping. A population of 400–500 for each of the five groups at the turn of the nineteenth century seems reasonable in light of Juan Antonio Padilla's claim that in 1820 the Cocos alone numbered about 400 individuals (1919:51).

This apparent slowing of population decline or even demographic stabilization during the latter half of the eighteenth century may be accounted for in various ways. An initial rapid decline during the early decades of contact would have reduced regional population densities, a phenomenon that in itself may have hampered the spread, and thus the severity, of later epidemics among coastal groups. Also probable is that surviving children became adults with immunity, so that the new generation was less severely affected and had lower mortality rates.

It is also likely that depleted population levels were bolstered by group mergers. Some interior Indian groups apparently moved to the coast during the eighteenth century to join with Karankawas. Morfi reports the merging of the Mayeyes, an interior group, with the Cocos by about 1780, stating that the "Cocos and the Mayeyes are two distinct nations that now live together and whose members have intermarried" (Morfi 1935:81). Also intriguing in this regard is the mention in the *Autos y Diligéncias* of Parilla (1767:21) that Culebras Island had been populated by Carancaguases, Copanes, and Pigiques. The latter group is never mentioned in eighteenth-century documents in discussions of the Karankawas and may in fact have been a separate sociocultural entity that had moved into Karankawan territory. For the early nineteenth century, Gatschet notes the presence of Tonkawas living among the Karankawas (Gatschet 1891:79–80).

During the eighteenth century, inland native groups in southern Texas were depopulated and displaced by southward moving Apaches, and later Comanches, in addition to disease and northward-moving Spaniards (Campbell 1988). As will be seen further on, the Karankawas themselves regarded the coast as a place of refuge from attacks by both Euro-Americans and Comanche, and perhaps interior groups shared that perception. With a drastically reduced population density, the Karankawas may have welcomed migration of interior Indians to the coast. Groups such as the Mayeyes were socially and economically integrated and ultimately probably became biologically absorbed into the coastal population.

During the 1820s, the Karankawan population appears to have rapidly declined to about half its size at the beginning of the century. An early Anglo-American settler, one Judge Duke, reported that "the Carancawa in 1822 could count between two and three hundred warriors" (Kuykendall 1903:250), implying a total population of between 800 and 1,200. That the larger Karankawan group is referred to is indicated by the size of the estimate and by the statement that "in this estimate he [Judge Duke] includes the Cokes and Cohannies—who were, in fact, but fragments of the same tribe" (ibid.). Duke's estimate is in accord with another for the same year, which places the total population of the Karankawas at about 1,000 individuals (Roessler 1883:616). For 1830 Berlandier (1969) estimated that the Cocos and Cujanes groups each consisted of about 50 families. Assuming that each of these groups had a population of about 200, a total population for all five groups of approximately 1,000 individuals can be extrapolated. However, it should be noted that nineteenth-century accounts no longer mention the Guapites and Copanes, so it is quite possible that they had ceased to exist as separate groups by 1830. If this was the case, then a total population of 1,000 is too high an estimate for that year. This may accord with another of Berlandier's observations that indicates that the 1820s were a decade of rapid demographic attrition among the Karankawas: "There are very few Carancahuases today, and their numbers diminish daily. Their tribe is composed at the most of from eighty to one hundred warriors with families" (Berlandier 1980:381).

In this particular passage, Berlandier is implying a total population for the Carancahuases group of some 320 to 400 people. The continued mention of the Cokes (Cocos) and Cohannies (Cujanes) suggests that they still existed as identifiable sociocultural populations. The Guapites and Copanes, however, may have merged with the Carancahuases by this time, which could account for the relatively large size of the latter group. If this was the case, then counting Berlandier's estimates of 200 each for the Cokes and Cohannies, a total Karankawan population of 720 to 800 is indicated for 1830.

In any event, the total Karankawan population appears to have been approximately halved during the 1820s. Padilla's (1919:51) estimate of 400 Cocos in 1820 was double Beranger's estimate for the same tribe in 1830, and if all five groups were extant at the beginning of the decade, a 50 percent reduction of total Karankawan population is indicated. While it is possible that the Karankawas had suffered population loss during the smallpox epidemic of 1815–1816, this seems questionable in light of the fact that the burial records for 1807–1825 at Refugio mission show no evidence for particularly high Indian mortality at that time (see Oberste 1942: 393).

Beginning around 1820, Anglo-Americans began to receive land grants for settlement on the coastal prairies just inland of traditional Karankawan territory. The Karankawas were generally regarded as a hindrance to settlement, and hostile relations quickly developed that were to drastically reduce the remaining native population. The following excerpts are typical of Anglo-American–Karankawan relations during the period:

Sometime during the same year [1824] he [Judge Duke] was one of a small party who were looking for Indians in the Colorado bottom; when they came upon a man and woman in their camp. They were Carancawas, and as they did not run on their approach the party resolved to make them prisoners.

> Capt. Robert Kuykendall was about to seize the squaw when she ran; the man also ran but did not get far as he was shot down by Daniel Rawls. . . .
>
> In the year 1826 Buckner defeated a party of Carancawas below Elbitt's crossing. In the winter of 1826 the families of Flowers and Cavanaugh were murdered by Carancawas. Capt. Buckner pursued them with a company. He found the Indians camped in a mot on the bay, about three miles east of the present town of Matagorda. He surprised them at daybreak and completely routed [them]—killing about thirty. This was the greatest loss the Indians ever sustained in any one fight with the colonists. (Kuykendall 1903:250)

Numerous similar incidents of the period have been recorded (e.g., Gatschet 1891:30–31; Newcomb 1983:361–362) and need not be repeated here. Suffice it to say that from about 1820 hostilities between Karankawas and Anglo-Americans were ongoing and must have contributed to a rapid decline in native population. To this can be added conflicts with Mexicans during the War of Texas Independence, during which some Karankawas chose to side with the Texans (Newcomb 1983:362).

By 1840 it was said that the Karankawas had only about 25 warriors and a population of no more than 100 individuals:

> They have once been a very powerful nation and were more celebrated for their bravery than any other tribe of the southwestern Indians; but their continued wars with Mexico and the wild Indians and the early American settlers of this country have reduced them to a mere handful, and their spirits have met with depression. They do not now number more than one hundred souls, with twenty-five warriors. (Bonnell 1840:137)

By the 1850s, the Karankawas had disappeared as an identifiable group. Hostilities and perhaps continued attrition caused by diseases were largely responsible. Survivors of these traumatic years appear to have in part dispersed into northern Mexico (Newcomb 1983:362).

The various population estimates discussed here are listed in Table 10 and graphically presented as a demographic curve in Figure 26. An initial rapid decline in population to around the mid-eighteenth century is followed by a period of near stabilization that lasted at least through the first decade of the nineteenth century.

The trajectory of this curve is in general very similar to that presented by Gerhard (1978:25) for general native depopulation on northern frontier of New Spain. It also agrees in its general configuration with the demographic curves constructed by Aten (1983: Figure 4) for various groups on the upper Texas coast during the historic period. In all cases, an initial precipitous drop in population is followed by either slowed decline, stabilization, or even slight recovery. The degree to which this is a biological phenomenon (i.e., reduced spread of disease resulting from markedly lowered population densities or increasing immunity of the adult population) or the result of sociocultural adaptations to colonial conditions remains to be elucidated.

## Karankawan Socioeconomic Organization during Historic Times: Evidence for Continuity amid Change

The information just reviewed clearly shows that epidemic diseases took a heavy toll on the original level of Karankawan population, causing about a 70 percent reduction in the six or seven decades following 1685. It is appropriate to ask: What were the changes in fundamental sociocultural organizational patterns within the context of such a dramatic change in overall demographic conditions?

Basic patterns of economy, settlement, and group mobility seem to have changed little during the eighteenth century. Given the continuity in these fundamental patterns, it can be expected that there would have been a similar continuity in patterns of human organization. The available data suggest that this was indeed so and that the native organizational structure was sufficiently resilient to operate under conditions of considerable depopulation.

Four scales of group organization are identifiable in native Karankawan culture. From the smallest to the largest, these were the band, the aggregate socioeconomic group or macroband, the tribe, and a larger network of closely related tribal groups. The characteristics of each during the historic period can be examined with reference to both the archaeological record and to continuity and change during the colonial era.

First, the term "band" is used here in the sense of the minimum group size that carried out a general range of economic activities. This definition corresponds with the "minimum band" concept previously posited for nonagricultural, hunter-gatherer peoples (Lee and DeVore 1968). While the minimum band is a normative concept and should not be automatically assumed to have operated in any

**Table 10.** *Historical Population Estimates for All Karankawan Groups*

| Total Population | Year | Source |
|---|---|---|
| 8,000 | 1685 | Extrapolated (see text) |
| 2,500 | 1751 | Piszina 1751 |
| 3,000 | ca. 1780 | Morfi 1935:79–80 |
| 2,400 | 1800 | Bollaert 1850 |
| 2,000 | 1807 | Sibley 1807 |
| 1,000 | 1822 | Roessler 1883:616 |
| 800–1,200 | 1822 | Kuykendall 1903:250 |
| 800 | 1830 | Berlandier 1969 |
| 100 | 1840 | Bonnell 1840:137 |
| 50 | 1843 | Roessler 1883:616 |
| 80 | 1850 | Bollaert 1850 |

given cultural context, the evidence for the Texas central coast does in fact indicate the existence of such an organizational unit. Specific historical references to small groups are listed in Table 11, along with documentations of larger-scale groupings. These were either observed operating within the coastal zone environment or were groups that came to or left the various coastal missions as traveling units. As noted at the bottom of Table 11, the average size of documented bands was 55.3 persons. The earliest available documentation for a band dates to 1751, but such small groups were doubtless a component of aboriginal organization much earlier. The mobile summer group documented by de Bellisle in 1719 (Folmer 1940) was probably this sort of band, and the prairie-riverine campsites of the late prehistoric Rockport Phase are generally too small in area to have been the residential camps of significantly larger groups.

It is probably significant that the documented sizes of such groups seem not to have changed substantially during the eighteenth century. Sizes fluctuate around the average of 55.36, with no discernible directional change. The band, as the most basic functioning socio-economic unit, was probably maintained as an essential adaptive unit regardless of changes in the sizes of larger-scale organizational groupings.

There is a dearth of data on the internal social organization of these groups. However, the observation by Cabeza de Vaca that "all who are of one lineage go about together" (Davenport 1924:232) suggests a socially integrated kin group, which is a basic feature of the normative concept of the minimum band. De Solís (Kress and Hatcher 1931:43) remarked in 1768 that the coastal Indians had two kinds of particularly influential individuals: "priests" called *conas* and "captains" called *tamas*. The later eighteenth-century documents refer to bands affiliated with particularly influential men, who held roles of leadership. References are made to specific individuals such as Frasada Pinta (Silva March 10, 1792) and Llano Grande (Garza June 13, 1791), each of whom was linked to a small group of people. Such individuals may have had some authority beyond the sphere of the small band, but if so, this is not documented in the presently known records. Beranger's observation to the effect that among a large shoreline aggregation of 500 people "they had no chief at all nor any subordination among them" (Carroll 1983:22) may reflect an absence of individuals with authority beyond the context of the smaller, constituent band groupings.

Second, "macroband" is the term preferred here for the aggregate group historically documented at shoreline locations and inferred for archaeological fishing campsites. As may be seen in Table 11, the

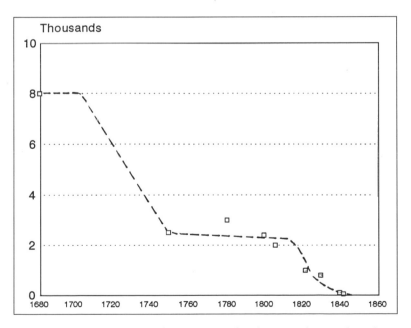

*Figure 26.* Historical population curve for the Karankawas, based on documentation discussed in the text and summarized in Table 10. Note precipitous decline to about 1750, subsequent relative stability, and final decline after about 1820.

**Table 11.** *Data on Sizes of Karankawan Bands, Macrobands, and Tribes*

| Band | Macroband | Tribe | Date | Source |
|------|-----------|-------|------|--------|
| | 400 | | 1528 | Cabeza de Vaca (Covey 1983) |
| | 400–500 | 1,600 | 1685 | Margry 1889:316 |
| | 500 | | 1720 | Beranger (Carroll 1983:21) |
| 54 | | 500 | 1751 | Piszina (letter of 12/26/1751) |
| | | 500–600 | 1780 | Morfi 1935:79–80 |
| 30+ | | | 1779 | Croix (letter of 10/17/1779) |
| 51 | | | 1789 | Treviño (diary entry 12/12/1789) |
| 86 | | | 1791 | Silva (letter of 4/26/1791) |
| 69 | | | 1791 | Silva (letter of 4/26/1791) |
| 41 | | | 1791 | Oberste 1942:32 |
| | 111 | | 1791 | Oberste 1942:36–37 |
| | 186 | | 1791 | Garza (letter of 12/15/1791) |
| 47 | | | 1791 | Oberste 1942:36 |
| | 208–161 | | 1793 | Garza (letter of 1/18/1793) |
| 52 | | | 1797 | Refugio census (Elquezabal 7/3/1797) |
| 47 | | | 1797 | Refugio census (ibid.) |
| 76 | | | 1797 | Refugio census (ibid.) |
| | | 400 | 1820 | Padilla 1919:51 |
| | | 320–400 | 1830 | Berlandier 1980:381 |
| | | 200 | 1830 | Berlandier 1969 |
| | | 80–120 | 1836 | Kuykendall 1903 |

*Note*: Average band = 55.3.

earliest historical records for macrobands estimate aggregates of around 400 or 500 people. By the late eighteenth century, these groups were smaller; in the three documented cases, the numbers of individuals were 111, 161 (208 prior to the splitting off of a group of 47 people), and 186. The relevant documentations indicate that in all three of these later examples, temporary aggregations of people were involved, rather than large groupings permanently maintained on a year-round basis.

Macrobands were apparently loosely organized and of flexible size. Beranger remarked that the large group of about 500 people he observed in the fall of 1720 was undergoing internecine conflict and that there was no apparent individual in authority (Carroll 1983: 21), an observation that suggests a group operating at the limit of its capacity for internal organizational stability. That group size fluctuated is suggested by the splintering of 47 people from the original group of 208 camped at the mouth of the Guadalupe River in the winter of 1791 (Garza to Muñoz January 18, 1793).

Macroband groupings have been documented elsewhere for hunter-gatherer societies (e.g., Lee and DeVore 1968; Birdsell 1953). In normative terms, they perform a crucial social function, insofar as they provide a context for viable mating networks, exchanges of information, and the performance of ritual activities that serve to link together the smaller socioeconomic units of their constituent bands (Wobst 1974; Hassan 1981:180–186).

Third, as used here, the term "tribe" refers to any of the five subgroups of the larger Karankawan entity (Cocos, Cujanes, Carancaguases, etc.). In terms of group size, at least, Newcomb (1983) has equated the tribe with what is here called the macroband. However, the sparse data suggest that two distinct scales of organization actually existed. For the late seventeenth century, we have the references to a camp of about 400 individuals observed by La Salle and to a larger group able to muster about 400 warriors, which indicate a population of about 1,600. As already discussed, this group was called Quelancouchis and probably is the same as the Clamcoets who sacked Fort Saint Louis (as noted by a captive French boy, Jean Baptiste Talon; see Weddle 1987). The group is generally equated with the Carancaguases of the eighteenth century (Bolton 1906; Newcomb 1983; T. N. Campbell, pers. comm.), a reasonable correlation on the basis of consistent location through time in the Matagorda Bay area.

The mechanisms that integrated macrobands within these larger tribal groupings are unclear. However, considering the apparently loose organization of the macroband and its apparent tendency to shifting band membership, it is possible that tribal identities derived from an analogous internal mixing of members within a commonly shared territory.

By the mid-eighteenth century, the tribal group contained about 500 people, a size that seems to have been more or less stable up to about 1820 when, as has been shown, the Karankawas began to experience final, catastrophic demographic collapse. Interestingly, this is the size of earlier documented macrobands, suggesting that the tribe was taking on the functional role previously performed by the macroband. This is supported by the fact that macrobands had become smaller by the late 1700s and thus may not have been optimal contexts for viable mating networks and information exchange. In effect, the critical hunter-gatherer organizational entities of the minimum band and the larger network of 400–500 people (see various discussions in Lee and DeVore 1968) were maintained within the context of reduced intraregional population.

At least by the 1820s, two of the tribal groupings—the Copanes and the Guapites—are no longer mentioned in contemporary accounts. Berlandier in 1830 still refers to the Cocos, Carancaguases, and Cujanes, and so these groups were apparently still extant and identifiable. The rapid demographic decline after 1820 probably required a merging of previously discrete tribal groupings for the purpose of maintaining biological and social viability. While the eighteenth century saw the once-more inclusive tribal entity fulfilling this function, during the nineteenth century the same organizational role could be played in some cases only by composite tribal entities.

Fourth, during the eighteenth century, the larger Karankawan grouping, as repeatedly mentioned, comprised five major tribal groupings, all interrelated through common language. The archaeological and ethnohistorical data combine to indicate that peoples of the central coast region followed one basic adaptive strategy, suggesting a common lifeway that, along with perhaps other shared language, customs, and sociocultural perceptions, may have been the foundation for a general sense of common ethnic identity.

By the 1840s, the Karankawas had a population of 100 or so individuals (Table 10). It is unclear whether this number refers to a remnant of the Karankawas proper or to the larger Karankawan group. In either case, the minimum population threshold for biological viability had probably been crossed, and the traditional forms of sociocultural organization, by necessity, would have broken down. Survivors of the catastrophic depopulation of the 1820s through 1840s probably dispersed—most likely into northeastern Mexico—to become absorbed into other, still viable native populations.

# Chapter 9
# The Karankawas on the Spanish Colonial Frontier: Seven Decades of Hostilities and the Resolution of Conflict

Throughout most of the eighteenth century, Karankawan relations with the Spaniards who settled the nearby interior were characterized by a tenuous and discontinuous link with the missions and by chronic hostilities (see general reviews in Newcomb 1961, 1983; Wolff 1969). The first Spanish effort to convert the coastal tribes ended in the Indian abandonment of Espíritu Santo mission, the relocation of that mission in 1726 further inland, and the redirection of missionary efforts toward interior Indian groups. In the fall of 1723, quarreling had broken out between the Indians and the soldiers at presidio La Bahía, which ended in fighting and the death of two Indians and Captain Domingo Ramón (Bolton 1906:117). The direct cause of the fighting was the attempt on the part of Ramón to massacre all the Indians, who had gathered together in the belief that they were about to partake in a feast (Castañeda 1936:182). The "Cocos, Cujanes, Guapites and Talancaguaches," little affected by the efforts of the Franciscans, "returned to their savage ways" (Ciprian 1979:20).

In 1728 Pedro Rivera reported that the Cujanes, Cocos, Guapites, and Carancaguases were hostile to La Bahía (cited in Bolton 1906: 20). In 1751 Fray Benito de Santa Ana wrote to the viceroy:

> Near the Bahía del Espíritu Santo, there have been some Indians called Cujanes [the mid-eighteenth-century generic term for the Karankawas], those same who used to be associated with the mission of La Bahía. For the past twenty years, they have been living in heathendom and with mortal hostilities between the Indians and the soldiers. The Cujanes were reputed to be irreducible for some thirty years, and this came to be (according to reports filed with the secretary of the government) the primary hindrance to the Presidio of La Bahía, preventing further goals. (Santa Ana to the Viceroy December 20, 1751, author's translation)

In the 1750s, a new round of relations was opened between the Spaniards and the Karankawas. At the end of March 1751, a group of 54 Indians approached presidio La Bahía, by then located on the banks of the lower San Antonio River. This encounter seemed to hold promise for more peaceful relations, since

> They [the Cuxanes] were so delighted by their treatment in the presidio and the mission, that they offered not only peace, but voluntarily offered to congregate in the mission and settle in the same way as had the Tamiques and Jaranames. (Pizsina to the Viceroy December 26, 1751, author's translation)

However, the situation did not work out amicably, and by fall all of the Indians had abandoned the mission, having found "strong new reasons for their old war" (Marqués de Altamira, February 29, 1752, quoting Santa Ana, author's translation).

Nonetheless, the new mission of Nuestra Señora del Rosario was established in 1754 for the express purpose of converting the Cujanes (see discussion in Bolton 1906). At the end of four years, only 21 souls had been baptized at Rosario, and those were in *articulo mortis*. By 1768, 200 persons had been baptized, but the Indians were noted for their inconstancy, and little had been accomplished toward the goal of Indian *reducción* to the Holy Faith and to colonial life (Bolton 1906:135–136). Thus upon a visit of inspection in 1767–1768, Fray Gaspar José de Solís noted that many of the Indians had fled "to the woods and the beach" prior to his arrival and assessed the Karankawan character in the following terms:

> The Indians among whom this mission (Rosario) was founded are the Coxanes, Guapites, Carancaguases and Copanes, although at the present time there are few of this nation [at the mission], since the greater number of them are in the woods. . . . They are all barbarians, given to idleness, lazy, indolent. They are very gluttonous and ravenous and eat meat almost raw, roasted and dripping with blood. . . . They are idle and given over to all kinds of vices, especially the vices of lasciviousness, robbery, systematic thieving and dancing. (Kress and Hatcher 1931:40)

This view seems to have become prevalent on the part of the Spaniards during the course of the eighteenth century. Fray Augustín Morfi reported that in the 1770s, the "Carancaguases or Carancagues nation [was] vile, cowardly, treacherous, and very cruel. . . .

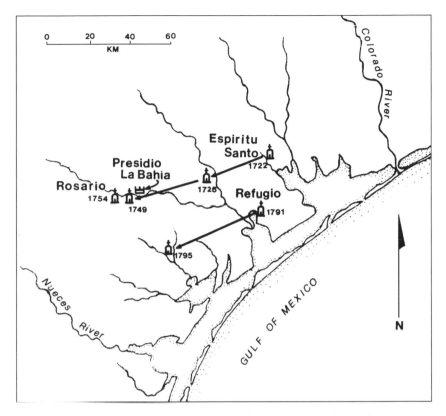

*Figure 27.* Map showing locations and relocations of eighteenth-century Spanish missions on the central coastal prairie of Texas.

Many of them speak Spanish with great fluency, being, in many instances, apostates from our missions" (Morfi 1935:79–80).

Taking the statements by de Solís and Morfi at face value, it might be assumed that Karankawan culture, and its individual participants, was imbued with a predisposition toward confrontation and conflict. Certainly these kinds of statements, along with the violent end of La Salle's colony at the hands of the Karankawas and the later conflicts with Anglo-American settlers, have been used to foster a modern popularization of this perception (e.g., Kilman 1959).

It is interesting, however, to note that in instances of initial Euro-American–Karankawan encounters that took place prior to any onset of hostilities or bad relations, the Indians appear to have had rather open attitudes to visitors to their lands. For example,

La Salle's party was well received by the Karankawas, who invited them to participate in a buffalo hunt. Only after La Salle had ordered some of his men to steal several Indian dugout canoes did conflict follow in which the retaliating Indians killed several Frenchmen (Joutel 1713). Jean Baptiste Talon, a boy who was adopted by the Indians after his capture during the Karankawan destruction of Fort Saint Louis suggested that

> M. de la Salle would never have had war with the Clamcoets if on arrival he had not high-handedly taken their canoes and refused them some little article that they asked him in return for them and for other services that they were ready to render to him. Nothing is easier than to win their friendship [than by giving them presents]. But also, as they give voluntarily of what they have, they do not like to be refused. And, while they are never aggressors, neither do they ever forget the pride of honor in their vengeance. (Weddle 1987:251)

An apparently analogous incident occurred in the area of the lower Colorado River—the eighteenth-century territory of the Cocos—during the 1687 exploration by Barroto. The Barroto party encountered some Indians who were gathering in mottes on the mainland; the Indians asked the Spaniards to lay down their arms and then "received them in a friendly fashion." The Spaniards later asked the Indians to board their ship, but the Indians did not want to do so. Captain Pedro de Yriarte then ordered three men to force one of the Indians onto the ship, but

> the three could not subdue him, because all these Indians are of great stature and very robust of limb. With the knife he had he wounded the three who had taken hold of him and thus freed himself. To his shouting many others came out who had concealed themselves in very tall grass and commenced shooting arrows at the captain and the rest. (Barroto 1987:162)

This incident resembles the sequence of events experienced by La Salle's party, insofar as an initial overture of friendship on the part of the Indians quickly devolved into conflict. In both cases, the Indians were quick to respond to what were clearly acts of aggression on the part of the Europeans.

On the other hand, there are indications in early accounts that when no such violations were committed, friendly relations between the Indians and Europeans ensued. Barroto's earlier visit with a group of Indians in the vicinity of present Aransas Pass was unmarked by hostilities. The Indians "came to the beach to play games next to the galley," and Captain Yriarte received gifts of fish from the Indian women and reciprocated with presents of beads (Barroto 1987:155). Similarly, in 1720 Beranger passed several days in the vicinity of a large shoreline camp and remarked that the Indians offered his men food and voluntarily helped them in gathering enough acorns to fill six casks (Carroll 1983:21–23).

These various accounts do not portray a people bent upon random or indiscriminate aggression, nor one that was unduly "vile, wicked, cowardly or treacherous." At the same time, they do suggest that, in the view of the Karankawas, violations of acceptable behavior were to be dealt with in no uncertain terms. Jean Baptiste Talon's observation that the Karankawas never forgot "the pride of honor in their vengeance" suggests that an offense, or something perceived as an offense, if sufficiently serious might have initiated ongoing and ultimately reciprocal animosities between Indians and Euro-Americans.

In the light of these observations, it can at least be suggested that catastrophes such as the Karankawan destruction of Fort Saint Louis and the attendant killing of the colonists were, in the perception of the Indians, acts of vengeance for some offense, real or perceived. It may not be coincidence, for instance, that the attack on Fort Saint Louis followed shortly after the outbreak of smallpox in the colony; if the sickness spread to the Indians, the settlers could conceivably have been held accountable. Perhaps relevant is the fact that Cabeza de Vaca and his fellow Spaniards were immediately held accountable for the outbreak of illness on Isla de Malhado and the ensuing death of half the Indians there; certainly the Indians seem to have had no difficulty in identifying the human vector of their misfortune.

None of this is meant to imply that the Karankawas were a consistently peace-loving people. They had their traditional tribal enemies, on whom they may have waged war on a more or less regular basis (Weddle 1987). Enemies killed in battle were at times apparently subjected to cannibalism, although this was probably similar to the ritualistic practices found among other aboriginal groups and should not in any way be regarded as peculiar to Karankawan culture (as has been the case in popular literature; see, e.g., Kilman 1959).

The key point here is that historical data suggest that the roots of Karankawan-European conflicts will be found in the nature of

initial Indian-colonial relations, rather than in an inevitable predisposition to conflict on the part of the Karankawas. Specific
instances of disagreement and misunderstanding doubtless contributed to hostile relations (e.g., the conflict, mentioned above,
that arose in 1723 at La Bahía and that was at least one contribut-
ing factor to years of subsequent hostilities). As suggested, the introduction of lethal diseases could well have been another catalyst for
acrimonious attitudes on the part of the Karankawas.

A third factor that can be suggested—one of a more fundamentally ecological nature—had its roots in the Spanish introduction of
cattle to the coastal prairies. There can be no doubt that the cattle
herds of the missions and associated ranches were frequently the
object of Indian depredations nor that the Karankawas were counted
among the various Indian groups responsible. As early as 1751,
Spaniards perceived the coastal Indians as a threat to their herds.
Captain Piszina writes from La Bahía that upon learning of the
approach of a group of Cuxanes, he sent his lieutenant

> with a squadron of men and some auxiliary Indians from the
> nearby Mission of Espíritu Santo, not to trouble them, but only
> to find out what they wanted and to prevent them from doing
> damage to the mission cattle, as they are known to have done in
> the past. (Piszina to the Viceroy December 26, 1751, author's
> translation)

The problem was a perennial one through the end of the eighteenth century. In 1785 Fray José Francisco López observed that
after the abandonment by the coastal Indians of Rosario mission,
"whose funds and wealth consisted mainly of cattle and horses,"
the herds were completely destroyed by the Apache and coastal
tribes (López 1940:15). As late as 1798, Fray Antonio Garavito
wrote from Refugio mission to Juan Elquezabal, commander at La
Bahía:

> I fear that if the Indians from Rosario do not have enough to eat
> in their mission, they will wander about doing damage. . . . the
> cattle will be destroyed, the herds driven off, the tame horses
> taken, and nothing will remain that they will not steal.
> (Garavito to Elquezabal March 25, 1798, author's translation)

Cattle, to the Spaniard, was property—in effect, a cultural artifact. To the Indian, it was a source of food that, though somewhat

novel, was little different from other major kinds of game in terms of its benefits. As the archaeological data have shown, bison were a highly significant source of meat for the Karankawas, and it can be assumed that cattle were readily substituted whenever it was convenient or necessary to do so. In fact, there is reason to believe that such a substitution became increasingly necessary to the Indians during the course of the eighteenth century, as cattle displaced the native bison through competition for prime grazing areas.

There is no doubt that bison were present in significant numbers on the Texas coastal prairies during the early decades of Euro-American occupation, since there are repeated references during this period to bison roaming the region. Joutel in 1685 refers to herds of bullocks, that had to have been the native bison, since this predates the earliest importation of domesticated Spanish animals (Cox 1905:81). Bison are referred to by Jean Baptiste Talon (Weddle 1987:227); De León documents their presence on the prairies near the coast in 1689 (West 1905:207); de Bellisle refers to bison hunting on the coastal prairie in 1719–1720 (Folmer 1940); and Beranger notes their presence on the mainland in 1720 (Carroll 1983:21). As late as 1768, de Solís remarked that bison abounded in the region and that they were a source of food for the Indians (Kress and Hatcher 1931:43).

On the other hand, once cattle were introduced to the region, they thrived and multiplied in numbers. By 1710 herds of cattle were well established in the vicinity of the early East Texas mission of San Francisco de los Tejas, and in 1721 the Marqués de Aguayo saw them roaming as far west as the Guadalupe River (Myers 1969: 11–14). The Texas missions were established as centers of ranching activity, and the largest and most important of the mission ranches was that associated with Espíritu Santo mission at La Bahía (ibid.).

In his Report of 1785, Fray López noted that "twelve years ago" [in 1773], there were more than 15,000 branded head of cattle at Espíritu Santo, "and of those unbranded there was an incomparably greater number." The rapid rate of expansion of the cattle herds of the coastal prairie missions can be seen clearly in the data presented in Table 12.

By 1775 cattle, mostly unbranded, were widely distributed across the region's grasslands (Jackson 1986:9). The once abundant bison, however, seem to have waned in numbers with the expansion of the cattle herds. The report of Corporal José Manuel Granados of 1793 lists many of the abundant floral and faunal resources of the coastal prairies but, unlike similar observations of earlier days, makes no

**Table 12.** *Cattle Herd Sizes, Coastal Prairie Missions*

| Year | Espíritu Santo (founded 1749) | Rosario (founded 1754) | Refugio (founded 1795) |
|------|-------------------------------|------------------------|------------------------|
| 1758 | 3,000 | 700 + | |
| 1759 | 4,000 | 1,000 + | |
| 1767–1768 | 16,000 | 4,000 + | |
| 1774 | 15,000[a] | | |
| 1780 | | 10,000 | |
| 1783 | | 30,000 (includes unbranded) | |
| 1797 | | | "too few" |
| 1808 | | | 5,000 (includes small stock) |

*Note:* [a]Plus "and incomparably greater number unbranded" (López 1940).
*Source*: Data from Ramsdell n.d., Linn 1883, and López 1940.

mention of bison when noting the region's edible animals (cited in Oberste 1942:83). Similarly, in a detailed and perceptive description of the environment in 1829, Jean Louis Berlandier mentions bison only in restricted locales (Berlandier 1980).

It is likely, therefore, that the Karankawas increasingly substituted cattle for bison as a major source of red meat during the eighteenth century, and that this was a common cause of conflict between Indians and Spaniards. The situation was probably not markedly different from that for the northern frontier of New Spain in general, as described by Campbell:

> They [the Spaniards] brought livestock that competed with wild grazing and browsing animals. Game animals were thinned or driven away by Spanish hunters with firearms. The Indians turned to livestock as a substitute for game animals, and loss of livestock brought punitive action by Spaniards. (Campbell 1988:42)

By the 1780s, hostilities between Karankawas and Spaniards were a chronic condition. Under the "bad influence" of an Indian known to the Spaniards as José María, Rosario mission had been abandoned (López 1940). As recorded in various documents of the period, the soldiers at La Bahía engaged in frequent overt conflict with the coastal groups that took the form of punitive expeditions in retaliation for Indian raids and thefts. By 1779 it was predicted that

. . . the said Carancaguases will cause the Presidio of La Bahía more trouble than is apparent, especially considering the apostate Joseph María, which fact I can do no less than expose to Your Lordship to warn of what contingencies may befall that presidio in the future. (Croix to Cabello October 17, 1779)

Punitive actions were not easily accomplished. The Spaniards did not have the equipment or the requisite knowledge of coastal geography with which to pursue the Karankawas, who customarily fled to the coast and disappeared in what seemed like a veritable maze of marshes and lagoons. Don Luis Cazorla, commander of La Bahía, in writing to Governor Rafael Martínez Pacheco in 1787, characterized the problem from the Spanish point of view:

[in pursuit of Carancaguases who had stolen horses from a Spanish ranch, the corporal sent by Cazorla to capture and punish the Indians] reported only having spotted some six canoes [filled] with many Carancaguases Indians near the mouth of these rivers [the San Antonio and Guadalupe Rivers]. They shouted at these Indians but in no way were able to get them within gunshot [range]. Since we do not have such boats available to enter the bays, it would prove illusory to make any attempt to render these pagans the just punishment which they deserve, unless they surrender, which is a point I have made repeatedly. (Cazorla to Pacheco January 22, 1787)

The following May, Cazorla again wrote to the governor regarding the situation with the Karankawas, this time more forcefully arguing his case for their eradication:

I am of the opinion—modifying the opinion of our commandant [but] without acting contrary to it in any manner whatsoever—that [we] could receive them [the Indians] in peace and put them in missions, sending them all the corresponding guarantees for this purpose. In this way, since at any time they will create provocations, at the first which is committed [we] could make a reprisal and expel them once and for all. With this, without violating our treaties with them (for which I can see no justification in humanity, hospitality, or natural law), we would achieve their extermination. And though some would remain in the woods, their surrender would be less difficult [to achieve]. This is the view which I have developed of the aforesaid coastal Indians—with no other purpose than that of serving God and the King and the public interest—based on experience which I have [in the matter]. (Cazorla to Pacheco May 2, 1788)

Even five years later, after general relations between the Spaniards and the Karankawas had begun to take a more peaceful turn, authority at La Bahía was inclined toward the view expressed by Cazorla. Captain Juan Cortes wrote to Governor Muñoz in 1793:

> In this emergency [of unrest at Refugio mission], if the many occupations of Your Lordship prevent you from coming, please send immediately as many troops as you can to punish these heathens, who deserve to be treated with all the rigor of war and not with the sympathy with which they have been treated since they asked, in my presence, for a mission. (Cortes to Muñoz December 5, 1793, author's translation)

Fortunately for the Indians at the mission, Muñoz replied that "the Carancahuaz tribe had given us cause to exterminate it many times, but the King's policy demands gentleness and encouragement that they should give up their heathen life" (Muñoz to Cortes December 13, 1793, author's translation).

In the 1790s the final phase of Franciscan missionary activity in Texas was initiated. The efforts of the padres during this decade were devoted largely to the establishment of the mission of Nuestra Señora del Refugio that, like the earlier mission of Rosario, was founded expressly for conversion of the Karankawan groups. For reasons that can at this time be only partly understood, Refugio was to be a more successful venture than was Rosario. During the early nineteenth century, Refugio mission became a focal point for Karankawan-Spanish interaction and a locus for a degree of Karankawan acculturation.

Fray Manuel de Silva, superior of all Franciscan missions of the Colegio de Nuestra Señora de Guadalupe de Zacatecas, visited Texas in 1791 to evaluate the feasibility of a new mission for the coastal tribes. Accompanied by Fray Juan Garza, Silva set out from La Bahía to speak directly with the Karankawas and to ascertain their receptivity to a new mission. The results of these efforts were, in Silva's view, sufficiently satisfactory to justify the effort and expense of the proposed enterprise. In his report to the king, he stated:

> Finally, in spite of their crudeness, they heard, without fear or intimidation, the high nature of the venerable mysteries of Our

Holy Faith. Nor did the subordination to the civil laws and mercies of Your Majesty appear too hard to them. In effect, Your Lordship, the seed fell (it seems) on good ground, so that later it began to bear fruit. Convinced of the sound reason of the truth, and attracted by the kindness with which my companion and I treated them, they would later come to establish and keep an inviolable peace with us Spaniards, a peace that so far they have not broken, whereas previously they made hostilities, committing robberies and murders. (Silva to the King March 3, 1793, author's translation)

Garza documented the actual response of one Karankawan leader to the idea of the new mission. It is particularly significant in that it shows that the Indians were open to the idea, provided that the mission was on the coast within the heart of their traditional territory:

Father, don't deceive yourself, for we don't want to go to the Mission [of Rosario]. We will do nobody harm, we will go our own way, and let the Spaniards come also to our country, with the assurance that we will receive them as friends, but we do not want to leave our country. If you want to, put a mission here on the coast for us. We will gather in it, all of us who are Christians, and we will bring with us all the heathens that are on this coast from the mouth of the Nueces to the Colorado River. . . . Father, if you put a mission there [at the mouth of the Guadalupe River] for us, then you can say that the whole coast is yours. Go and see if it pleases you . . . and send us word when we may gather there. (Garza to Muñoz June 13, 1791, in Oberste 1942:29)

On the whole, the new mission was to provide a peaceful bridge between the Karankawas and the Spaniards. In 1797 Elquezabal, interim commander at La Bahía, was able to write:

From what I have seen of their [the Karankawas'] manners and ways of doing things, there does not appear to be any bad intention, or anything that one could find suspicious, or any artfulness in their thinking. (Elquezabal to Muñoz July 3, 1797, author's translation)

Elquezabal's words seem to reflect a marked shift in stated perceptions of Karankawan character, one that likely emerged from the

period of peace that began around the time of the founding of Refugio mission.

By the first decade of the nineteenth century, a stable interaction between the Karankawas and the Spaniards had emerged. In 1806 Manuel Antonio Cordero, governor of the Province of Tejas, wrote to Nemesio Salcedo, commandant general of the Interior Provinces:

> West of the Colorado, roving along the coast, southward as far as the San Antonio River, were the Karankawas. These fierce tribes had been cannibalistic, but they are now civilized and report regularly to the commander at La Bahía and the missionary at Refugio everything that occurs on the coast. (Cordero to Salcedo January 16, 1806)

In his later Reminiscences, John Linn, an early Anglo-American settler, wrote that

> Father Díaz, who was the last of the missionaries, gave me quite a history of the different Texas missions. He stated that in the year 1808 the mission of Refugio possessed fully five thousand head of livestock of various kinds; the "flat" in front of the church was their cultivated field. Up to this period they had all the necessaries . . . and were making rapid progress in the path of civilization, when the war of Mexican Independence came and destroyed . . . the work and fruits of many years of arduous toils. . . . [The] Indians relapsed into barbarism . . . and was again the savage that he was at first. The Carankua women, too, learned the use of the spinning wheel, and manufactured a very good article of cotton cloth, and also blankets of superior quality. (Linn 1883:334)

Referring to the late 1820s, Berlandier notes of the Karankawas:

> The Carancahuases of today are less ferocious than those of the past century. They can be considered as mission Indians, half-tamed. Transformed into mariners on the bays, they lead an itiophage [fishing] life, hunting and more often fishing for their needs. Before the wars of independence, when Mexico was flourishing, almost all the Carancahuases lived at their mission. Now living most of the time on the coast, they come only occasionally to visit the presidio, where the authorities sometimes give them small presents. Following the example of other indigenes,

they have some horses, although their travels are much more frequently over the bays than over the land. . . . Although vagabonds, all call themselves Christians. Some wear a cross hung around their neck, and all their newborn are carried with ceremony to the Franciscan father who leads them, in order to receive the waters of baptism from him. I have questioned several of them on the religion of their ancestors, but they never wished to answer. (Berlandier 1980:380–381)

The observations of Elquezabal, Fray Díaz, as recorded by Linn, as well as those of Cordero and Berlandier, show that by the first decades of the nineteenth century the Karankawas had experienced a marked shift in attitudes and actions vis-à-vis the Spanish colonial frontier. It is clear that the hostilities that characterized the previous century had abated, giving way to peaceful interaction at the focal points of the mission and the presidio. It is also apparent that within this context the Karankawas had undergone a significant degree of acculturation to the previously resisted Christian ideology, as well as to behavioral patterns derived from European culture. Fray Díaz' mention of "rapid progress in the path of civilization," particularly the practice of the cottage industries of spinning and weaving of cotton cloth, completely foreign to traditional Karankawan culture, are telling in this regard. Berlandier's observation that the Indians maintained ties with the mission is highly significant, since it shows an important shift in ideology and the maintenance of associated modes of behavior even after the mission system had been weakened by the onset of the Mexican War of Independence. Berlandier's statement that the Karankawas, who numbered at least 2,000 in the early 1800s, were almost all living in the mission, is doubtless an exaggeration. It can, however, probably be taken to reflect particularly strong ties between Indians and Spaniards during that period and may indicate that most of the Karankawas were associated with the mission at one time or another.

The specific causes for the shift from confrontation and hostility to peaceful interaction and acculturation, beginning in the early 1790s, are difficult to identify precisely. It is clear from the letters of the professional soldiers, Cazorla and Cortes, that those Spaniards charged with policing the situation were becoming exasperated with the chronic conflict with the Karankawas, to the point of advocating a policy of extermination. It may be that, in general, the Karankawas, too, were weary of chronic conflict by about 1790.

Also, the Indians may have been aware of the increasingly genocidal viewpoint at the presidio, concluding that it was in their own best interests to come to a more amicable understanding with the Spaniards.

The Karankawas perhaps also responded to a fundamentally new cultural and demographic geography in the larger Texas region. By 1790 the native Coahuiltecans and other groups of the interior had virtually disappeared, having undergone heavy mortality from disease, large-scale displacements due to Apache and later Comanche incursions, and *reducción* within the missions at San Antonio and La Bahía (Campbell 1988). Such a situation could have begun to seriously affect Karankawan security, insofar as it resulted in the removal of buffer groups between the coast and the intrusive Comanches, who were, by the late eighteenth century, perceived as a serious threat (e.g., Elquezabal to Muñoz July 3, 1797; Berlandier 1980:381). Also, the disappearance of the indigenous inland native population meant the eradication of a source of demographic rejuvenation for coastal groups, and this could have contributed to a perceived need for a reduction of hostilities. Finally, peace with the Spaniards may have been deemed advisable because the Karankawas had no desire to maintain hostilities on two major fronts, that is, between both the Spaniards and the Comanches.

In light of available information on Karankawan defensive strategy, it is unlikely that the coastal groups turned to the mission simply as an immediate refuge from Comanche attacks. For the Karankawas, maximum security was always obtained by losing themselves among the lagoons, islands, and marshes of the coastline. This was clearly the case during conflict with the Spaniards, as indicated by Fray Silva's observation that the soldiers could not follow the Indians once they reached the coast, "which only the Indians have known, and which fact has allowed them to make war . . . thus mocking the Spaniards who have been unable to follow them to the islands" (Silva to Muñoz April 26, 1791). As early as 1768, Fray de Solís noted that the Karankawas, when threatened by inland Indians, took refuge on the coast, "imagining that in these parts they are free and secure" (Kress and Hatcher 1931:44). In 1797 the Karankawas clearly stated their preference for Refugio mission over Rosario mission because at Refugio they would be within "proximity of the coast for fishing in time of urgent necessity, as well as the greatest distance from their enemies, the Comanche" (Elquezabal to Muñoz July 3, 1797, author's translation). The very same reasons were given for avoiding congregation in the missions at San Antonio (ibid.). A letter from Fray Antonio Garavito at Refugio mission,

written to José Moral, commander at La Bahía, reveals the Karankawan perception of security most precisely:

> I say that the Indians of this mission are more motivated to
> retire to the coast with their families, because of the fear that
> the Comanche might come to avenge the grievance of having
> two of their number wounded while in the houses of Spaniards
> at that presidio [La Bahía]. They [the coastal Indians] judge
> themselves more secure from attack in the bays, and it being
> best to flee, even in disregard of the reasonings of the minister
> who has always persuaded them otherwise. But then, they
> are Indians. (Garavito to Moral October 13, 1798, author's
> translation)

Thus, while the missions served as refuges for interior groups
(Campbell 1988:43), who in effect had no place else to go, this does
not seem to have been a primary attraction for the Karankawas.
What was important to the Karankawas, however, was that the mission be so situated that a fast retreat to the coast, when required,
could be readily accomplished.

Whatever might have been the precise motive, or complex of
motives, for the Karankawa peace with the Spaniards, as well as the
new gravitation toward the missions, viable change did occur, and
the change was probably related to the variables just discussed. It
would be erroneous to view the new relationship as the only option
open to a defeated people who were merely accepting an inevitable
subjugation. In 1790 the Karankawas were far from that state. Their
population level had been more or less stable for forty years, and at
around 2,000 or 2,500 was two and one-half to three times as great
as the combined Indian and Spanish populations at La Bahía (see
Tjarks 1974). The Karankawas doubtless could still regard the coast
as a viable defensive location when it was necessary to do so. Their
traditional cultural ecology and internal organizational structures
were intact, though in modified forms. The transition to peace, and
attendant acculturation, was not made from desperation, but rather
must have involved some measure of choice, and probably should be
viewed as an adaptive decision made within the context of a changing sociocultural environment.

In a sense, it is rather remarkable that such a transition was
effected at all. As the combination of archaeological and ethnohistorical data has here shown, the Karankawan lifeway, as grounded in
a basic adaptive system, was both deeply rooted in prehistory and
resilient under the impacts of European colonization. At least from

the late Archaic, circa 2000 B.P., life on the Texas central coast was characterized by continuity in basic patterns of subsistence, settlement, and seasonal mobility. Given the distinctive language and the apparently common general ethnic identity of the Karankawan groups, it is inferable that these continuities also involved significant cultural-cognitive correlates, rooted in a traditional lifeway, and shared by participant peoples. Such cognitive dimensions are difficult to define with the available data, but, as will be seen in what follows, it is at least possible to point to a strong sense of the coastal environment as traditional place, as well as a space defined by known boundary conditions. The critical point is that the traditional lifeway must have provided the basis for a consensual cognition, with traditional values and culturally derived perceptions acting as filters through which change had to have been evaluated.

How, then, was the change in Karankawan attitudes and relations with the Spaniards effected, given the Indians' adherence to traditional adaptive strategies and patterns of sociocultural organization? By what means did the Karankawas accomplish the shift from resistance to the Spaniards to an acceptance of their presence and, to some degree, of the institution of the mission as the embodiment of a foreign ideology? Documentary information to be discussed in the following chapter suggests that these changes were possible precisely because they did not represent, at least initially, a Karankawan conformity to Spanish culture but rather the integration of the mission into *Karankawan* culture. The mission was quite strategically incorporated into traditional native life at the basic level of an ecological resource, and its acceptance in this fundamental sense provided the groundwork for subsequent partial acculturation to Spanish behavioral and cognitive patterns.

# Chapter 10
# The Mission as an
# Ecological Resource

From its sixteenth-century beginnings, the mission in the Spanish New World served as a focal point of cultural change as well as a locus of religious conversion (e.g., McAlister 1984:170–173). *Reducción* of the Indians entailed, at least in its idealized conceptualization, the acculturation of native peoples to Spanish lifeways as well as baptism and conversion in the Holy Faith. In order to provide a proper context for cultural transformation, the mission was to be a self-sufficient economic unit in which Indian neophytes learned to live and work within a microcosmic Christian community. In the case of many of the missions of New Spain's northeastern frontier, *reducción* had, by necessity, to involve transmission of the practices of agriculture and animal husbandry within the novel setting of sedentary life. The missionaries' task was a formidable one that required habituating the neophytes, accustomed to a mobile, hunting, and gathering lifeway, to an entirely new set of behavioral patterns. The frustrations of the task are apparent in the words of Father José Mariano Reyes, written at Rosario mission in 1790:

> In this province, one cannot found a mission, nor resurrect those that have been abandoned, in the same way that Mexican settlements are established, where the Indians, prior to their conquest, already lived in society, with some cleanliness and with commerce between kingdoms. With the nations of the north, it is impossible because they live dispersed in their heathendom, without loyalty to any monarch, since they have none. These nations have no fixed abode and are always wandering about. (Reyes to the Viceroy May 1, 1790, author's translation)

This difficulty must have been compounded when dealing with the Karankawas, who, unlike many interior Indian groups, were not forced to accept the mission as a place of last refuge against the marauding Apaches and Comanches.

In the face of these obstacles, the missionaries and their compatriots relied heavily on enticements of gifts and food to bring the Indians into the missions. Piszina writes in 1751:

> Solely to bind [to the mission and presidio] this portion of them [a group of Cuxanes], I gave them gifts, at a cost of three hundred pesos, of beef, corn, tobacco, rope, bayeta, hats, and other trifles that appealed to them. (Piszina to the Viceroy December 26, 1751, author's translation)

Similarly, Padres Silva and Garza, when visiting the coast in the early 1790s, opened the way to dialogue with the Karankawas by making presents and offering gifts of food:

> They received us very well. We gave them what we could, considering our poverty, of ears of maize, maize flour, tobacco, and some perigosos [?]. (Silva to Muñoz April 26, 1791, author's translation)

> [We visited the Indians] in their rancherías, . . . communicating with them and obtaining, with attentions, presents, industry, and good means, their good will. (Silva to the King March 3, 1793, author's translation)

Once a group of Indians arrived at the mission, the primary task facing the missionaries was to provide the new arrivals with basic necessities. As long as this could be accomplished, the Indians had reason to stay at the mission. However, when provisions were inadequate, they felt that something of a contractual agreement had been broken and left the mission. The Indians' primary expectation that the mission provide sustenance, and their predisposition to leave when provisions were depleted, is highlighted by events of 1798. Two Karankawan groups, one of Carancaguases and the other of Cocos, were sent from Rosario mission to Refugio mission when supplies of food ran out at Rosario. This put an insuperable strain on Refugio's provisioning capacities, creating an untenable situation. Commander Elquezabal of La Bahía wrote to Governor Muñoz:

> The eighth of this month, I left this presidio [La Bahía] for Refugio, and, before I arrived at that mission, I received news that the Cujanes and Carancahuas Indians, with their families

from Rosario, which had been gathered in that mission, had left for the coast of Bergantín [a general term for the coast along Matagorda and San Antonio Bays]. I then dispatched two soldiers to call the capitancillos Andres and Nicolás, who briefly gave me the explanation of Fr. Antonio de Juan Garavito [regarding the Indians' leaving]. He said that, there being insufficient supplies for everyone, and therefore inadequate sustenance for the Indians, they had gone to the coast to sustain themselves. It was for this reason that they were obliged to leave the mission, so that they could go and feed themselves on fish. (Elquezabal to Muñoz January 17, 1798, author's translation)

Regarding the same situation, Father Garavito wrote, in a letter to Elquezabal:

I have notified you that the Indians of this mission [of Refugio] have already gone to the coast. Though they did not force me, all have gone. The reasons given to me by them are "Father, we must go to the coast. The Indians from Rosario have been eating our cattle, which are now all gone, so we the Indians of this mission must now go out to look for something to eat." . . . I fear that if the Indians from Rosario do not have enough to eat in their mission, they will wander about doing damage . . . the cattle will be destroyed, the herds driven off, the tame horses taken, and nothing will remain that they will not steal. [The failure to receive new provisions] would bring about the collapse of the two missions and end the peace, quietude, and calm on the whole coast. I say the whole coast because the Indians from Rosario went from here to there angry, seeing that the Indians of Refugio mission did not want them [at Refugio], even though they speak the same language. It so vexed the Indians of Refugio to see what was happening to that mission's goods, that they are considering joining up with the great chief Frasada Pinta. This may come about if God and Our Blessed Lady Mary do not prevent it. (Garavito to Elquezabal March 25, 1798, author's translation)

It is clear, then, that the most immediate attraction of the mission for the Indians was the possibility of receiving sustenance. In return, they had to remain at the mission, participate in daily activities, receive appropriate instruction in Christian ideology, and, when they were judged ready by the missionary fathers, baptism in the Holy Faith. The efforts of the padres were readily interrupted

when the basic requirement of sufficient food for the resident neophytes could not be met. Father Reyes, writing to Governor Muñoz,
again summed up the situation as follows:

> You must well know that for these neophytes the Gospel enters
> through the mouth, not through the ears, and if you are think-
> ing that they will come later from the coast [to the mission] to
> work for a living, this is an illusion, and I can give twenty rea-
> sons why after five years they have not taken to work. (Reyes
> to Muñoz November 18, 1790, author's translation)

*Funny
Quote*

In the light of these bits of information, it might be concluded
that the Karankawas turned to a dependence on the mission when
traditional subsistence strategies proved inadequate, or simply went
to the missions as a relatively easy way of temporarily meeting subsistence needs. Given the primary motivation of receiving food,
such a conclusion doubtless has some merit. It provides, however,
only a very partial understanding of how the Karankawas perceived,
and dealt with, the mission from the perspective of their traditional
lifeway.

The archaeological information from the Texas central coast,
dealt with here at some length, has provided a key to the spatial and
seasonal patterns of resource use by the region's native people.
Seasonality data have indicated that settlement focused at highly
productive shoreline locations during the fall and winter. The relatively large size and archaeological density of shoreline fishing sites,
and the abundance of estuarine faunal remains, indicate that these
camps supported sizable groups that relied heavily on fishing,
which was supplemented by hunting and shellfish gathering. A
spring-summer dispersal of population, with emphasis on procurement of terrestrial game, is indicated by the relatively small size,
the seasonality, and the kinds of faunal remains at the numerous
prairie-riverine sites, all of which are in proximity to the region's
coastal prairie environment. In short, the archaeology indicates a
clear seasonal dichotomy between large fall-winter shoreline camps
and smaller, more dispersed spring-summer camps on the prairies
of the adjacent interior. As has been shown, documented firsthand
European observations of group locations, camp sizes, and subsistence patterns support the archaeological conclusions and indicate that the basic adaptive strategy of precontact times operated
through the Colonial Period.

From the archaeological data, it appears that the shift in settlement and subsistence patterns from shoreline fishing to dispersed

terrestrial resource procurement generally took place sometime between the end of March and the end of April. This period represents the early end of the seasonal range of *Rangia cuneata* seasonality estimates at prairie-riverine sites. These are, of course, only estimated ranges, but their consistency suggests that initial occupation of these camps generally took place at this time of the year. This is also supported by the ethnohistorical data that document shoreline occupations between October and March but suggest shoreline abandonment and occupation of riverine zones by April.

Given these lines of information, it is probably highly significant that the Karankawas most frequently showed interest in the missions between the end of March and early May. Examination of available documents has produced sixteen instances in which the exact or approximate date of Karankawan arrival at the missions was documented. Of these, eleven, or 69 percent, indicate Indian arrivals at dates from mid-March through May (see Figure 28).

The Karankawas were thus approaching and/or entering the missions almost exclusively at just the time of year that traditionally involved a major shift in settlement and subsistence strategies. The close correspondence between documented dates of arrivals at the missions and the archaeological evidence for seasonal shifts in occupation between shoreline fishing locales and prairie-riverine campsites is indicated graphically in Figure 29.

It is interesting to note too that, while most instances of the Karankawas coming to the missions were in the spring, the next most frequent time of the year was the fall (four, or 25 percent of the cases). According to the model of settlement and subsistence mobility based upon the archaeological and ethnohistorical data, the fall was the time when Karankawan groups would have returned to favored coastal fishing localities from summers spent on the coastal prairies. The fall season, then, would have required, as did the spring, decisions concerning residential locations. Some bands may occasionally have opted at this time for spending the winter at the mission. As noted earlier, a band-sized group of forty-seven people split from the large winter camp on Guadalupe Bay in January 1793, suggesting the shoreline locales did not invariably support all of the population that might otherwise have congregated. Some bands, perhaps anticipating this kind of situation—or possibly perceiving other less tangible problems, such as social tensions—may have seen the mission as a viable winter residence.

The recorded instances of Karankawan arrivals at the missions, spanning the years between 1722 and 1798, are listed in Table 13. Basically, there were two kinds of approaches to the mission: either

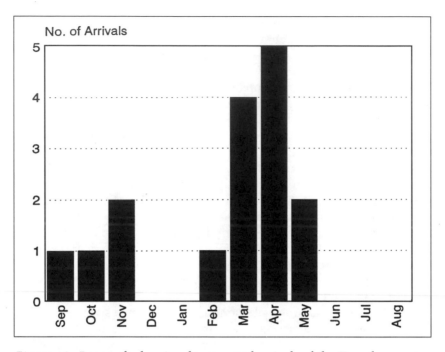

*Figure 28.* Bar graph showing documented arrivals of the Karankawas at coastal prairie missions, according to number of arrivals per month (see Table 13 for specific arrival dates and information on the circumstances and group sizes involved).

(1) a leader, usually accompanied by a retinue of warriors, came to scout the mission to see whether supplies were sufficiently abundant to justify bringing the rest of his people to the mission or (2) a family or band group entered the mission and stayed for an indefinite period of time, leaving when provisions became inadequate.

In either case, it is apparent that the time of the year during which the Karankawas were most interested in the mission was just the time that traditionally involved a major shift in residential patterns and attendant subsistence activities. This move is hardly likely to have been coincidence and strongly suggests that the Indians were scheduling visits to the mission within their long-established pattern of seasonally oscillating subsistence strategy. These visits, which were sometimes followed by group entries into, and residence at, a given mission, were therefore not random or haphazard events but were strategically incorporated into the traditional seasonal round.

It can be noted too that the kinds of foods that were available at the missions were analogous to those that had been traditionally sought and procured during the spring and summer. Cattle, the mainstay of the mission diet (e.g., Oberste 1942), took the place of bison, while maize was a high starch supplement that partially replaced the plant foods doubtless traditionally gathered during the spring and summer (for which there is no direct archaeological evidence but that can be inferred to have been a dietary necessity and that are indicated by the reference to the gathering of "wild potatoes" in de Bellisle's "Relation" [Folmer 1940]).

Along these same lines, it is probably significant that Refugio, the mission that was to have the most sustained influence on the Karankawas in terms of conversion and acculturation, was located within the traditional operational area of coastal groups. With the exception of the short-lived original location of Espíritu Santo on Garcitas Creek, other coastal prairie missions were located beyond the inland margin of Karankawan home territory. Refugio was

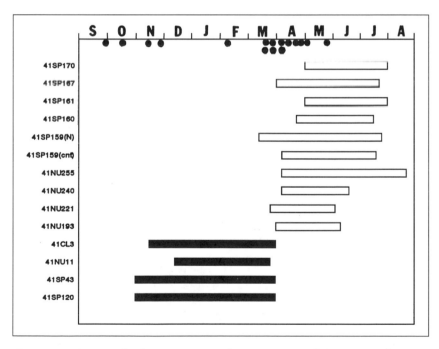

*Figure 29.* Bar graph showing seasonality estimates of Group 1 and Group 2 Rockport Phase sites, along with documented dates of arrival (black dots) of Karankawas at coastal prairie missions.

**Table 13.** *Data Pertaining to Documented Instances of Karankawas Coming to Coastal Prairie Missions*

| Year | Date | Number of People, Circumstances | Source |
|------|------|-------------------------------|--------|
| 1722 | Around May 4 | A number of Coco families come to new site of Espíritu Santo, leave soon after due to lack of provisions. | Testimonio de la Mission de N. Sra. de Loreto, A.G.I., Audiencia de Guadalajara, cited in Castañeda 2:167 |
| 1722 | Late May | Chiefs of Coco and Cujane nations come to new Espíritu Santo mission with their families, again leave due to inadequate provisions. | Ibid. |
| 1722 | March 16 | Many coastal Indians arrive at Espíritu Santo, stay an indefinite time. | Ibid. |
| 1751 | End of March | Group of 54 Cujanes arrive at Espíritu Santo, stay about 2-1/2 months. | Piszina to the Viceroy 12/16/1751 |
| 1789 | October through November | Karankawas come to Rosario and stay for indefinite period of time. | Espadas to Pacheco 12/29/1789 |
| 1791 | April 7 | Chief Frasada Pinto arrives at Rosario with some of his people. | Silva to the Viceroy 3/10/1792, cited in Oberste 1942:20 |
| 1791 | April 20 | Chief Manuel Allegre and his family go to Rosario. | Silva to Muñoz 4/26/1791 |
| 1791 | November | Five families of Karankawas arrive at Rosario. | Jaudenes to Muñoz 11/30/1791 |
| 1793 | March | Chief Frasada Pinta arrives at Refugio with 8 Cocos men, representing 55 people; they leave due to low provisions. | Garza to Muñoz 6/10/1793, cited in Oberste 1942:82 |
| 1793 | April | Frasada Pinta returns to Refugio, again leaves due to low provisions. | Ibid. |
| 1793 | February 10 | Frasada Pinta and 5 of his men arrive at Refugio, promise to bring their families "when weather improves." | Oberste 1942:67 |
| 1794 | April 28 | Frasada Pinta and his people arrive at Refugio to receive meat and maize. | Muñoz to Cortes 6/10/1794 |

**Table 13.** (Continued)

| Year | Date | Number of People, Circumstances | Source |
|---|---|---|---|
| 1795 | September | Frasada Pinta arrives at Refugio. | Silva to Muñoz 9/30/1795 |
| 1796 | April 5 | Combined group of 97 Karankawas and Cocos arrive at Refugio. | Castañeda 5:191 |
| 1797 | Late March | Combined group of Cocos and Carancaguases arrive at Rosario. | Cortes to Muñoz 3/24/1797 |
| 1798– 1799 | November– January | Indians who had left Refugio in March because of lack of provisions return to mission. | Moral to Muñoz 11/21/1798, 1/18/1799 |

initially situated near the coast, in proximity to the mouth of the Guadalupe River. It was soon moved to the north bank of the Mission River, at present-day Refugio, Texas. Even at the more inland location, the mission was closer to the coast than either Rosario or Espíritu Santo. It was in fact located 38 kilometers from the mainland shoreline, along the inland boundary zone of Karankawan territory as represented archaeologically by the inland distribution of Rockport sites and historically by the previously cited reference to the proposed Karankawan reserve that was to extend 40 kilometers from the shoreline. That the final location of Refugio suited the Karankawa far better than the more inland locations is indicated by Elquezabal, who in a letter to Governor Muñoz noted that the Cocos and Carancaguases, when asked if they would consider settling in the San Antonio missions, replied that

> for no reason would they settle in the missions around San Antonio, this because of the presence of the Comanches, as well as because of the distance from the coast. [At the Refugio mission they could] be happy, without so much hunger [as at Rosario], and where the climate suited them perfectly, and there was the proximity of the coast for fishing in time of urgent necessity, as well as the greatest distance from their enemies, the Comanches. . . . They ask to live in the mission as Christians and to be worthy to receive the water of baptism, and to be left quiet and at peace at Refugio, where they can be content, and in harmony, Cocos and Carancaguases. (Elquezabal to Muñoz July 3, 1797, author's translation)

The statement of a Karankawan spokesman to Father Garza, already cited, is quoted here again because it suggests that the success of Refugio mission would in fact depend upon its location within the traditional operational area:

> Father, don't deceive yourself, for we don't want to go to the mission [of Rosario]. . . . If you want to, put a mission here on the coast for us. We will gather in it, all of us who are Christians, and we will bring with us all the heathens that are on this coast from the mouth of the Nueces to the Colorado River. . . . if you put a mission there [at the mouth of the Guadalupe River] for us, then you can say that the whole coast is yours. (Garza to Muñoz June 13, 1791, cited in Oberste 1943:29)

Thus the Karankawan strategy was to incorporate, when feasible, the mission into the traditional seasonal round as a source of meat and grain. This cycle involved visiting or entering the mission during the spring, that time of the year when traditional fishing camps were abandoned in favor of inland terrestrial resource procurement, and encouraging the Spaniards to place a mission within the bounds of the traditional operational area, presumably in part so that it would be accessible within the spatial patterning of traditional group mobility.

The location of the Refugio mission made this strategy particularly feasible, since it suited the requirements of established Karankawan subsistence strategies. This fact, coupled with the apparent desire on the part of the Indians to reach a peaceful accommodation with the Spaniards, doubtless contributed to the limited success of the Refugio mission. In effect, the mission became a component in the traditional human ecosystem of the Karankawa: it provided the kinds of subsistence upon which the Indians had always relied during the spring and summer, and it was spatially accessible, being located within traditional territorial boundaries. Inferably, it was the extent to which the Karankawa could utilize the mission according to established behavioral patterns that provided the measure of its acceptability within the cognitive filter of traditional culture, thus providing a viable adaptive bridge between known cultural patterns and the Spanish colonial frontier.

# Chapter 11
# The Long-Term Ecological Roots
# of Adaptive Change

In the preceding pages, the culture of the natives of the central coast of Texas, as an adaptive system, has been examined from prehistoric times through the Colonial Period of Spanish occupancy of the coastal prairies. The available data suggest that the structure of the late prehistoric adaptive system had emerged at least by later Archaic times, about 2,000 years ago. The limited data for the Archaic has suggested the same characteristic pattern of fall-winter emphasis on estuarine resource exploitation, documented for the late prehistoric and early historic periods.

It can be concluded, then, that the lifeway of people on the central coast at the time of European contact was a highly traditional one that revolved around basic adaptive patterns that were deeply rooted in prehistory. Furthermore, traditional patterns were resilient under the impacts of early Euro-American colonization of the region. Patterns of economy and settlement, and probably scales of group organization, were maintained from at least later prehistory up to and through the Colonial Period. While the early decades of European contact resulted in high mortalities from introduced diseases and a major reduction in regional population, overall population appears to have stabilized by the mid-eighteenth century, and the organizational units of the band, the macroband, and the tribe were maintained until the period of final cultural and demographic collapse beginning by around 1820.

In contrast to the maintenance of traditional adaptive patterns during the Spanish Colonial Period, later Anglo-American settlement expansion was a force with which the Karankawas could not effectively cope. During the period of early Anglo-American settlement, the Karankawas suffered catastrophic depopulation and attendant sociocultural breakdown. Unlike the Spaniards, who were concerned with maintaining a political frontier and who generally maintained a policy toward native groups of acculturation (Butzer

1990), the Anglo settlers were bent on permanent land acquisition and settlement, processes that were intended ultimately to exclude Indian peoples. Further documentary research may shed light on the cultural breakdown and demographic collapse of the Karankawas after 1830, when at least three of the five tribal groups were still more or less intact and each still was represented by several hundred people. At least one documentation of a Karankawan band fleeing to northeastern Mexico has been noted (Gatschet 1891; Newcomb 1983). While a sizable number of Indians must have perished in conflicts during the 1820s and 1830s, it is also likely that other small groups made their way to Mexico under the insuperable strains of Anglo-American pressures.

Since it was to the Spanish frontier culture of the mission and presidio complex that the Karankawas were in fact able to adapt, it is advisable to make a clear distinction between the cultural interactions of the Colonial Period, on the one hand, and those of the post-colonial decades of Anglo-American settlement, on the other. While the former period was characterized by initial conflict, it ultimately saw the emergence of a viable interaction between Indians and Spaniards and some degree of Karankawan acculturation to colonial Spanish culture. The latter period, marked by an entirely different set of goals on the part of Anglo-American settlers, was one to which the Karankawas could not adjust, largely because interaction with a viable Indian population was not on the settlers' agenda.

Compared to the rapid sociopolitical reorganization of Indian societies in central Mexico, which was accomplished in about two decades (McAlister 1984:103), the *reducción* of the Karankawas was a slow process. Partial success in converting these people to Christian ideology and peaceable relations came only after some seventy years of frustrated missionary activities and chronic hostilities. Whereas in the heart of New Spain conquest could be rapidly effected in large part by a displacement of ruling Indian elites of sedentary societies (ibid.:104), on the northeastern frontier the numerous hunter-gatherer groups had no elites to displace and no sedentary communities in which the Spaniards could assume a mantle of sociopolitical authority. The task facing the missionaries was a trying one, though in general, they found the indigenous interior groups somewhat more tractable than the Karankawas (e.g., Ciprian Report of 1749; Kress and Hatcher 1931:47).

The particular difficulty in converting the Karankawas probably derived at least in part from their lack of dependency on the mission for refuge during periods of Apache and Comanche raids. Rooted in their coastal environment, the Karankawas were to a degree insulated from the demographic displacements that severely impacted indigenous interior groups during the eighteenth century. This difficulty was probably compounded by a perceptual corollary of a long tradition of coastal adaptation, namely, a deeply rooted Karankawan sense of home place, as marked by distinct and long-maintained territorial boundaries. As already noted, the most complete missionary success was attained at Refugio mission, which was located first in the heart of, and shortly thereafter at the inland margin of, Karankawan territory. It is significant that in Karankawan perception this mission could succeed only if it were situated within the traditional coastal territory; in spite of their apparent desire for peace, the Indians made it quite clear that they had no desire to go as far inland as Rosario mission, since they did not want to leave their own country (Garza to Muñoz June 13, 1791, in Oberste 1943:29). While the earlier mission establishments of Espíritu Santo and Rosario, located further inland, obviously had little lasting success due to chronic hostilities, it is also apparent that a precondition of success at Refugio—and the peaceable Karankawan acculturation for which the Spaniards had worked for decades—was the mission's location within the traditional Karankawan homeland. That the distinct nature of the inland boundary had considerable time depth is indicated by the archaeological data for the late prehistoric period. As previously discussed, the data from Site 41RF21 in Refugio County and from the San Patricio County sites along the Aransas River evidence a discrete cultural boundary zone that saw interdigitation of coastal Rockport Phase sites and generally contemporaneous sites of the interior Toyah Horizon. The apparent interface of radiocarbon-dated coastal and interior archaeological remains at Site 41RF21 permits the placement of this boundary at least as early as the late thirteenth century A.D. (whether it can be traced back into the Archaic will depend on whether future research can distinguish coastal from interior artifact assemblages, in the absence of the diagnostic ceramics of late prehistoric times). All of the pertinent sites are located about 40 kilometers from the shoreline, the very same distance inland at which the Mexican government was prepared to draw the boundary of a Karankawan reserve in the early nineteenth century. Significantly, the second and final location of the Refugio mission was 38 kilometers from the mainland shoreline, as compared to over 70 kilometers in the case of mission Rosario.

It can be inferred, then, that the Karankawas perceived the inland limits of their home territory in quite definite terms and that this perception was the cognitive correlate of the operational area that traditionally marked the spatial bounds of the native ecosystem. To carry this line of inference a bit further, it can be suggested that centuries of adaptation to, and within, a particular environmental context had produced a strong perceptual identification with territory as home place. Long-term relations between people and environment yielded a perception of place that had emerged as a historically contingent process, in the sense formulated by Pred (1984).

From the highly traditional patterns of life and concomitant perceptions of place, the Karankawas were finally able to adapt to the pressures exerted by the Spanish colonial frontier. The adaptive process in this case did not involve major reformulations of tradition but was rather effected through the integration of novel sociocultural factors into the structure of the traditional cultural ecology. The Karankawas' treatment of the mission as an ecological resource, analogous in terms of both its spatial location and economic function to the aboriginal use of the coastal prairies, permitted this foreign institution to pass through the cognitive filter of tradition. This approach to the mission was, in effect, a form of stabilizing selection (Kirch 1980), in which new sociocultural input was integrated into established patterns in a way that maintained, rather than disrupted, those patterns.

This arrangement doubtless entailed some perceptible benefits for the Karankawas and probably some real costs. The advantages to the Indians would have been amelioration of a previously volatile sociopolitical relation with the Spaniards and an attendant alleviation of the effects of overt conflict, in addition to the immediate economic gain to be had from drawing upon the mission's stock of provisions. On the cost side, traditional ideological patterns would have had to be sacrificed, or at least modified, since the price of benefiting from the mission was some degree of acceptance of its underlying Euro-Christian worldview. That the Indians did in fact conform to this expectation, at least in part, is indicated by Jean Louis Berlandier's observation of 1829, already noted, that all the Karankawas called themselves Christians and took their newborn with ceremony to the Franciscan father at Refugio to receive baptism.

Thus the initial stabilizing selection that incorporated the mission into a traditional cultural-ecological framework opened the way for a directional selection (Kirch 1980), involving a progressive acceptance of European ideology and behavioral patterns. That this acculturative process was entering into the nonideological dimensions of Indian life by the early 1800s is indicated by the fact that Karankawan women were learning the foreign skills of spinning cotton and weaving cloth "of superior quality" and that, in general, "rapid progress in the path of civilization" was under way (Linn 1883:334).

The key point is that the pathway to directional change was set upon from the vantage point of known and long-accepted ways of doing things; the transition to new modes of ideology and behavior was facilitated by first absorbing novelty into the realms of securely established, and thoroughly fundamental, patterns of human-environmental relations and concomitant perceptions of traditional place. Judging from the fact that traditional tribal identities were still in existence by 1830 (though as already noted, some tribes were perhaps forced to merge with others because of post-1820 demographic decline), it is apparent that the acculturative changes of the late eighteenth and early nineteenth centuries left traditional organizational and ethnic structures intact. This is in accord with the observation that viable change was of a transitional nature, emerging from a synthesis of old and novel elements, rather than a disruptive displacement of the old by the new. The historical sequence of these processes is schematically summarized in Figure 30.

There are implications here for a general understanding of the fundamental processes by which relatively small-scale communities may adapt to changing conditions, as exerted across sociocultural frontiers by the expansion of larger cultural systems. In the case of the Karankawas, viable adaptation to novel frontier conditions was possible through synthesizing foreign elements within the patterns of known and accepted tradition. The initial efforts of the Spaniards to promote a direct and immediate acceptance of change among the coastal tribes led only to misunderstandings and conflict. Nondisruptive change and an incipient intercultural viability were possible only when the Karankawas (1) perceived the need for such interaction and (2) achieved it through incorporation of new cultural elements into a traditional cultural-ecological framework.

In our contemporary world, after decades of often disruptive or even disastrous attempts at intercultural viability (often couched in terms of various approaches to "Third World development"; e.g., Tobis 1974; Britton 1980), it has become increasingly apparent that adaptation on the part of smaller-scale systems must be predicated upon an understanding of, and due attention to, traditional cultural ecologies (e.g., Knight 1974:237–261; Mabogunje 1981:333–345). The Karankawas case, though only a single study, appears to offer support from a long-term historical perspective for the view that

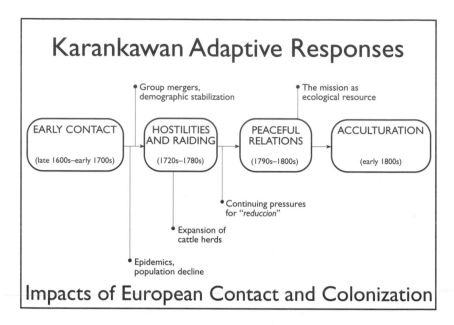

*Figure 30.* Diagram indicating Karankawan responses to Spanish colonization of the coastal prairies, as inferred from a synthesis of archaeological and ethnohistorical data.

viable change can occur only within the framework of ecological tradition. If modern processes of global interaction are irreversible, then the viable (i.e., humane) approach to intercultural relations will be based on real needs, as perceived by members of the communities in question, and on careful considerations as to how change can be introduced into the context of traditional ecological variables. If the present inferences drawn from the archaeological and ethnohistorical data have merit, then it follows that cultural perceptions and human ecology are inextricably interwoven and that change is viable only to the extent that it is integrated with these kinds of fundamental cognitive and behavioral patterns.

Despite the inherent limitations of archaeology for examining the subtler issues of human decision making, and despite the fragmentary nature of the ethnohistorical record, it is felt that one cultural group's ways of adjusting to novel conditions have been elucidated. Fresh perspectives on how contemporary communities may effectively respond to changing conditions can benefit from such historical studies, which have the advantage of highlighting traditional patterns as long-term processes and of investigating the role of these processes in adaptive transformations. Parallel studies of other Native American groups and examination of the nature of their responses to the impacts of Euro-American colonization can contribute to a cumulative understanding of the articulation of tradition and novelty within a wide range of cultural and human ecological contexts. The empirical foundations of such particular case studies will be an essential ingredient in the construction of a sound conceptual framework of long-term roots of sociocultural adaptation.

After a century or so of archaeological and ethnohistorical research into the various native cultures of the New World, substantial bodies of both prehistorical and historical information exist for many areas. These methodologically and empirically disparate databases, usually only tangentially linked, are susceptible to a productive synthesis within a historical human-ecological paradigm, and further insights into the ways people adapt to change across cultural boundaries are in store for the interested researcher. The field is wide open for further work.

# Appendix A
# Defining the Geographical and Chronological Parameters of the Rockport Phase through Ceramic Analysis

## Rockport Ware Pottery as an Indicator of Culture Area Boundaries

As an archaeological culture area during the Rockport Phase, the central coast of Texas is bounded on the north and west, respectively, by the Texas upper coast area and interior South Texas. Each of these areas is characterized by its own distinguishable ceramic tradition (there appears to be little or no native ceramic tradition to the south on the lower Texas coast). Sites on the upper coast have yielded abundant sandy paste and grog-tempered pottery of the Goose Creek, San Jacinto, and Baytown series (Aten 1983). While Goose Creek ware is made of the same basic sandy clay as is Rockport ware, it does not bear the asphaltum-painted decorations and/or surface coating so typical of the latter. Also, the small-mouthed, often constricted-neck olla forms commonly found on the central coast are rare on the upper coast, where nearly all reported pottery pertains to widemouthed jars or deep bowls (e.g., Suhm and Jelks 1962; Aten 1983; Howard 1990; Ricklis 1994). Rockport ware can, therefore, be distinguished from upper Texas coast pottery by the common use of asphaltum surface treatment and, to some extent, by a different proportional use of vessel forms. The criterion of presence/absence of asphaltum was in fact successfully used by Gayle Fritz (1975) to place the boundary between the central and upper coast areas, at least during ceramic times, in the vicinity of the east end of Matagorda Bay and the lowermost Colorado River.

The prolific use of asphaltum surface treatment also distinguishes Rockport ware, at a general level, from contemporaneous pottery of the inland Toyah Phase or Horizon. At interior sites such as Hinojosa in Jim Wells County (Black 1986) and Berclair in Goliad County (Hester and Parker 1970), the overwhelming majority of potsherds are plain. Asphaltum is found on only a few pieces, and in some cases it was used only to patch cracks in pots. The characteristic decorative motifs of Rockport painted pottery—lip banding and vertical squiggles—are nearly absent: none are reported from the Hinojosa Site, and only one specimen was documented in the collection of over 800 sherds from the Berclair Site.

Also, the interior plainware ceramics are noted for the common inclusion of abundant crushed bone temper. While some Rockport ware does contain bone temper (e.g., Story 1968), it was less consistently used and was added to the potter's clay in much less profuse quantities.

Since Fritz (1975) has effectively delineated the boundary zone between Rockport pottery and upper coast wares, the sole concern here is to quantify the differences between Rockport ware and interior bone-tempered plainware, so that the boundary between the operational areas of interior groups and the coastal Karankawas can be delineated.

The pottery sample from the Holmes Site (41SP120) is the starting point for this analysis, since the site is obviously coastal and a relatively large sample of potsherds remain to work with. Once critical attributes have been defined and quantified in terms of their proportional representations in the sample, ceramics from other late prehistoric sites in the study area can be compared on the basis of those same attributes, and the degree of similarity in the ceramics from the Holmes Site can be assessed.

The ideal attributes to consider, in light of the goal of determining spatial distributions, are those that are readily discernible in even the smallest fragments. This is the case simply because at many sites samples are relatively small and contain very few large pieces. Thus, decorative attributes such as particular design motifs are of limited use because a given motif is likely not to be represented on a small fragment, even if it were placed on some part of the pot. The vertical squiggles typical of Rockport Black-on-Gray, for instance, were rather widely spaced and so will appear on only a fraction of the sherds from vessels of the type. Similarly, the asphaltum lip banding will be seen only on rim fragments.

This problem is dealt with here by lumping asphaltum decoration of all kinds, as well as asphaltum coating, into a single "asphaltum surface-treated" category. Since the combined quantities of coated and decorated sherds are quite high on Rockport Phase sites, there should be enough examples in even relatively small samples to distinguish a site producing predominantly Rockport pottery from one yielding a predominance of interior plainware.

However, generally about half the sherds from a Rockport Phase site are devoid of any asphaltum surface treatment. They pertain either to vessels of the Rockport Plain type or to plain sections of decorated or perhaps partially coated vessels. Tempering material, which can be discerned in even the smallest sherds, is thus employed as a second basic attribute category. Since interior plainware is noted for its relatively consistent and heavy use of crushed bone temper, and Rockport ware by its fine sandy paste with only occasional bone temper, the presence or absence of bone tempering in various quantities (none, sparse, moderate, profuse) within sherd samples should indicate which of the two ceramic traditions is represented by a given sherd sample. Sparse shell, occasionally found in Rockport sherds, is not considered to be an intentional temper because the lagoonal clays within the vicinity of shoreline sites contain natural inclusions of minute shell fragments similar to those seen in sherds (see Story 1968). For the sake of comparability, the definitions of sparse, moderate, and profuse bone temper here follow Black's (1986) criteria for pottery from the interior Hinojosa Site in Jim Wells County: bone temper is sparse when it constitutes less than an estimated 5 percent of the clay body; moderate and profuse constitute 5–25 percent and over 25 percent, respectively.

Thus the spatial distributions of sites of coastal or interior cultural affiliation should be determinable on the basis of two sets of attributes, with each treated analytically in terms of the dichotomy of presence/absence.

The basic unit of analysis here is the ceramic vessel rather than the individual potsherd, since attribute analyses based on the latter can easily be skewed by the vagaries of cultural debris deposition and/or the partial sampling inherent in virtually all archaeological recovery. Quite conceivably, a single vessel may be represented by only a single sherd. In such a case, assessment of the proportional representations of particular attributes based on individual sherd analysis would obviously be misleading.

The attribute analysis presented here for the Holmes Site (41SP120), and for all sites discussed in this book, is thus based on sherd groups, each of which is believed to represent a single vessel. Each sherd has been placed within a group based on its attributes of color, thickness, surface treatment, completeness of firing, general surface hardness, and, most definitively, characteristics of aplastic (nonclay) inclusions such as tempering and the quantity, size, and color of inclusive sand grains. All paste characteristics were determined by examining fresh edge breaks under a 20X or 30X binocular microscope.

The analyses for the Holmes Site were conducted on sherds from two contiguous 1-meter-square excavation units, and all pottery-producing 10-centimeter levels within those units. Because of the large sample size, only the larger sherds were used. A consistent minimum size of 3 centimeters in length was the criterion for inclusion in the sample.

A total of 189 examined specimens fell into 80 sherd groups. In terms of the stated key attributes, the sherd groups broke down as follows:

Asphaltum Surface Treatment
Present:       42      (52.5 percent)
Absent:        38      (47.5 percent)

Bone Tempering
None:          49      (61 percent)
Sparse:        16      (20 percent)
Moderate:       9      (11.5 percent)
Profuse:        6      (7.5 percent)

If the ceramic sample from the Holmes Site is assumed to be, in terms of the selected attributes, generally representative of Rockport Phase ceramics, then the proportional breakdowns of these attributes should be similar at other Rockport sites and, at the same time, should contrast with proportional representations of the same attributes at non-Rockport Phase sites. In order to test this assumption, ceramics from several other sites have been examined along the same lines as was the Holmes Site sample. For the Rockport Phase, samples were chosen from sites situated either on bay/lagoon shorelines or within a few kilometers of shorelines to maximize the probability that the sites represent occupation by late prehistoric people operating within a coastal adaptive system. This is a reliable criterion, since, as indicated by ethnohistorical information, the territory of the Karankawas extended inland approximately 40 kilometers from the mainland shoreline.

Sherd group samples were thus analyzed, in terms of proportional representations of bone-tempered vessels, from six additional coastal zone sites (41NU37, 41NU221, 41NU255, 41SP11, 41SP103, and 41CL3). Samples from three of these sites were included in the analysis to determine proportions of asphaltum surface-treated pots; the other three were excluded because the sherds, which were surface-collected, often showed weathering that precluded reliable identification of surface treatment.

These analyses produced results that were consistently similar to those from the Holmes Site (see Figures 31, 32). In all cases, the majority of vessels had no added temper and contained only the apparently natural sand inclusions. Bone-tempered vessels account for between about 20 and 40 percent of the total at each site, with sparse bone temper predominating, followed proportionally by moderate, then profuse, bone tempering. In terms of the layout of variables on the graphs in Figure 31, a graphic "signature" emerges for Rockport ware samples. As may be seen in Figure 32, the percentages of vessels with asphaltum surface treatment hover rather closely around 50 percent in all site samples examined.

The ceramics from the Hinojosa Site, as reported by Black (1986), form the basis for a comparison of these results with a non-Rockport, interior Toyah Horizon site, located in Jim Wells County, well inland of the Rockport Phase area. Black's analysis was based on a "select sample" of 100 sherds culled from a total of over 700 found at the site. While vessel sherd groups were not used, the data are probably sufficiently representative of the site for comparative purposes, since the sherds came from an extensive excavation at what was apparently a recurrently occupied locus. The breakdown of percentages of sherds with sparse, moderate, profuse, and no bone temper presents a marked contrast to the Rockport sites. Sherds with no bone temper constitute only 4 percent of the sample, as compared to 60 to 80 percent in the Rockport samples. Sparse, moderate, and profuse bone-tempered sherds represent 27 percent, 53 percent, and 16 percent of the sample, respectively. In graphic terms, a very different "signature" is indicated for Toyah pottery (see Figure 33).

Black (1986) reports the use of asphaltum surface treatment on 11 percent of the sherds in the select sample. I have examined these sherds, housed at the Center for Archaeological Research, University of Texas at San Antonio. Several exhibit asphaltum banding that does not conform to typical Rockport decorative motifs. The banded decoration at Hinojosa is on the vessel body exterior; in Rockport ware, banding is confined to vessel lips, and wavy lines or squiggles are the only linear lines painted on vessel bodies. Also, interior asphaltum coating of pots, characteristic of Rockport vessels with exterior body decoration, is absent on the Hinojosa sherds.

The percentage breakdowns of these key ceramic attributes can be used as a basis for distinguishing occupational loci of inland, as opposed to coastal, groups. The characteristic attribute percentage signatures of the two ceramic traditions occur independently of one another, on separate, discrete late prehistoric site components, indicating that (1) the two traditions are separable on the basis of

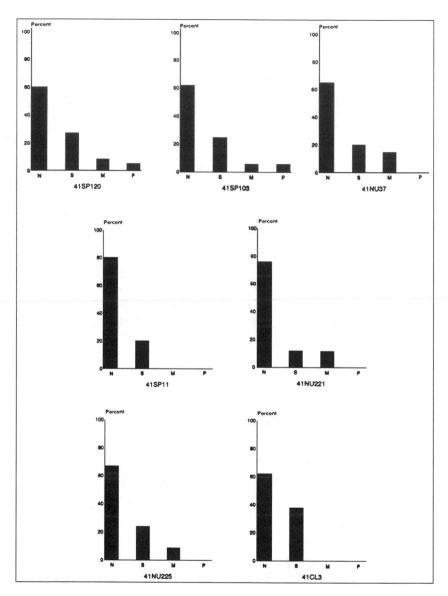

*Figure 31.* Bar graphs showing relative percentages of ceramic vessels with no bone temper (N), sparse (S), moderate (M), and profuse (P) bone temper, Rockport Phase sites.

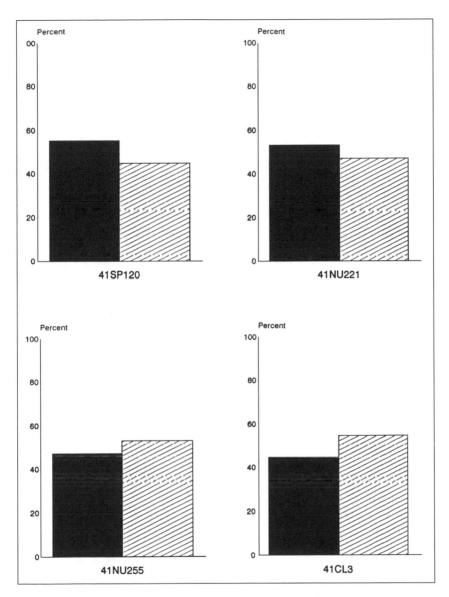

*Figure 32.* Bar graphs showing relative percentages of ceramic vessels with (black) and without (hachured) asphaltum surface treatment, at four Rockport Phase sites.

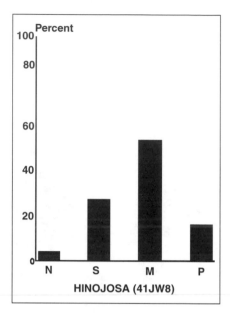

*Figure 33.* Bar graph showing relative percentages of ceramic sherds with no bone temper (N), sparse (S), moderate (M), and profuse (P) bone temper for the Toyah Horizon Hinojosa Site (41JW8) (based on data in Black 1986).

these two key attribute criteria and (2) that little mixing of the two traditions occurred.

This is most clearly indicated in Figure 34, which contrasts percentages of bone-tempered sherd groups from sites on the Aransas River. It will be seen that the percentages in the samples from Rockport Phase Sites 41SP167 and 41SP170 are virtually identical to the percentages at the Holmes Site. In contrast, the percentage breakdowns from non-Rockport Site 41SP169 and the non-Rockport component at 41SP170 are similar to those for the inland Hinojosa site.

That this is a recurrent spatial pattern, reflecting different occupations by interior and coastal groups, as opposed to a temporal change within a single tradition, is indicated by the contemporaneity of the two traditions at the Melon Site (41RF21). As discussed in Chapter 5, there were two late prehistoric components at this site: the northern half of the site yielded pottery of the inland Toyah Horizon, while the southern half produced pottery of coastal

Rockport ware. The percentages of the two key attributes at the north and south components of this site are shown in Figure 35. The attributes for the southern half of the site show percentage breakdowns that are essentially the same as those at other Rockport

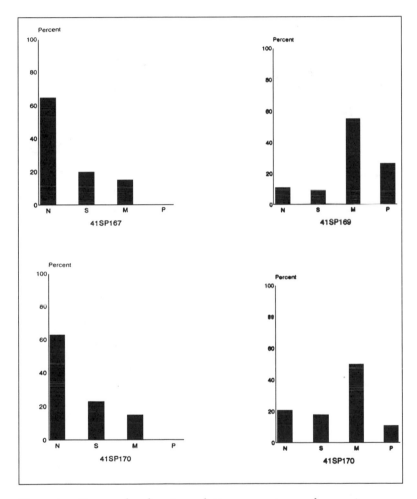

*Figure 34.* Bar graphs showing relative percentages of ceramic vessels with no bone temper (N), sparse (S), moderate (M), and profuse (P) bone temper from four sites near the Aransas River. Note that Sites 41SP167 and 41SP170 (Rockport Phase component) match graphs for the same attribute from other Rockport Phase sites, whereas data from 41SP169 and the southern or Toyah component at 41SP170 are similar to graph shown in Figure 33 for the inland Hinojosa Site.

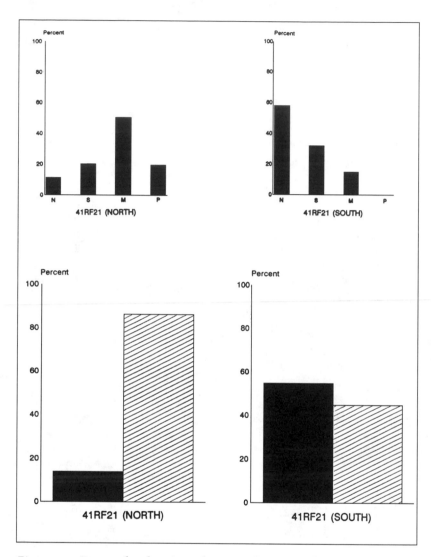

*Figure 35.* Bar graphs showing relative percentages of ceramic vessels with no bone temper (N), sparse (S), moderate (M), and profuse (P) bone temper from the north and south parts of the Melon Site (41RF21) (top) and relative percentages of vessels with (black) and without (hachured) asphaltum surface treatment from the north and south parts of the site (bottom).

Phase sites. Those from the northern half of the site are similar to the breakdowns from Hinojosa and the non-Rockport Phase sites on the Aransas River.

Using these kinds of ceramic analyses in conjunction with a consideration of the spatial distributions of sites with one or the other attribute signatures, it is possible to geographically define the boundary of the Rockport Phase operational area. Discrete site components with either Rockport ware or interior bone-tempered plainware are found about 40 kilometers from the mainland shoreline. When combined with the ethnohistorical information discussed in the text, this line apparently represents a distinct cultural boundary zone.

## Temporally Significant Ceramic Attributes at the Holmes Site (41SP120)

The relatively deep and stratified cultural deposits at the Holmes Site provide a good context for examination of change in regional ceramics through time. Several ceramic attributes show frequency changes according to arbitrary or stratigraphic levels, suggesting evolution in ceramic style and/or technology. This observation is based on a select sample of 300 sherds made up of all sherds in the total sample with lengths of greater than 3 centimeters. Smaller sherds, often no more than 1 to 2 centimeters, were apparently more susceptible to vertical displacement within the deposits, since they were found within old burrow channels in the lower excavation levels. Also, it was noted that a disproportionately high percentage of the decorated pieces found in the lower levels were very small sherds, suggesting downward displacement of smaller pieces from the upper levels, where decorated sherds tended to be larger.

The attributes considered, and their proportional numerical significance by level, are shown in Table 14. These data must be viewed with some caution, as the samples of sherds from the topmost and lower levels are rather small. However, a set of time-related trends does appear. The attribute of surface scoring (apparently executed with a ribbed bivalve shell; see Calhoun 1961) appears to increase in significance through time. The Rockport Black-on-Gray II type, typified by thin vessel walls with light-colored (oxidized) exteriors, interior asphaltum coating, and exterior vertical wavy lines or squiggles, shows an increase through time. There is a hint that asphaltum lip banding on widemouthed vessels (Rockport Black-on-Gray I) was proportionally more significant in earlier times than

**Table 14.** *The Holmes Site (41SP120): Numerical Occurrences of Selected Attributes of Larger Potsherds by Excavation Levels, South Block*

| Level | Scored | Lip Band[a] (rim sherds) | Rockport B-on-G II[b] | Crenelated Lip | Incised Rim | All Others[c] |
|---|---|---|---|---|---|---|
| 1 | 0 | 1 (6%) | 2 (13%) | 1 (6%) | 0 | 12 (75%) |
| 2 | 2 (2%) | 6 (6%) | 22 (22%) | 2 (2%) | 0 | 69 (68%) |
| 3 | 6 (5%) | 4 (4%) | 17 (15%) | 1 (1%) | 2 (2%) | 84 (74%) |
| 4 | 6 (15%) | 4 (10%) | 2 (5%) | 0 | 1 (3%) | 26 (66%) |
| 5 | 1 (11%) | 0 | 0 | 0 | 0 | 8 (89%) |
| Shell | 3 (30%) | 0 | 0 | 0 | 0 | 7 (70%) |
| Below shell | 3 (25%) | 0 | 0 | 0 | 0 | 9 (75%) |

[a] Rockport Black-on-Gray I

[b] Includes rim and body sherds with interior asphaltum coating and exterior vertical asphaltum squiggles, as well as body sherds assigned to the type on the basis of diagnostic combination of typological attributes (thinness, exterior oxidized surface, interior asphaltum coating, and sandy paste with absence of added temper).

[c] Includes plain body and rim sherds as well as body sherds with asphaltum coating that cannot be assigned to the Rockport Black-on-Gray II type.

later. Also faintly suggested is a relatively early presence of incised rims (Rockport Incised type) and a later introduction of crenelated rims. An increase in lip crenelation with time may be supported by the strong presence of the style at the Live Oak Point Site (41AS2) on Copano Bay (Ricklis 1990), where at least some of the Rockport ware pottery was associated with European trade material (Campbell 1958a).

In general these trends are in accord with the postulated introduction of a basically undecorated, sandy paste pottery from the upper Texas coast (Campbell 1961; Story 1968:64; Shafer and Bond 1985) and a subsequent in situ development of the indigenous, asphaltum-decorated wares of the central coast. Asphaltum was already in use as a coating agent on basketry during the Archaic (as evidenced by basketry imprinted asphaltum fragments at Kent-Crane and the late Archaic shell stratum at the Holmes Site), and its application to ceramic surfaces, as coating and later also as decoration, would seem to be a logical development. While the data presented in Table 14 should be augmented with analyses of additional ceramic samples, they do suggest some degree of intraregional stylistic evolution of ceramics.

# Appendix B
# Methods of Seasonality Analysis

The important interpretations of seasonal movements of the late prehistoric Karankawas discussed in this book are based on three methods of analysis, each developed respectively for fish otoliths, *Rangia cuneata* clamshells, and oyster shells. Each method involves determination of the amount of growth in the fish otolith or mollusk shell beyond a visible growth interruption that is related to seasonally low winter temperatures; when ambient water temperature drops below a certain threshold, growth of the organism temporarily ceased or is greatly retarded.

## Otoliths

Otoliths are small concretions found in pairs in the neurocrania of many marine fish species and are believed to aid fish in maintaining equilibrium (Casteel 1976). Each species has otoliths of a distinctive, easily identifiable shape (Zimmerman et al. 1988). Otoliths are formed of proteins and calcium carbonate in the form of aragonite (Casteel 1976:18–20), and their growth is directly related to growth of the fish. During the first year, the otolith develops as a small nucleus; during each successive growth year, an annulus, or growth band, is deposited on the otolith. Each annulus consists a single narrow band and a much wider, darker-colored band. When thin-sectioned, the narrow bands are opaque, and the wider bands are translucent (Beckman et al. 1988a, 1988b). The narrow bands represent slowed or suspended growth associated with reduced water temperatures during the winter months; the wide bands reflect the rapid growth during the warmer months (ibid.; C. Wilson, pers. comm.). Because of the seasonal periodicity of their formation, otoliths have long been used as a basis for determining age in fish (Casteel 1976). More recently, they have been employed in archaeological situations on the Texas coast to determine seasonality (e.g., Smith 1983; Prewitt 1987; Ricklis 1988, 1994; Eling et al. 1993).

The method employed on otolith samples from the sites discussed here is basically simple and straightforward. Each otolith to be examined was transversely cross-sectioned to show the internal growth rings of annuli. The most completely opaque part of final (outer) narrow, lighter-colored band was located, and the amount of growth subsequent to formation of the final narrow band was estimated as a percentage of the average of the widths of the two previous annuli. If the final growth band represented less than 33 percent of the average annulus width, the otolith was recorded as representing a spring fish death. If the final growth band represented between 33 and 66 percent, a summer death was recorded; if the band width was more than 66 percent of the average annulus width, and a new winter opaque band had not begun to form, a fall death was recorded. A winter death was recorded if the narrow opaque band was at the outer edge of the otolith.

This method is not without its imprecisions. The placement of each otolith in a seasonal category assumes an even spring through fall growth rate, which may not be the case either with fish populations or with individual fish. Probably, some variability in growth rates takes place because of both yearly differences in water temperatures and individual growth rates in fish. On the other hand, most otoliths showed rather uniform widths in their annuli, suggesting that yearly growth was not sufficiently uneven to seriously detract from the method's usefulness. To minimize inaccuracies associated with uneven growth rates, otoliths with markedly uneven annulus widths, or with particularly nebulous bands, were relegated to an indeterminate category and eliminated from final consideration. As a matter of course, specimens with eroded outer surfaces were eliminated, as were otoliths representing deaths prior to the third growth year, since at least one complete annulus was the minimal criterion for estimation of season of death.

To determine the validity of this method, samples of otoliths from marine fish with known dates of harvest are necessary. For this purpose, five samples of fish of known dates of catch were obtained from commercial fishers in the Corpus Christi area. All fish (consisting of a mix of black drum, redfish, and trout) were caught either in Corpus Christi or Aransas Bays. One otolith was extracted from the cranium of each fish and then cross-sectioned and examined according to the procedure just discussed. The amount of growth of each otolith was then estimated and expressed as a percentage of the width of the penultimate (and completed) growth annulus. The results of these analyses are presented in Figure 36, where each vertical bar represents the percentage of growth in a single otolith beyond the final winter growth interruption ring. If growth had stopped on the winter ring, the specimen was graphed as having completed its final growth cycle, that is, at 100 percent.

The results of these analyses are satisfactory in that an expectable pattern of seasonal otolith growth is indicated. As is evident in Figure 36, the sample with the greatest number of winter deaths (i.e., otoliths that stopped growing on the winter interruption ring) is from a January fish catch. The other samples, representing fish catches in late spring through fall, show an expectable and fairly linear increase in the amount of growth beyond the final winter interruption, with the least growth in the late spring and the most in the fall sample. Though time permitted the procurement of only five samples, the conformity of the results to expectations indicates that (1) otoliths do in fact show a predictable seasonal growth cycle and (2) that the method used for estimating seasonal growth on archaeological samples is sufficiently accurate to identify basic patterns of seasonality in fishing activities.

### *Rangia cuneata*

Shells of the brackish water clam, *Rangia cuneata* are used in seasonality analysis according to a method developed by Lawrence Aten (1981) during his archaeological research on the upper Texas coast. The method involves macroscopic examination of the shell surface and is based on the fact that *Rangia cuneata* clam shells experience a temperature-dependent growth interruption during the winter. The method has been used effectively by a number of researchers working in the Texas upper and central coast regions (e.g., McGuff 1978; Aten 1983; Hamilton 1988; Ricklis 1988). On the basis of the amount of growth subsequent to the final winter interruption ring, shells are assigned to one of three growth categories: early, middle, or late, each of which represents one-third of the width of the final complete growth band. If shell growth terminated on a winter interruption ring, the shell is placed in the interrupted growth category. Those that cannot be placed confidently in any of these categories, due to unclear or uneven growth patterns, are placed in an indeterminate category, which generally accounts for between 5 and 15 percent of any given sample. A sample of 20 shells is considered the minimum size for reliable results.

Once the sample has been separated into the five growth categories, the various category percentages are plotted graphically in a

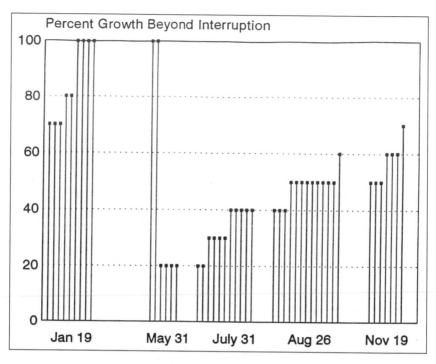

*Figure 36.* Graph showing amount of growth beyond final winter interruption ring in otoliths of fish of known dates of harvest from Corpus
Christi and Aransas Bays. Each bar represents 1 otolith from each of 47
fish (species include black drum, redfish, and spotted sea trout).

histogram that can be compared with a series of histograms similarly derived by Aten from samples gathered from living clam populations at 2-week intervals. Theoretically, then, the method is
accurate to within 2-week intervals.

This level of accuracy has been questioned (Monks 1981) on the
grounds that the variability in clam growth is too great for such a
high degree of precision. However, Carlson (1988), in scrutinizing
the method, using a FORTRAN computer program designed to test
the fit between modern and archaeological samples, arrived at some
interesting and highly encouraging results. In general, he found that
most archaeological samples showed good fits with Aten's modern
sample histograms. He also determined that combined samples
from two different seasonal periods were recognizable as such; com-
bining fall and spring samples, for instance, did not result in a histogram that mimicked a winter sample but rather resulted in a
bimodal pattern, recognizably representing separate fall and spring

harvests. On the other hand, Carlson did find that a sample representing a full season was nearly identical to the 2-week interval histogram for the middle of that season. Thus, for example, the combined 2-week histograms for the full spring season are nearly indistinguishable from the single 2-week histogram for either the end of April or the middle of May. On this basis, Carlson (ibid.: 211) concludes that "the accuracy of this technique for seasonality estimates may be as good as ±1.5 months. Considering the simplicity of the technique and our current understanding of seasonal exploitation by prehistoric populations, this level of accuracy is impressive."

Because the combined seasonal samples mimic midseason, single 2-week intervals, seasonality estimates derived here from archaeological samples will be expressed as a range. When a sample analysis yields a histogram that replicates that of any single modern 2-week sample, the range will be expressed as extending forward and backward in time from the modern sample date by 1.5 months, according to Carlson's findings. When the archaeological sample produces a clearly unimodal, but less temporally focused histogram, the range will be derived from the dates of those modern 2-week samples whose growth category percentages, when averaged, produce a unimodal histogram of similar configuration. Finally, when the histogram is bimodal, it will be assumed that two seasons are represented, and a bipartite range will be determined, again by averaging growth category percentages for the relevant modern samples.

## Oyster

Finally, a method for determining season of death in oysters (*Crassostrea virginica*) has been recently developed by researchers working on the Atlantic Coast (Kent 1988; Lawrence 1988). Again, the method is based on the identification of winter growth interruptions and determination of the relative amount of growth subsequent to the final winter interruption. While growth interruptions are recorded on the exterior surface of oyster valves, the irregularity of external shell growth precludes accurate determination of seasonality from observation of outer shell surfaces. The interior dorsal (umbonal) portion of the lower valve of oysters does, on the other hand, exhibit a regular growth pattern. Winter growth interruptions appear as raised ridges that transect the prominent anterior and posterior nymphae and the intervening depressed chondrophore. Less prominent but regular transverse ridges represent growth retardation due to summer heat shocks and summer spawning, while random growth interruptions can occur as a result of severe storms (Kent 1988:68).

The techniques of estimating seasonality as presented by Kent (1988:64–69) and Lawrence (1988:269–270) differ in detail but derive from the same principle. Kent suggests expressing the amount of growth subsequent to the final winter interruption as a numerical ratio of the average width of the two previous complete annual growth increments, as measured by the distance between winter interruption ridges. Lawrence's approach simply identifies the point at which umbonal shell accretion ceased relative to previous annual growth increments: cessation subsequent to the final winter interruption, but prior to the secondary summer heat shock ridge, is interpreted as a spring-summer death; cessation well beyond the heat shock ridge but prior to the formation of an additional winter interruption ring is considered a fall death.

Since Kent's approach is recommended in conjunction with a series of modern oyster samples with known gathering dates from within any given study area, and since these are presently unavailable for the Texas coast, it would be pointless here to attempt analysis with the level of precision sought by Kent's technique. While Lawrence's approach yields only general seasonality estimates, it is employed in this study as a means of roughly approximating seasonality of oyster gathering.

It should be mentioned that Kent believes "southern oysters" will exhibit the greatest degree of growth interruption during the summer heat shock rather than during the winter, thus requiring a complete reversal in the interpretation of seasonality in a given sample. Kent does not, however, specify the geographical extent of what he considers southern oyster (his analyses are performed on archaeological and modern samples from Chesapeake Bay).

Lawrence's studies were carried out on oysters from South Carolina, where the greatest growth interruption evident is again unambiguously associated with winter growth interruption (Lawrence 1988:270). The author examined a sample of oysters gathered in Galveston Bay at the end of October 1989 and found that, when the most prominent growth interruption ridges were considered to represent the winter season, all shells recorded a fall harvest. Similarly, a sample of 15 shells gathered in mid-January in San Antonio Bay all produced consistent winter readings. Thus, the general method as outlined seems to be applicable for the northwest Gulf coast, though refinement through additional analyses of modern samples is called for (see also discussions and data in Cox and Cox 1993 and Cox 1994).

# References Cited

Altamira, Marqués de

1752    Letter of El Marqués de Altamira to the Viceroy, February 29, 1752. Archivo General de la Nación (Mexico), Bolton Transcriptions, vol 287. Center for American History, University of Texas at Austin.

Andrews, J.

1977    *Shells and Shores of Texas*. Elma Dill Russell Spencer Foundation Series 5. Austin: University of Texas Press.

Aten, L. E.

1981    Determining Seasonality of *Rangia Cuneata* from Gulf Coast Shell Middens. *Bulletin of the Texas Archeological Society* 52:179–200.

1983a    *Indians of the Upper Texas Coast*. New York: Academic Press.

1983b    *Analysis of Discrete Habitation Units in the Trinity River Delta, Upper Texas Coast*. Occasional Papers 2. Austin: Texas Archeological Research Laboratory, University of Texas.

Barroto, E.

1987    The Enrique Barroto Diary. Trans. Robert S. Weddle. In *La Salle, the Mississippi, and the Gulf*. Ed. Robert S. Weddle. Pp. 149–171. College Station: Texas A&M University Press.

Becker, J.

1964    About Trout. *Texas Game and Fish* 22(5):11–30.

Beckmann, D. W., A. L. Stanley, J. H. Render, and C. A. Wilson

1988    *Age and Growth of Black Drum in Louisiana Gulf of Mexico Waters*. Baton Rouge: Coastal Fisheries Institute, Center for Wetland Resources, Louisiana State University.

Beckman, D. W., C. A. Wilson, and A. L. Stanley

1988    *Age and Growth Structure of Red Drum, "Sciaenops Ocellatus," from Offshore Waters of the Northern Gulf of Mexico*. Baton Rouge: Coastal Fisheries Institute, Center for Wetland Resources, Louisiana State University.

Berlandier, J. L.

1969    *The Indians of Texas in 1830*. Ed. J. C. Ewers. Trans. P. R. Leclercq. Washington, D.C.: Smithsonian Institution Press.

1980    *Journey to Mexico during the Years 1826 to 1834*. 2 vols. Trans. S. M. Ohlendorf, J. M. Bigelow, and M. M. Standifer. Austin: Texas

State Historical Association and the Center for Studies in Texas History.

Birdsell, J. B.
1953    Some Environmental and Cultural Factors Influencing the Structuring of Aboriginal Australian Populations. *American Naturalist* 87:171–207.

Binford, L. R.
1980    *Bones: Ancient Men and Modern Myths.* New York: Academic Press.

Black, S. L.
1986    *The Clemente and Herminia Hinojosa Site, 41JW8: A Toyah Horizon Campsite in Southern Texas.* Special Report 18. San Antonio: Center for Archaeological Research, University of Texas at San Antonio.

Blair, W. F.
1950    The Biotic Provinces of Texas. *Texas Journal of Science* 2(l): 93–117.

Bogusch, E. R.
1952    Brush Invasion in the Rio Grande Plain of Texas. *Texas Journal of Science* 4(1):85–91.

Bollaert, W.
1850    Observations on Indian Tribes of Texas. *Journal, Ethnological Society of London* 2:262–283.

Bolton, H. E.
1906    The Founding of Mission Rosario: A Chapter in the History of the Gulf Coast. *Quarterly of the Texas State Historical Association* 10(2):113–139.

1915    *Texas in the Middle Eighteenth Century: Studies in Spanish Colonial History and Administration.* Berkeley: University of California Press.

Bonnell, G. W.
1840    *Topographical Description of Texas; To Which is Added an Account of the Indian Tribes.* Austin: Clark, King and Brown.

Britton, R.
1980    Shortcomings of World Tourism. In *Dialectics of Third World Development.* Ed. I. Vogeler and A. R. de Souza. Pp. 231–240. Montclair, N.J.: Allanheld, Osmun.

Brown, L. F., J. L. Brewton, J. H. McGowen, T. J. Evans, W. L. Fisher, and C. G. Groat.
1976    *Environmental Geologic Atlas of the Texas Coast: Corpus Christi Area.* Austin: Bureau of Economic Geology, University of Texas.

Buckley, E. C.
1911    The Aguayo Expedition into Texas and Louisiana, 1719–1722. *Quarterly of the Texas State Historical Association.* 15:1–65.

Bureau of Economic Geology
1975    *Geologic Atlas of Texas: Corpus Christi Sheet.* Austin: Bureau of Economic Geology, University of Texas.

Butzer, K. W.

1982    *Archaeology as Human Ecology: Method and Theory for a Contextual Approach.* Cambridge: Cambridge University Press.

1990    Change and Continuity in New Spain. Paper presented at the annual meeting of the Association of American Geographers, Toronto, Canada, April 20.

Cabello, D.

1779    Letter from Domingo Cabello, Governor of the Province of Tejas, to Commandant General Cavallero de Croix, October 17, 1779. Bexar Archives Translations, Series I. Center for American History, University of Texas at Austin.

Calhoun, C. A.

1961    Scored Pottery of the Texas Coastal Bend. *Bulletin of the Texas Archeological Society* 32:321–326.

Calnan, T. R.

1980    *Molluscan Distribution in Copano Bay, Texas.* Report of Investigations 103. Austin: Bureau of Economic Geology, University of Texas.

Campbell, T. N.

1947    The Johnson Site: Type Site of the Aransas Focus of the Texas Coast. *Bulletin of the Texas Archeological and Paleontological Society* 18:40–75.

1952    The Kent-Crane Site: A Shell Midden on the Texas Coast. *Bulletin of the Texas Archeological Society* 23:39–77.

1956    Archeological Materials from Five Islands in the Laguna Madre, Texas Coast. *Bulletin of the Texas Archeological Society* 27:7–46.

1958a   Archeological Remains from the Live Oak Point Site, Aransas County. *Texas Journal of Science* 10(4):423–442.

1958b   Probable Function of Perforated Oyster Shells Found in Aransas Focus Sites. *Texas Archeology* 2:7.

1960    Archeology of the Central and Southern Sections of the Texas Coast. *Bulletin of the Texas Archeological Society* 29 (for 1958): 145–175.

1988    The Coahuiltecans and Their Neighbors. In *The Indians of Southern Texas and Northeastern Mexico: Selected Writings of Thomas Nolan Campbell.* Austin: Texas Archeological Research Laboratory, University of Texas.

Campbell, T. N., and T. J. Campbell

1981    *Historic Indian Groups of the Choke Canyon Reservoir and Surrounding Area, Southern Texas.* Choke Canyon Series 1. San Antonio: Center for Archaeological Research, University of Texas at San Antonio.

Carlson, D. L.

1988    *Rangia Cuneata* as a Seasonal Indicator for Coastal Archeological Sites in Texas. *Bulletin of the Texas Archeological Society* 58 (for 1987): 201–214.

Carr, J. T., Jr.
1967    *Climate and Physiography of Texas.* Report 53. Austin: Texas Development Board.

Carroll, W., trans.
1983    *Beranger's Discovery of Aransas Pass.* Papers of the Corpus Christi Museum 8. Corpus Christi: Corpus Christi Museum.

Castañeda, C. E.
1936    *The Mission Era: The Winning of Texas, 1692–1731.* Vol. 2 of *Our Catholic Heritage in Texas.* Austin: Von Boeckman–Jones.

1942    *The Mission Era: The End of the Spanish Regime.* Vol. 5 of *Our Catholic Heritage in Texas.* Austin: Von Boeckmann–Jones.

Casteel, R.
1976    *Fish Remains in Archaeology and Paleoenvironmental Studies.* New York: Academic Press.

Cazorla, L.
1787    Letter of Don Luís Cazorla, Commander of Presidio La Bahía, to Governor Don Rafael Martínez Pacheco, January 22, 1787. Bexar Archives Translations, Series I. Center for American History, University of Texas at Austin.

1788    Letter of Don Luís Cazorla, Commander of Presidio La Bahía, to Governor Don Rafael Martínez Pacheco, May 2, 1788. Bexar Archives Translations, Series I. Center for American History, University of Texas at Austin.

Ciprian, Fr. I. A.
1979    *Report of Fr. Ignacio Antonio Ciprian, 1749, and Memorial of the College to the King, 1750.* Transcript of the Spanish Original and English Translation by Fr. B. Leutenegger. Old Spanish Missions Historical Research Library at San Jose Mission, San Antonio.

Compton, H.
1975    Texas Saltwater Fishes. *Texas Parks and Wildlife* 33(10):33.

Comuzzie, A. G., M. Marek, and D. G. Steele
1986    Analysis of Human Skeletal Remains from the Palm Harbor Site on the Central Gulf Coast of Texas. *Bulletin of the Texas Archeological Society* 55 (for 1984): 213–247.

Cook, S. F.
1973    The Significance of Disease in the Extinction of the New England Indians. *Human Biology* 45(3):485–508.

1976    *The Indian Population of New England in the Seventeenth Century.* Publications in Anthropology 12. Berkeley: University of California.

Corbin, J. E.
1974    A Model for Cultural Succession for the Coastal Bend Area of Texas. *Bulletin of the Texas Archeological Society* 45:29–54.

Cordero, M. A.
1806    Letter from Manuel Antonio Cordero, Governor of the Province of Texas, to Nemesio Salcedo, Commandant General of the Interior Provinces, June 16, 1806. Bexar Archives, General Manuscript

Series. Center for American History, University of Texas at Austin.

Cortes, J.

1793     Letter from Juan Cortes, Commander at Presidio La Bahía, to Governor Don Manuel Muñoz, December 5, 1793. Bexar Archives, General Manuscript Series. Center for American History, University of Texas at Austin.

1795     Census of Indians at the Mission of Nuestra Señora del Refugio, October 23, 1795. Bexar Archives, General Manuscript Series. Center for American History, University of Texas at Austin.

1797     Letter from Juan Cortes to Governor Muñoz, March 24, 1797. Bexar Archives, General Manuscript Series. Center for American History, University of Texas at Austin.

Covey, C.

1983     *Adventures in the Interior of America by Alvar Nuñez Cabeza de Vaca.* Albuquerque: University of New Mexico Press.

Cox, I. J., ed.

1905     *The Journeys of René Robert Cavelier de la Salle.* 2 vols. New York: Barnes.

Cox, K. A.

1994     Oysters as Ecofacts. *Bulletin of the Texas Archeological Society* 62 (for 1991): 219–47.

Cox, K. A., and S. Cox

1993     Oyster Analysis at White's Point. In *A Model of Environmental and Human Adaptive Change on the Central Texas Coast: Geoarchaeological Investigations at White's Point, Nueces Bay, and Surrounding Area.* Ed. R. A. Ricklis. Pp. 81–122. Corpus Christi: Coastal Archaeological Studies.

Cox, K. A., and H. A. Smith

1988     Kent-Crane Revisited. *La Tierra* 15(3):24–38.

Croix, T.

1779     Letter of Teodoro Croix to Governor Domingo Cabello, October 17, 1779. Bexar Archives Translations, Series I. Center for American History, University of Texas at Austin.

Crosby, A. W.

1972     *The Columbian Exchange.* Westport, Conn.: Greenwood Press.

Davenport, H., ed.

1924     The Expedition of Pánfilo de Narváez by Gonzalo Fernandez Oviedo y Valdez. *Southwestern Historical Quarterly* 27(2): 217–241.

Day, D. W., J. Laurens-Day, and E. R. Prewitt

1981     *Cultural Resources Surveys and Assessments in Portions of Hidalgo and Willacy Counties, Texas.* Reports of Investigations 15. Austin: Prewitt and Associates.

Denevan, W., ed.

1976     *The Native Population of the Americas in 1492.* Madison: University of Wisconsin Press.

DeVos, G. A., and L. Romanucci-Ross
1975     Ethnic Identity: Cultural Continuities and Change. Palo Alto, Calif.: Mayfield Publishing.
Dobyns, H. F.
1966     Estimating Aboriginal American Population: An Appraisal of Techniques with a New Hemispheric Estimate. Current Anthropology 7:395–444.
1983     Their Numbers Became Thinned: Native American Population Dynamics in Eastern North America. Knoxville: University of Tennessee Press.
Drawe, D. L., A. D. Chamrad, and T. W. Box
1978     Plant Communities of the Welder Wildlife Refuge. Contribution 5, Series B, Revised. Sinton, Tex.: Rob and Bessie Welder Wildlife Foundation.
Dreiss, M. L.
1994     Marine and Freshwater Shell Artifacts. In Aboriginal Life and Culture on the Upper Texas Coast: Archaeology at the Mitchell Ridge Site, 41GV66, Galveston Island. Ed. R. A. Ricklis. Corpus Christi: Coastal Archaeological Research.
Duffen, W. A.
1941     Report on Site 72D913, Kent and Crane Place, Aransas County, Texas, Work Project no. 16770, March 1941. Manuscript, Texas Archeological Research Laboratory, University of Texas at Austin.
Dyer, J. O.
1916     Historical Sketch: Comparisons of Customs of Wild Tribes near Galveston a Century Ago with Ancient Semitic Customs. Galveston: Privately printed.
1917     The Lake Charles Atakapas (Cannibals): Period of 1817–1820. Galveston: Privately printed.
Eling, H. E., S. A. Turpin, and J. F. Powell
1993     Limited Test Excavations at the Horse Island Site, 41CF29, Cameron County, Texas. Technical Report 32. Austin: Texas Archeological Research Laboratory, University of Texas.
Elquezabal, J. B.
1797     Letter of Juan Bautista Elquezabal, Interim Commander at Presidio La Bahía, to Governor Don Manuel Muñoz, including census of Indians at Mission Nuestra Señora del Refugio, July 3, 1797. Bexar Archives, General Manuscript Series. Center for American History, University of Texas at Austin.
1798     Letter of Juan Bautista Elquezabal, Interim Commander at Presidio La Bahía, to Governor Don Manuel Muñoz, January 17, 1798. Bexar Archives, General Manuscript Series. Center for American History, University of Texas at Austin.
Ensor, H. B.
1987     The Cinco Ranch Sites, Barker Reservoir, Fort Bend County, Texas. Reports of Investigations 3. College Station: Archeological Research Laboratory, Texas A&M University.

Erlandson, J. M.
1988    The Role of Shellfish in Prehistoric Economies: A Protein
        Perspective. *American Antiquity* 53(1):102–109.
Espadas, M.
1789    Letter of Manuel Espadas, Commander at Presidio La Bahía, to
        Governor Martínez Pacheco, December 29, 1789. Bexar Archives,
        General Manuscript Series. Center for American History, Uni-
        versity of Texas at Austin.
Ewers, J. C.
1973    The Influence of Epidemics on the Indian Populations and Cul-
        tures of Texas. *Plains Anthropologist* 18(60):104–115.
Fenneman, N. M.
1938    *Physiography of the Eastern United States.* New York: McGraw-
        Hill.
Folmer, H.
1940    De Bellisle on the Texas Coast. *Southwestern Historical Quarterly*
        44(2):204–231.
Fritz, G.
1975    *Matagorda Bay Area, Texas: A Survey of the Archeological and
        Historical Resources.* Research Report 45. Austin: Texas Archeo-
        logical Survey, University of Texas.
Gadus, E. F., and M. A. Howard
1990    *Hunter-Fisher-Gatherers on the Upper Texas Coast: Archeo-
        logical Investigations at the Peggy Lake Disposal Area, Harris
        County, Texas.* Reports of Investigations 74. Austin: Prewitt and
        Associates.
Garavito, A.
1798    Letter from Fr. Antonio Garavito to Juan Elquezabal, Interim Com-
        mander at Presidio La Bahía, March 25, 1798. Bexar Archives,
        General Manuscript Series. Center for American History, Uni-
        versity of Texas at Austin.
1798    Letter from Antonio Garavito to José Moral, October 13, 1798.
        Bexar Archives, General Manuscript Series. Center for American
        History, University of Texas at Austin.
Garza, J.
1791    Letter from Fr. Juan Garza to Don Manuel Muñoz, Governor of the
        Province of Tejas, June 13, 1791. Bexar Archives, General Manu-
        script Series. Center for American History, University of Texas at
        Austin.
1791    Letter from Fr. Juan Garza to Don Manuel Muñoz, Governor of
        the Province of Tejas, December 15, 1791. Bexar Archives, General
        Manuscript Series. Center for American History, University of
        Texas at Austin.
1793    Letter from Fr. Juan Garza to Don Manuel Muñoz, Governor of the
        Province of Tejas, January 18, 1793. Bexar Archives, General Manu-
        script Series. Center for American History, University of Texas at
        Austin.

1793    Letter of Fr. Juan Garza to Don Manuel Muñoz, June 10, 1793.
        Bexar Archives, General Manuscript Series. Center for American
        History, University of Texas at Austin.

Gatschet, A. S.
1891    *The Karankawa Indians: The Coast People of Texas.* Archaeo-
        logical and Ethnological Papers of the Peabody Museum. Cam-
        bridge: Harvard University.

Geiger, E., and G. Borgstrom
1962    Fish Protein: Nutritive Aspects. In *Fish as Food.* Vol. 2 of *Nutri-
        tion, Sanitation, and Utilization.* Ed. G. Borgstrom. Pp. 29–65.
        New York: Academic Press.

Gerhard, P.
1978    *The North Frontier of New Spain.* Princeton: Princeton University
        Press.

Gilmore, K.
1984    La Salle's Fort St. Louis in Texas. *Bulletin of the Texas Archeo-
        logical Society* 55:61–72.

Goddard, I.
1979    The Languages of South Texas and the Lower Rio Grande. In *The
        Languages of Native America: A Comparative Assessment.* Ed.
        L. Campbell and M. Mithun. Austin: University of Texas Press.

Grayson, D. K.
1979    On the Quantification of Vertebrate Archaeofaunas. *Advances in
        Archaeological Method and Theory* 2:199–237.

Gunter, G.
1945    *Studies of Marine Fishes of Texas.* N.p.: Institute of Marine Sci-
        ence, University of Texas.

Hackett, C. W., ed.
1934    *Pichardo's Treatise on the Limits of Louisiana and Texas.* Vol. 2.
        Austin: University of Texas Press.

Hale, T. H., and M. D. Freeman
1978    A Reconnaissance Survey and Assessment of Prehistoric and
        Historic Resources, Cypress Creek Watershed, Harris and Walker
        Counties, Texas. Manuscript, Texas Archeological Survey, Uni-
        versity of Texas at Austin.

Hall, G. D.
1989    Long-Bone Implements from Some Prehistoric Sites in Texas:
        Functional Interpretations Based on Ethnographic Analogy. *Bul-
        letin of the Texas Archeological Society* 55 (for 1988): 157–176.

Hall, G. D., S. L. Black, and C. Graves
1982    *Archaeological Investigations at Choke Canyon Reservoir, South
        Texas: Phase I Findings.* San Antonio: Center for Archaeological
        Research, University of Texas at San Antonio.

Hamilton, D. L.
1988    Archeological Investigations at Shy Pond, Brazoria County, Texas.
        *Bulletin of the Texas Archeological Society* 58 (for 1987): 77–146.

Harrington, R. A., G. C. Matlock, and J. E. Weaver
1979    *Length — Weight and Dressed — Whole Weight Conversion Tables for Selected Saltwater Fishes.* Management Data Series 6. Austin: Coastal Fisheries Branch, Texas Parks and Wildlife Department.

Hassan, F. A.
1981    *Demographic Archaeology.* New York: Academic Press.

Hayes, M. O.
1965    Sedimentation on a Semiarid, Wave-Dominated Coast, with Emphasis on Hurricane Effects. Ph.D. dissertation, University of Texas at Austin.

Headrick, P. J.
1991    *The Archeology of 41NU11, the Kirchmeyer Site, Nueces County, Texas: Long-Term Utilization of a Coastal Clay Dune.* Studies in Archeology. Austin: Texas Archeological Research Laboratory, University of Texas.

Heffernan, T. L., A. W. Green, L. W. McEachron, M. G. Weixelman, P. C. Hammerschmidt, and R. A. Harrington
n.d.    *Survey of Finfish Harvest in Selected Texas Bays.* Washington, D.C.: National Marine Fisheries Service, U.S. Department of Commerce.

Heidenreich, C.
1971    *Huronia: A History and Geography of the Huron Indians, 1600 to 1650.* Toronto: McClelland and Stewart.

Henley, D. E., and D. G. Rauschuber
1981    *Freshwater Needs of Fish and Wildlife Resources in the Nueces— Corpus Christi Bay Area, Texas: A Literature Synthesis.* Albuquerque: Biological Services Department, U.S. Fish and Wildlife Service.

Hester, T. R.
1977    *Archaeological Research at the Hinojosa Site (41JW8), Jim Wells County, Southern Texas.* Survey Report 42. San Antonio: Center for Archaeological Research, University of Texas at San Antonio.
1980    *Digging into South Texas Prehistory: A Guide for Amateur Archaeologists.* San Antonio: Corona Publishing.

Hester, T. R., and T. J. Hill
1975    *Some Aspects of Late Prehistoric and Protohistoric Archaeology in Southern Texas.* Special Report 1. San Antonio: Center for Archaeological Research, University of Texas at San Antonio.

Hester, T. R., and R. Parker
1970    The Berclair Site: A Single Component in Goliad County, Texas. *Bulletin of the Texas Archeological Society* 41:1–24.

Highley, C. L.
1980    Archaeological Materials from the Alazan Bay Area, Kleberg County, Texas. In *Papers on the Archaeology of the Texas Coast.* Ed. T. R. Hester and C. L. Highley. Special Report 11. San Antonio: Center for Archaeological Research, University of Texas at San Antonio.

1986    *Archaeological Investigations at 41LK201, Choke Canyon Reservoir, Southern Texas.* Choke Canyon Series 11. San Antonio: Center for Archaeological Research, University of Texas at San Antonio.

Hoese, D. H., and R. H. Moore
1977    *Fishes of the Gulf of Mexico.* College Station: Texas A&M University Press.

Hole, F., and R. G. Wilkinson
1973    Shell Point: A Coastal Complex and Burial Site in Brazoria County, Texas. *Bulletin of the Texas Archeological Society* 44:5–50.

Howard, M. A.
1990    Ceramic Analysis. In *Prehistoric Hunter-Fisher-Gatherers on the Upper Texas Coast: Archaeological Investigations at the Peggy Lake Disposal Area, Harris County, Texas.* Reports of Investigations 74. Austin: Prewitt and Associates.

Jackson, B. E., J. L. Boone, and M. Henneberg
1987    Possible Cases of Endemic Treponematosis in a Prehistoric Hunter-Gatherer Population on the Texas Coast. *Bulletin of the Texas Archeological Society* 57 (for 1986): 183–193.

Jackson, H. E.
1990    The Trouble with Transformations: Effects of Sample Size and Sample Composition on Meat Weight Estimates Based on Skeletal Mass Allometry. *Journal of Archaeological Science* 16:601–610.

Jackson, J.
1986    *Los Mesteños: Spanish Ranching in Texas, 1721–1821.* College Station: Texas A&M University Press.

Janota, B.
1980    A Preliminary Study of the Shell Ornaments of the Texas Coast between Galveston Bay and the Nueces River. In *Papers on the Archaeology of the Texas Coast.* Special Report 11. San Antonio: Center for Archaeological Research, University of Texas at San Antonio.

Jaudenes, J.
1791    Letter from Fr. José Jaudenes to Governor Muñoz, November 30, 1791. Bexar Archives, General Manuscript Series. Center for American History, University of Texas at Austin.

1794    Census of Indians at Rosario Mission by Fr. José Jaudenes, September 26, 1794. Bexar Archives, General Manuscript Series. Center for American History, University of Texas at Austin.

Jennings, F.
1975    *The Invasion of America: Indians, Colonialism, and the Cant of Conquest.* New York: W. W. Norton.

Jochim, M. A.
1981    *Strategies for Survival: Cultural Behavior in an Ecological Context.* New York: Academic Press.

Johnson, L.
1987    A Plague of Phases: Recent Sociocultural Taxonomy in Texas Archeology. *Bulletin of the Texas Archeological Society* 57 (for 1986): 1–26.

1994     *The Life and Times of Toyah-Culture Folk: The Buckhollow Encampment, Site 41KM16, Kimble County, Texas.* Office of the State Archeologist Report 38. Austin: Texas Department of Transportation and Texas Historical Commission.

Johnston, M. C.

1963     Past and Present Grasslands of Southern Texas and Northeastern Mexico. *Ecology* 44(3):456–466.

Jones, F. B.

1983     *The Flora of the Texas Coastal Bend.* Sinton, Tex.: Rob and Bessie Welder Wildlife Foundation.

Joutel, H.

1713     *Journal Historique d'un Voyage de l'Amerique.* Paris.

Kent, B. W.

1988     *Making Dead Oysters Talk: Techniques for Analyzing Oysters from Archaeological Sites.* St. Mary's City, Md.: Maryland Historical Trust, Jefferson Patterson Park and Museum.

Kie, J. G., M. White, and D. L. Drawe

1983     Condition Parameters of White-Tailed Deer in Texas. *Journal of Wildlife Management* 47(3):583–594.

Kilman, E.

1959     *Cannibal Coast.* San Antonio: Naylor Company.

Kinnaird, L., trans.

1958     *The Frontiers of New Spain: Nicolás La Fora's Description, 1766–1769.* Berkeley, Calif.: Quivira Society.

Kirch, P. V.

1980     The Archaeological Study of Adaptation: Theoretical and Methodological Issues. *Advances in Archaeological Method and Theory* 3:101–156.

Klein, R. G., and K. Cruz-Uribe

1984     *The Analysis of Animal Bones from Archeological Sites.* Chicago: University of Chicago Press.

Knight, C. G.

1974     *Ecology and Change: Rural Modernization in an African Community.* New York: Academic Press.

Knowlton, F. F., M. White, and J. G. Kie

1978     Weight Patterns of Wild White-Tailed Deer in Southern Texas. In *Proceedings of the First Welder Wildlife Foundation Symposium.* Ed. D. L. Drawe. Pp. 55–64. Sinton, Tex.: Rob and Bessie Welder Wildlife Foundation.

Kress, M. K., and M. A. Hatcher

1931     Diary of a Visit of Inspection of the Texas Missions Made by Fray Gaspar de Solís in the Year 1767–68. *Southwestern Historical Quarterly* 35(1):28–76.

Kuykendall, J. H.

1903     Reminiscences of Early Texans. *Quarterly of the Texas State Historical Association* 6:236–253.

Landar, H.
1968    The Karankawa Invasion of Texas. *International Journal of American Linguistics* 34(4):242–258.
La Salle, M. W., and A. A. de la Cruz
1985    *Common Rangia.* Biological Report 82. Washington, D.C.: Fish and Wildlife Service, U.S. Department of the Interior.
Lassuy, D. R.
1983    *Atlantic Croaker.* Species Profiles: Life Histories and Environmental Requirements (Gulf of Mexico). Washington, D.C.: Fish and Wildlife Service, U.S. Department of the Interior and U.S. Army Corps of Engineers.
Lawrence, D. R.
1988    Oysters as Geoarchaeologic Objects. *Geoarchaeology* 3(4):267–274.
Lee, R. B., and I. DeVore
1968    *Man the Hunter.* Chicago: Aldine.
Linn, J. J.
1883    *Reminiscences of Fifty Years in Texas.* New York: Sadlier.
Lopez, J. F.
1940    *The Texas Missions in 1785.* Trans. J. A. Dabbs. Preliminary Studies of the Texas Catholic Historical Society. Austin: Texas Knights of Columbus Historical Commission.
McAlister, L. N.
1984    *Spain and Portugal in the New World, 1492–1700.* Minneapolis: University of Minnesota Press.
McClellan, W. S., and E. F. DuBois
1930    Clinical Calorimetry, 45: Prolonged Meat Diets with a Study of Kidney Function and Ketosis. *Journal of Biological Chemistry* 93:419–434.
McGilvery, R. W.
1983    *Biochemistry: A Functional Approach.* London: W. B. Saunders.
McGowen, J. H., C. V. Procter, Jr., T. J. Evans, W. L. Fisher, and C. G. Groat
1976    *Environmental Geologic Atlas of the Texas Coastal Zone: Port Lavaca Area.* Austin: Bureau of Economic Geology, University of Texas.
McGuff, P. R.
1978    *Prehistoric Archeological Investigations at Palmetto Bend Reservoir: Phase I.* Research Report 58. Austin: Texas Archeological Survey, University of Texas.
Mabogunje, A. L.
1981    *The Development Process: A Spatial Perspective.* New York: Holmes and Meier Publishers.
Mallouf, R. J., B. J. Baskin, and K. L. Killen
1977    *A Predictive Assessment of Cultural Resources in Hidalgo and Willacy Counties, Texas.* Office of the State Archeologist Survey Report 23. Austin: Texas Historical Commission.

Martin, G. C.
1930    Two Sites on the Callo del Oso, Nueces County, Texas. *Bulletin of the Texas Archeological and Paleontological Society* 2:7–17.
1931    Texas Coastal Pottery. *Bulletin of the Texas Archeological and Paleontological Society* 3:53–56.
Matlock, G. C., and J. E. Weaver
1979    *Fish Tagging in Texas Bays during November 1975–September 1976.* Management Data Series 1. Austin: Coastal Fisheries Branch, Texas Parks and Wildlife.
Margry, P.
1886    *Decouvertes et Etablissements Françaises dans L'Ouest et dans le Sud de L'Amerique Septentrionale, 1614–1698.* Vol. 4. Paris: Maisonreuve et Cie.
Mayhall, M. P.
1939    The Indians of Texas: Atakapa, Karankawa, Tonkawa. Ph.D. dissertation, University of Texas at Austin.
Milner, G. R.
1980    Epidemic Disease in the Postcontact Southeast: A Reappraisal. *Midcontinental Journal of Archaeology* 5(1):39–56.
Minet
1987    Journal of Our Voyage to the Gulf of Mexico. Trans. L. Bell. In *La Salle, the Mississippi, and the Gulf: Three Primary Documents.* Ed. R. S. Weddle. Pp. 83–126. College Station: Texas A&M University Press.
Monks, G. G.
1981    Seasonality Studies. In *Advances in Archaeological Method and Theory* 4:177–219.
Mooney, J.
1928    *The Aboriginal Population of America North of Mexico.* Miscellaneous Collections 80. Washington, D.C.: Smithsonian Institution.
Moral, J.
1798    Letter of José Moral to Governor Manuel Muñoz, November 21, 1798. Bexar Archives, General Manuscript Series. Center for American History, University of Texas at Austin.
1799    Letter of José Moral to Manuel Muñoz, January 18, 1799. Bexar Archives, General Manuscript Series. Center for American History. University of Texas at Austin.
Morfi, J. A.
1935    *History of Texas, 1673–1779.* Trans. C. E. Castañeda. N.p.: Quivira Society.
Muñoz, M.
1793    Letter from Don Manuel Muñoz, Governor of the Province of Tejas, to Captain Juan Cortes, Commander of Presidio La Bahía, December 13, 1793. Bexar Archives, General Manuscript Series. Center for American History, University of Texas at Austin.

Muñoz, M.
1794    Letter from Don Manuel Muñoz to Juan Cortez, June 10, 1794.
Bexar Archives, General Manuscript Series. Center for American
History, University of Texas at Austin.

Myers, S. L.
1969    *The Ranch in Spanish Texas.* Social Science Series 2. El Paso:
University of Texas at El Paso.

Neumann, G. K.
1952    Archeology and Race in the American Indian. In *Archeology of
Eastern North America.* Ed. J. B. Griffin. Chicago: University of
Chicago Press.

Newcomb, W. W., Jr.
1961    *The Indians of Texas: From Prehistoric to Modern Times.* Austin:
University of Texas Press.
1983    Karankawa. In *Handbook of North American Indians.* Vol. 10. Ed.
A. Ortiz. Pp. 359–367. Washington, D.C.: Smithsonian Institution.

Noli, D., and G. Avery
1988    Protein Poisoning and Coastal Subsistence. *Journal of Archaeological Science* 15:395–401.

Oberste, W. H.
1942    *History of Refugio Mission.* Refugio, Tex.: Refugio Timely Remarks.

O'Connor, K. S.
1966    *The Presidio La Bahía del Espiritu Santo de Zuniga, 1721 to 1846.*
Austin: Von Boeckmann–Jones.

Odum, E. P.
1971    *Fundamentals of Ecology.* Philadelphia: W. B. Saunders Company.

Orton, R.
1969    *Map of Texas Showing Normal Precipitation Deficiency in Inches.*
Austin: Weather Bureau, Environmental Sciences Administration,
U.S. Department of Commerce.

Padilla, J. A.
1919    Texas in 1820: Report of the Barbarous Indians of the Province of
Texas. Trans. M. A. Hatcher. *Southwestern Historical Quarterly*
23:47–68.

Parilla, D. O.
1767    Autos y Diligéncias por el Coronel D. Diego Ortiz Parilla, Sobre las
Circunstancias de la Isla de los Malaguitas, que Communmente
han Llamado Isla Blanca. Archivo General de las Indias, Audiéncia
de Guadalajara 104-6-13. Dunn Transcripts. Center for American
History, University of Texas at Austin.

Parker, R. L.
1959    Macro-Invertebrate Assemblages of Central Texas Coastal Bays.
*Bulletin of the American Association of Petroleum Geologists*
43(9):2100–2166.

Parmalee, P., and W. Klippel
1974    Freshwater Mussels as a Prehistoric Food Source. *American
Antiquity* 39(3):421–434.

Pearson, J. C.

1929    Natural History and Conservation of Redfish and Other Sciaenids on the Texas Coast. *Bulletin of the U.S. Bureau of Fisheries* 49:1–73.

Piszina, M. R.

1751    Letter of Manuel Ramírez de la Piszina to the Viceroy, December 26, 1751. Archivo General de la Nación. Vol. 287. Bolton Transcription. Center for American History, University of Texas at Austin.

Potter, W. H.

1930    Ornamentation on the Pottery of the Texas Coastal Tribes. *Bulletin of the Texas Archeological and Paleontological Society* 2: 41–44.

Powell, J. F.

1988    Stress and Survival Models of Adaptive Success in the Texas Late Prehistoric. *Bulletin of the Texas Archeological Society* 58 (for 1987): 249–266.

1989    An Epidemiological Analysis of Mortality and Morbidity in Five Late Prehistoric Populations from the Upper and Central Texas Coast. M.A. thesis, Department of Anthropology, University of Texas at Austin.

Pred, A.

1984    Place as Historically Contingent Process: Structuration and the Time-Geography of Becoming Places. *Annals of the Association of American Geographers* 74(2):279–297.

Prewitt, E. R.

1981    Cultural Chronology in Central Texas. *Bulletin of the Texas Archeological Society* 52:65–89.

1985    From Circleville to Toyah: Comments on Central Texas Chronology. *Bulletin of the Texas Archeological Society* 54 (for 1983): 201–238.

1987    Observations on Seasonality of Selected Fish Remains from 41AS16. In *National Register Assessments of the Swan Lake Site, 41AS16, on Copano Bay, Aransas County, Texas,* by E. R. Prewitt, S. V. Lisk, and M. A. Howard. Pp. 259–268. Reports of Investigations 56, Austin: Prewitt and Associates.

Prewitt, E. R., S. V. Lisk, and M. A. Howard

1987    *National Register Assessments of the Swan Lake Site, 41AS16, on Copano Bay, Aransas County, Texas.* Reports of Investigations 56. Austin: Prewitt and Associates.

Prewitt, E. R., and J. G. Paine

1988    The Swan Lake Site (41AS16) on Copano Bay, Aransas County, Texas: Settlement, Subsistence, and Sea Level. *Bulletin of the Texas Archeological Society* 58 (for 1987): 147–174.

Price, W. A.

1933    Role of Diastrophism in Topography of Corpus Christi Area, South

Texas. *American Association of Petroleum Geologists Bulletin* 17(8):907–962.

Quast, W. D., T. S. Searcy, and H. R. Osburn

1988     *Trends in Texas Commercial Fishery Landings, 1977–1987.* Management Data Series 149. Austin: Coastal Fisheries Branch, Texas Parks and Wildlife Department.

Ramenofsky, A.

1987     *Vectors of Death: The Archaeology of European Contact.* Albuquerque: University of New Mexico Press.

Ramsdell, C. W., Jr.

n.d.     Spanish Goliad. Manuscript. Center for American History, University of Texas at Austin.

Reitz, E. J., I. R. Quitmeyer, S. Hale, Sylvia Scudder, and E. Wing

1987     Application of Allometry to Zooarchaeology. *American Antiquity* 52:304–307.

Reyes, J. M.

1790     Letter from Fr. José Mariano Reyes to the Viceroy, May 1, 1790. Bexar Archives, General Manuscript Series. Center for American History, University of Texas at Austin.

1790     Letter from Fr. José Mariano Reyes to Governor Don Manuel Muñoz, November 18, 1790. Bexar Archives, General Manuscript Series. Center for American History, University of Texas at Austin.

Rice, P. M.

1987     *Pottery Analysis: A Sourcebook.* Chicago: University of Chicago Press.

Ricklis, R. A.

1986     A Late Prehistoric Activity Locus in the Texas Coastal Bend: A Preliminary Report on Findings at the McKinzie Site (41NU221), Zone I. *La Tierra* 13(4):5–14.

1988     Archeological Investigations at the McKinzie Site (41NU221), Nueces County, Texas: Description and Contextual Interpretations. *Bulletin of the Texas Archeological Society* 58 (for 1987): 1–76.

1989     Preliminary Observations on a Late Prehistoric Bison-Processing Site (41RF21) on the Central Part of the Texas Coastal Plain. *Texas Archeology* 33(2):12–13.

1990     A Historical Cultural Ecology of the Karankawan Indians of the Central Texas Coast: A Case Study in the Roots of Adaptive Change. Ph.D. dissertation, Department of Geography, University of Texas at Austin.

1992a    Aboriginal Karankawan Adaptation and Colonial Period Acculturation: Archeological and Ethnohistorical Evidence. *Bulletin of the Texas Archeological Society* 63:211–243.

1992b    The Spread of a Late Prehistoric Bison-Hunting Complex: Evidence from the South-Central Coast Prairie of Texas. *Plains Anthropologist* 37(140):261–273.

1993     *A Model of Holocene Environmental and Human Adaptive*

Change on the Central Texas Coast: Geoarchaeological Investigations at White's Point, Nueces Bay, and Surrounding Area. Corpus Christi: Coastal Archaeological Research.

1994    *Aboriginal Life and Culture on the Upper Texas Coast: Archaeology at the Mitchell Ridge Site, 41GV66, Galveston Island.* Corpus Christi: Coastal Archaeological Research.

Ricklis, R. A., and M. B. Collins

1995    *Archaic and Late Prehistoric Human Ecology in the Middle Onion Creek Valley, Hays County, Texas.* Studies in Archeology 19. Austin: Texas Archeological Research Laboratory, University of Texas.

Ricklis, R. A., and K. A. Cox

1993    Examining Lithic Technological Organization as a Dynamic Cultural Subsystem: The Advantages of an Explicitly Spatial Approach. *American Antiquity* 58(3):444–461.

Rivera, P.

1736    Proyecto y Visita de Presidios Hecho en el Año 1728 por Pedro Rivera. Archivo General de la Nación, Províncias Internas. Vol. 29. Center for American History, University of Texas at Austin.

Rodriguez, M.

1793    Letter from Sergeant Mariano Rodrigues to Captain Juan Cortes, May 31, 1793. Bexar Archives, General Manuscript Series. Center for American History, University of Texas at Austin.

Roessler, A. R.

1883    *Antiquities and Aborigines of Texas.* Annual Report for 1881. Pp. 613–616. Washington, D.C.: Smithsonian Institution.

Russo, M.

1991    Archaic Sedentism on the Florida Coast: A Case Study from Horr's Island. Ph.D. dissertation, University of Florida.

Sayles, E. B.

1935    *An Archaeological Survey of Texas.* Medallion Papers 17. Globe, Ariz.: Gila Pueblo.

Santa Ana, B.

1751    Letter from Fr. Benito de Santa Ana to the Viceroy, December 20, 1751. Archivo General de la Nación. Bolton Transcription. Vol. 287. Center for American History, University of Texas at Austin.

Schaedel, R. P.

1949    The Karankawa of the Texas Gulf Coast. *Southwestern Journal of Anthropology* 5(2):117–137.

Schmidly, D. J.

1983    *Texas Mammals East of the Balcones Fault Zone.* College Station: Texas A&M University Press.

Shafer, H. J., and C. Bond

1985    An Archeological Review of the Central Texas Coast. *Bulletin of the Texas Archeological Society* 54 (for 1983): 271–285.

Shew, D. M., R. H. Baumann, T. H. Fritts, and L. S. Dunn

1981    *Texas Barrier Islands Region Ecological Characterization: Environmental Synthesis Papers.* Washington, D.C.: Biological Services Program, Fish and Wildlife Service, U.S. Department of the Interior.

Sibley, J.

1807    Historical Sketches of the Several Indian Tribes in Louisiana South of the Arkansas River and Between the Mississippi and River Grand. In *Travels in the Interior Parts of America: Communicating Discoveries Made in Exploring the Missouri, Red River and Washita by Captains Lewis and Clark, Doctor Sibley and Mr. Dunbar.* London.

Silva, M.

1791    Letter from Fr. Manuel Silva to Governor Muñoz, April 26, 1791. Bexar Archives, General Manuscript Series. Center for American History, University of Texas at Austin.

1792    Letter from Fr. Manuel Silva to the King, March 10, 1792. Bexar Archives, General Manuscript Series. Center for American History, University of Texas at Austin.

1793    Letter from Fr. Manuel Silva to the King, March 3, 1973. Bexar Archives, General Manuscript Series. Center for American History, University of Texas at Austin.

1795    Letter from Fr. Manuel Silva to Governor Muñoz, September 30, 1795. Bexar Archives, General Manuscript Series. Center for American History, University of Texas at Austin.

Simmons, E. G., and J. P. Breuer

1962    *A Study of Redfish, "Sciaenops ocellata Linnaeus," and Black Drum, "Pogonias cromis Linnaeus."* Publication 5. Austin: Institute of Marine Science, University of Texas.

Smith, E. A.

1981    The Application of Optimal Foraging Theory to the Analysis of Hunter-Gatherer Group Size. In *Hunter-Gatherer Foraging Strategies: Ethnographic and Archeological Analyses.* Ed. B. Winterhalder and E. A. Smith. Pp. 36–65. Chicago: University of Chicago Press.

Smith, H. A.

1983    Determination of Seasonality in Archaeological Sites through Examination of Fish Otoliths. *Journal of Field Archaeology* 10: 498–500.

Smithwick, N.

1900    *The Evolution of a State; or Recollections of Old Texas Days.* Austin: Gammel.

Snow, D. R., and K. M. Lamphear

1988    European Contact and Indian Depopulation in the Northeast: The Timing of the First Epidemics. *Ethnohistory* 35(1):15–33.

Solís, R. F.

1981    *Upper Tertiary and Quaternary Depositional Systems, Central Coastal Plain, Texas: Regional Geology of the Coastal Aquifer and Potential Liquid–Waste Repositories.* Report of Investigations 108. Austin: Bureau of Economic Geology, University of Texas.

Speth, J. D.
1983    *Bison Kills and Bone Counts: Decision Making by Ancient Hunters.* Chicago: University of Chicago Press.

Steele, D. G.
1988    Utilization of Marine Mollusks by Inhabitants of the Texas Coast. *Bulletin of the Texas Archeological Society* 58 (for 1987): 215–248.

Steele, D. G., and E. R. Mokry, Jr.
1985    Archeological Investigations of Seven Prehistoric Sites along Oso Creek, Nueces County, Texas. *Bulletin of the Texas Archeological Society* 54 (for 1983): 287–308.

Story, D. A.
1968    *Archeological Investigations at Two Central Gulf Coast Sites.* Archeological Program Report 13. Austin: State Building Commission.

Stuiver, M., and G. W. Pearson
1986    High-Precision Calibration of the Radiocarbon Time Scale, A.D. 1950–500 B.C. *Radiocarbon* 28(2B):805–838.

Suhm, D. A., and E. B. Jelks
1962    *Handbook of Texas Archeology: Type Descriptions.* Austin: Texas Archeological Society and Texas Memorial Museum.

Suhm, D. A., A. D. Krieger, and E. B. Jelks
1954    An Introductory Handbook of Texas Archeology. *Bulletin of the Texas Archeological Society* 25.

Swanton, J. R.
1952    *The Indian Tribes of North America.* Bulletin 145. Washington, D.C.: Bureau of American Ethnology.

Tjarks, A. V.
1974    Comparative Demographic Analysis of Texas, 1777–1793. *Southwestern Historical Quarterly* 77:291–338.

Tobis, D.
1974    United Fruit Is Not Chiquita. In *Guatemala.* Ed. S. Jonas and D. Tobis. Pp. 122–131. New York: North American Congress on Latin America.

Továr, F.
1768    Letter of Captain Francisco Továr, Commander at Presidio La Bahía, to Governor Don Hugo Oconor, June 6, 1768. Bexar Archives Translations, Series I. Center for American History, University of Texas at Austin.

Treviño, A.
1789    Diary of Sergeant Antonio Treviño's exploration of the coast, December 12, 1789. Bexar Archives, General Manuscript Series. Center for American History, University of Texas at Austin.

Troike, R. C.
1987    Karankawa Linguistic Data. In *La Salle, the Mississippi, and the*

*Gulf.* Ed. R. S. Weddle. Pp. 288–301. College Station: Texas A&M University Press.

Tull, D.
1987    *A Practical Guide to Edible and Useful Plants.* Austin: Texas Monthly Press.

Turner, E., and T. R. Hester
1993    *Stone Artifacts of the Texas Indians.* 2d ed. Houston: Gulf Publishing Company.

Watt, B. K., and A. L. Merrill
1975    *Composition of Foods.* Washington, D.C.: U.S. Department of Agriculture.

Weddle, R. S., ed.
1987    *La Salle, the Mississippi, and the Gulf: Three Primary Documents.* College Station: Texas A&M University Press.

West, E. H., trans. and ed.
1905    De Leon's Expedition of 1689, an Annotated Translation. *Quarterly of the Texas State Historical Association* 8(3):203–224.

Weinstein, R. A.
1992    *Archaeology and Paleogeography of the Lower Guadalupe River/ San Antonio Bay Region: Cultural Resources Investigations along the Channel to Victoria, Calhoun, and Victoria Counties, Texas.* Baton Rouge: Coastal Environments.

1994    *Archaeological Investigations along the Lower Lavaca River, Jackson County, Texas: The Channel to Red Bluff Project.* Baton Rouge: Coastal Environments.

White, T. E.
1953    A Method of Calculating the Dietary Percentage of Various Food Animals Utilized by Aboriginal Peoples. *American Antiquity* 28(4):396–398.

White, W. A., T. R. Calnan, R. A. Morton, R. S. Kimble, T. G. Littleton, J. H. McGowen, H. S. Nance, and K. E. Schmedes
1983    *Submerged Lands of Texas, Corpus Christi Area: Sediments, Biochemistry, Benthic Macroinvertebrates, and Associated Wetlands.* Austin: Bureau of Economic Geology, University of Texas.

Whittaker, R. H.
1975    *Communities and Ecosystems.* 2d ed. New York: Macmillan.

Wing, E. S., and A. B. Brown
1980    *Paleonutrition: Method and Theory in Prehistoric Foodways.* New York: Academic Press.

Winterhalder, B.
1981    Optimal Foraging Strategies and Hunter-Gatherer Research in Anthropology: Theory and Models. In *Hunter-Gatherer Foraging Strategies: Ethnographic and Archeological Analyses.* Ed. B. Winterhalder and E. A. Smith. Pp. 13–35. Chicago: University of Chicago Press.

Wobst, H. M.
1974    Boundary Conditions for Paleolithic Social Systems: A Simulation
        Approach. *American Antiquity* 39(2):147–178.
Wolff, T.
1969    The Karankawa Indians: Their Conflict with the White Man in
        Texas. *Ethnohistory* 16(1):1–32.
Woodbury, G., and E. Woodbury
1935    *Prehistoric Skeletal Remains from the Texas Coast.* Lancaster,
        Penn.: Lancaster Press.
Wright, S. S.
1980    Seismic Stratigraphy and Depositional History of Holocene Sedi-
        ments on the Central Texas Gulf Coast. M.S. thesis, Department
        of Geology, University of Texas at Austin.
Zimmerman, L. S., D. G. Steele, and J. D. Meyer
1988    A Visual Key for the Identification of Fish Otoliths. *Bulletin of the
        Texas Archeological Society* 58 (for 1987): 175–200.

# Index